AN ANSWER FOR
EVERYTHING

200 INFOGRAPHICS
TO EXPLAIN THE WORLD

ROB ORCHARD | CHRISTIAN TATE | MARCUS WEBB

From *Delayed Gratification* magazine

BLOOMSBURY PUBLISHING

LONDON · OXFORD · NEW YORK · NEW DELHI · SYDNEY

TO OUR FAMILIES AND FRIENDS, WHO HAVE
THE ANSWER FOR EVERYTHING ELSE

BLOOMSBURY PUBLISHING

Bloomsbury Publishing Plc
50 Bedford Square, London, WC1B 3DP, UK
29 Earlsfort Terrace, Dublin 2, Ireland

BLOOMSBURY, BLOOMSBURY PUBLISHING and the Diana logo are trademarks of Bloomsbury Publishing Plc

First published in Great Britain, 2021

A catalogue record for this book is available from the British Library
Library of Congress Cataloguing-in-Publication data has been applied for

ISBN: HB: 978-1-5266-3364-4; eBook: 978-1-5266-3363-7

2 4 6 8 10 9 7 5 3 1

Printed and bound in Italy by L.E.G.O. S.p.A.

Bloomsbury Publishing Plc makes every effort to ensure that the papers used in the manufacture of our books are natural, recyclable products made from wood grown in well-managed forests. Our manufacturing processes conform to the environmental regulations of the country of origin.
To find out more about our authors and books visit
www.bloomsbury.com and sign up for our newsletters

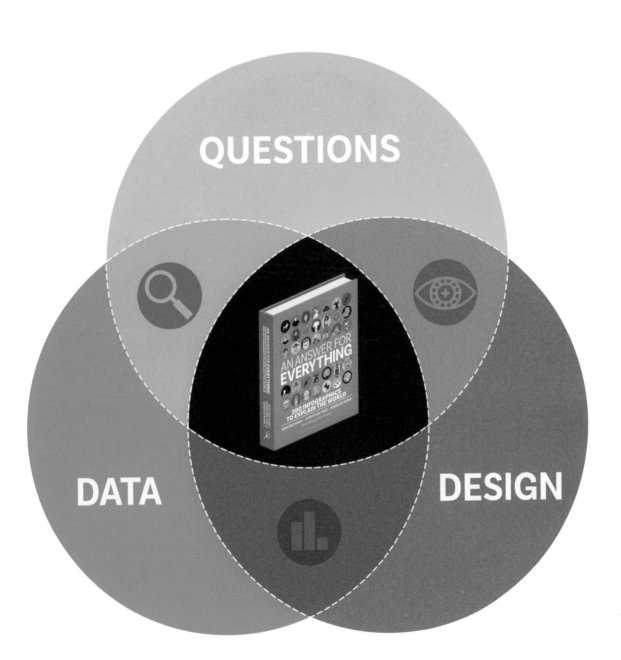

What's it all about?

The world is a delightful, baffling, wondrous and worrisome place...

...and for over a decade we've been using data to try to make sense of it, turning research from expert sources into beautiful infographics for our Slow Journalism magazine, *Delayed Gratification*.

This book gathers together updated versions of the best of our infographics alongside a whole host of brand new data visualisations we've created to answer questions ranging from the serious to the silly.

You may want to celebrate the highs – the incredible achievements of elite athletes (p052), the towering feats of human engineering (p064) and the unexpected and pleasing reappearance of knobbled weevils after decades of presumed extinction (p116).

You may wish to engage with the lows – the overheating of the Earth (p244), the scourge of mass shootings (p274) and the troubling appearance of locust swarms three times the size of New York City (p255).

You may simply be keen to answer some of the questions that have long vexed humanity – what the best thing since sliced bread is (p030), what war is good for (p278) and whether worse things do in fact happen at sea (p252).

In answering these questions and scores of others we have been helped by the unprecedented access to high-quality information enjoyed by the nerdier fringes of 21st-century humanity. We owe a large debt to the bands of meticulous people across the world compiling detailed reports on the widest range of subjects.

There are the archivists at NASA who've detailed everything astronauts have left on the moon, from golf balls to falcon feathers (p180). There are the admirably precise record-keepers of the UN Food and Agriculture Organization who helped us identify the country which is home to 39 chickens for every person (p123). Then there are the people who've tallied every war and major conflict (p264), every sighting of the Loch Ness monster (p184) and the favourite tipple of every nation on Earth (p080). It's been a joy to dive into their rich ocean of data.

We hope that you find *An Answer For Everything* to be a stimulating read which piques your curiosity, tickles your ribs and leads you into impassioned debates around the dinner table, down the pub or in your favourite corner of the internet. If nothing else, if we leave you creditably well informed about what UFOs look like (p168), how much it would cost to buy everything in *Vogue* (p071) and where babies come from (p032) then we'll have done our job.

Enjoy the book!

Rob, Christian and Marcus

What's in this book?

A guide to everything

WHO ON EARTH ARE YOU?
P014

? Questions about life as a human being

WHO'S THE GREATEST?
P038

? Questions about sport, cities and superstructures

WHERE DO I START?

? How to navigate this book

You can flip straight to the index on p302 and pick a topic that appeals to you. Alternatively, here are a couple of additional questions which will set you off on a solemn or lighthearted journey through the book:

Can we be serious for a moment?
The gravest and weightiest questions in each chapter

Can we be silly for a moment?
The daftest and most frivolous questions in each chapter

WHAT
DO WE WANT?
P068

? Questions about vices, desires and puggles

HOW DO
WE SAVE THE
PLANET?
P086

? Questions about flying, energy and mass veganism

WHAT'S IN
OUR NATURE?
P104

? Questions about fauna, flora and the rising tide of chickens

ARE YOU NOT ENTERTAINED?
P126

? Questions about films, music and murderous soap operas

IS THERE ANYBODY OUT THERE?
P166

? Questions about UFOs, space and conspiracy theories

HOW DO I MAKE FRIENDS AND INFLUENCE PEOPLE?
P188

? Questions about power, politics and Putin's poses

AM I LIVING MY BEST LIFE?
P214

WHAT'S THE WORST THAT COULD HAPPEN?
P236

WHY CAN'T WE ALL JUST GET ALONG?
P262

ANY OTHER QUESTIONS?
P282

? Questions about odds,
sods and miscellanea

WHAT CAN YOU TELL ME ABOUT...?
P302

? An index
to everything

3,139 topics, from **A-ha** (musical act)
to **Zürich** (picnicking potential of)

WHO ON EARTH ARE YOU

Questions about life as
a human being

How many of us have there been?

There have been a lot of humans in the last 192,000 years

How it works:
Each figure represents ten million people

Source: Population Reference Bureau

An estimated

116.76 billion

'modern' humans* have lived on Earth
in the last 192,000 years

You are one of 7.86 billion people alive today

For every **human alive today** ▶
there are almost 15 **dead people** ◀

*Only counting 'modern' *Homo sapiens*, the definition of which is the subject of academic debate centred around markers including anatomy, language
and the use of technologies. The Population Reference Bureau's estimated numbers are based on 'modern' *Homo sapiens* emerging in 190,000 BC

By 2050 it is estimated that another 4.21 billion people will have been born

How did we get here?

A lot has happened in the history of the universe – here are the highlights so far

How it works: We've charted key events since The Big Bang over a series of seven timelines.
Each timeline after the one on this page 'zooms in' on a section of the previous one, to look at a particular period in more depth

Sources: BBC, British Library, The Guardian, History, New Scientist, 'Social Development' by Ian Morris, Smithsonian National Museum of Natural History

THE LAST
**FOURTEEN
BILLION**
YEARS

The Big Bang

**The theoretical origin
of the universe
occurred around 13.8
billion years ago**

14   13   12   11   10   9

WHEN DID LIFE ON EARTH BEGIN?

The Earth was formed

Around 9.3 billion years after the 'Big Bang', gravity pulled together swirling gas and dust to form a hot, rocky planet

First organisms

Bacteria first appeared in the oceans between 3 and 4 billion years ago

First animals

Sea sponges were probably the planet's first animals to evolve, around 800 million years ago

Today

 8
 7
 6
 5
4
 3
 2
 1

BILLIONS OF YEARS AGO

WHEN DID THE DINOSAURS ARRIVE?

First animals

THE LAST
ONE BILLION
YEARS

1,000 — 900 — 800 — 700 — 600

WHEN DID OUR ANCESTORS EVOLVE?

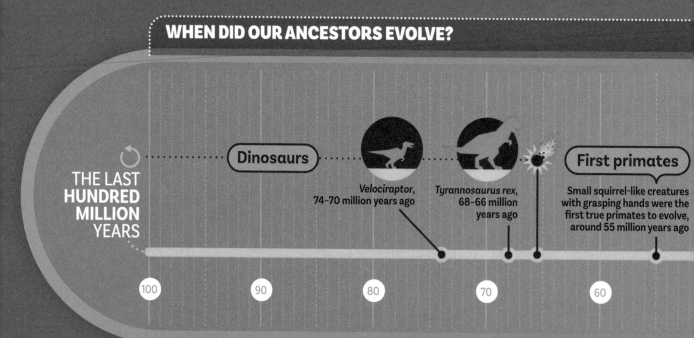

Dinosaurs

First primates

THE LAST
**HUNDRED
MILLION**
YEARS

Velociraptor,
74–70 million years ago

Tyrannosaurus rex,
68–66 million
years ago

Small squirrel-like creatures
with grasping hands were the
first true primates to evolve,
around 55 million years ago

100 — 90 — 80 — 70 — 60

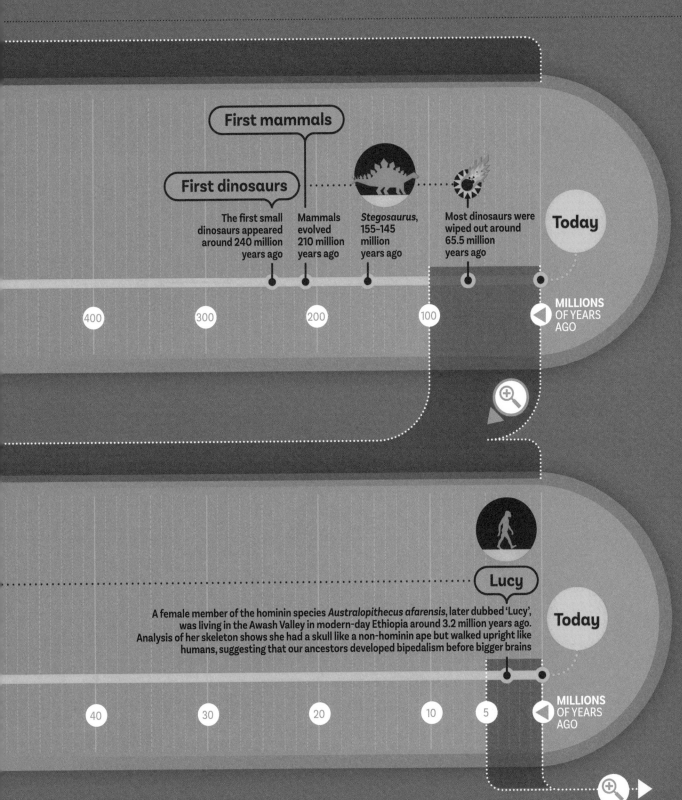

First mammals

First dinosaurs

The first small dinosaurs appeared around 240 million years ago

Mammals evolved 210 million years ago

Stegosaurus, 155–145 million years ago

Most dinosaurs were wiped out around 65.5 million years ago

Today

MILLIONS OF YEARS AGO

400 300 200 100

Lucy

A female member of the hominin species *Australopithecus afarensis*, later dubbed 'Lucy', was living in the Awash Valley in modern-day Ethiopia around 3.2 million years ago. Analysis of her skeleton shows she had a skull like a non-hominin ape but walked upright like humans, suggesting that our ancestors developed bipedalism before bigger brains

Today

MILLIONS OF YEARS AGO

40 30 20 10 5

WHEN DID *HOMO SAPIENS* ARRIVE?

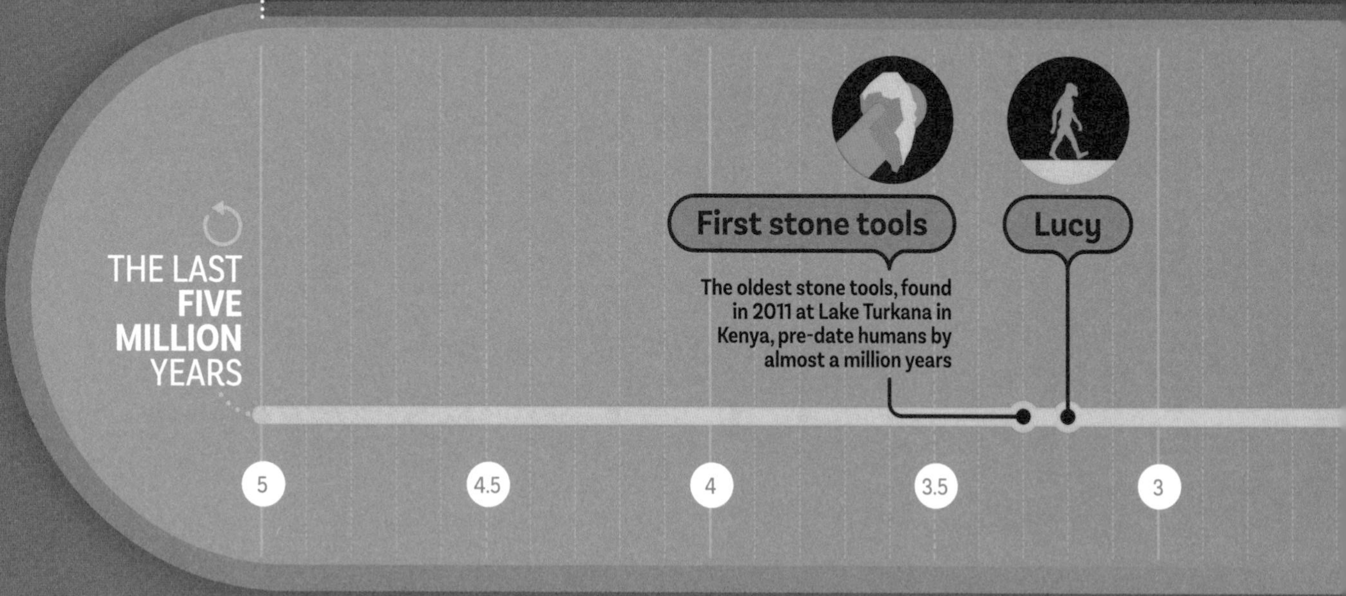

THE LAST **FIVE MILLION** YEARS

First stone tools

The oldest stone tools, found in 2011 at Lake Turkana in Kenya, pre-date humans by almost a million years

Lucy

5   4.5   4   3.5   3

WHEN DID WE TURN UP?

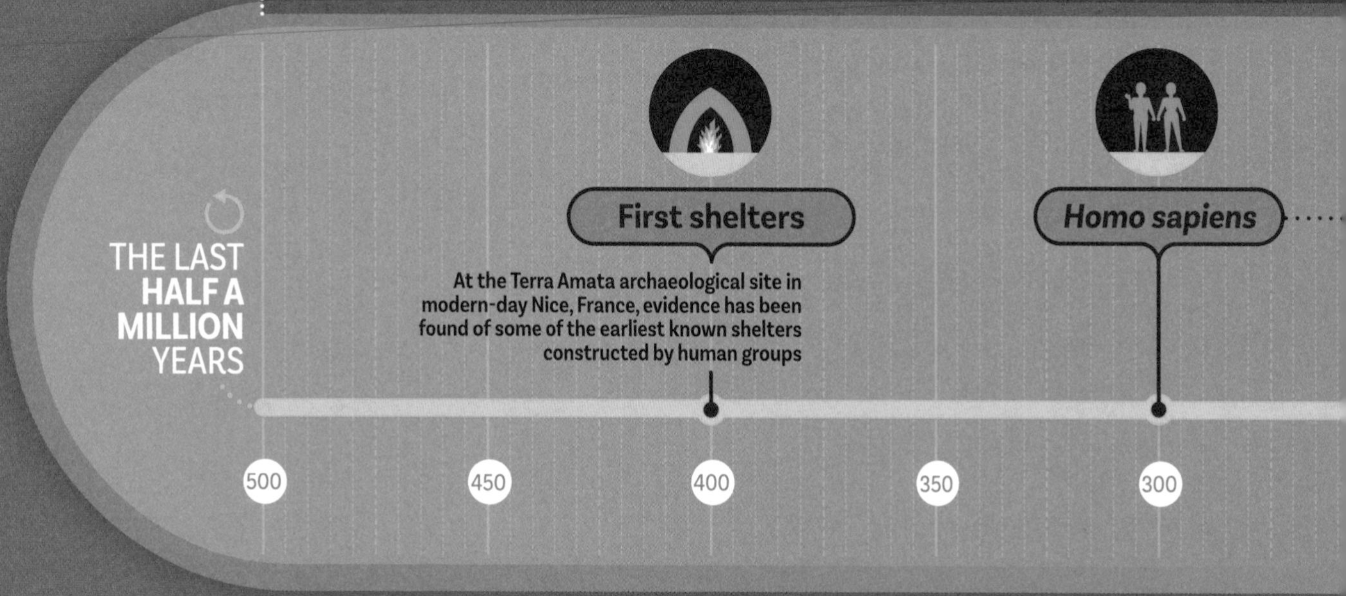

THE LAST **HALF A MILLION** YEARS

First shelters

At the Terra Amata archaeological site in modern-day Nice, France, evidence has been found of some of the earliest known shelters constructed by human groups

Homo sapiens

500   450   400   350   300

First humans

The earliest known humans, *Homo habilis*, lived between 2.4 and 1.4 million years ago

Other humans who arrived before us were:
Homo rudolfensis – 1.9 million to 1.8 million years ago
Homo erectus – 1.89 million to 110,000 years ago
Homo heidelbergensis – 700,000 to 200,000 years ago
Homo neanderthalensis – 400,000 to 40,000 years ago
Homo naledi – 335,000 to 236,000 years ago

Use of fire

Charred wood at the Gesher Benot Ya'aqov site in Israel is seen as evidence of controlled use of fire by humans

Homo sapiens

Fossil evidence of our own species has been found in Africa, dating back around 300,000 years

Today

2   **1.5**   **1**   **0.5**

MILLIONS OF YEARS AGO

Modern humans

It has been argued that recognisably 'modern' *Homo sapiens* emerged around 192,000 years ago

Other humans

Some species of human evolved later than us:
Homo longi – c. 146,000 years ago (under classification)
Homo floresiensis – 100,000 to 50,000 years ago
Homo luzonensis – 67,000 to 50,000 years ago

Today

200   **150**   **100**   **50**

THOUSANDS OF YEARS AGO

WHEN DID WE SETTLE DOWN?

Modern humans

↻
THE LAST
**TWO
HUNDRED
THOUSAND**
YEARS

Expanded diets

Evidence of *Homo sapiens* enlarging their diet by harvesting shellfish on the coast of Africa

Trade

The presence of materials in areas in which they do not naturally appear suggests that *Homo sapiens* were trading resources over substantial distances by this time

200   180   160   140   120

WHEN DID THE MODERN WORLD BEGIN?

Agriculture

↻
THE LAST
**TEN
THOUSAND**
YEARS

Çatalhöyük

First city

Around 9,000 years ago the proto-city of Çatalhöyük in Turkey had a population of around 1,000 people

Sumer

First urban civilisation

Humans settled in Sumer, between the Tigris and Euphrates rivers in Mesopotamia, modern-day Iraq. They initiated major elements of modern civilisation with innovations in architecture, government and agriculture

Writing

Cuneiform writing on clay tablets developed in Mesopotamia

10   9   8   7   6

Cave paintings

The oldest known cave painting, of a wild warty pig, was found on the Indonesian island of Sulawesi in 2017

Agriculture

The 'Neolithic revolution' 10-12,000 years ago saw humans begin raising crops and rearing animals. Farming is likely to have begun in the 'Fertile Crescent' covering modern-day Egypt, Syria, Palestine, Israel and Lebanon

Today

80 60 40 20

THOUSANDS OF YEARS AGO

The Iron Age

The Iron Age saw the replacement of bronze weapons and implements, which had dominated for the previous 2,000 years

The Industrial Revolution

Beginning in Britain in the mid 18th century, the Industrial Revolution ushered in machine manufacturing and triggered an explosion in the size of the human population

Today

4 3 2 1

THOUSANDS OF YEARS AGO

Vaccines
Edward Jenner founded modern vaccinology in 1796 by inoculating a 13-year-old boy with cowpox to protect him from smallpox

The refrigerator
The first vapour-compression refrigerator was patented in 1835 by US inventor Jacob Perkins

Photography
The exposure on the first photo – a view from the window of a French estate – took eight hours. As a result, the sun looks like it's shining on both sides of the building

The cotton gin
Used to separate cotton seeds and fibres

The combine harvester
Automated the reaping, threshing and winnowing of wheat

Electric batteries   Steam trains

Stephenson's *Rocket* locomotive

1780 • • • • • • • 1790 • • • • • • • 1800 • • • • • • • 1810 • • • • • • • 1820 • • • • • • • 1830 • • • • • • • 1840

What have we been
up to lately?

Humans have been busy in the 260 years since the beginning of the Industrial Revolution. Here are some of the best inventions they've created along the way

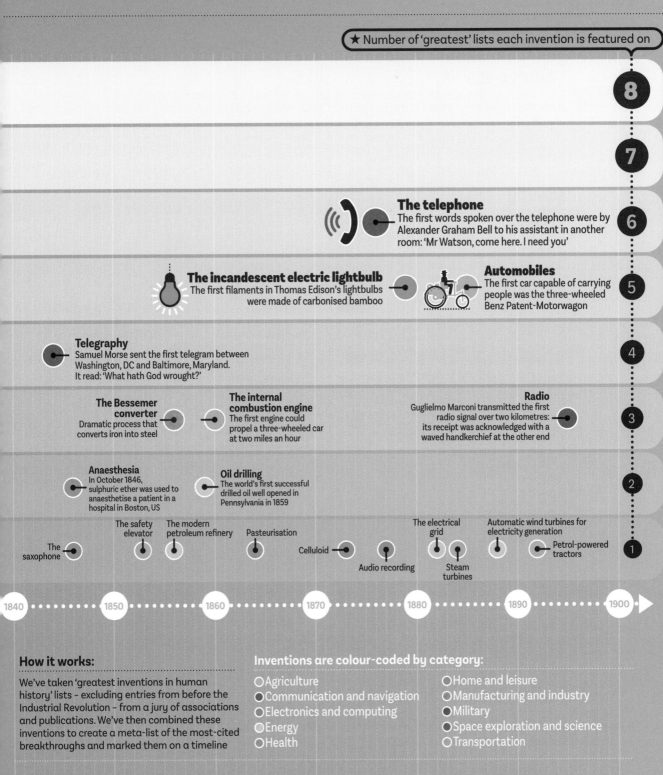

★ Number of 'greatest' lists each invention is featured on

8

7

6

The telephone
The first words spoken over the telephone were by Alexander Graham Bell to his assistant in another room: 'Mr Watson, come here. I need you'

5

The incandescent electric lightbulb
The first filaments in Thomas Edison's lightbulbs were made of carbonised bamboo

Automobiles
The first car capable of carrying people was the three-wheeled Benz Patent-Motorwagon

4

Telegraphy
Samuel Morse sent the first telegram between Washington, DC and Baltimore, Maryland. It read: 'What hath God wrought?'

3

The Bessemer converter
Dramatic process that converts iron into steel

The internal combustion engine
The first engine could propel a three-wheeled car at two miles an hour

Radio
Guglielmo Marconi transmitted the first radio signal over two kilometres: its receipt was acknowledged with a waved handkerchief at the other end

2

Anaesthesia
In October 1846, sulphuric ether was used to anaesthetise a patient in a hospital in Boston, US

Oil drilling
The world's first successful drilled oil well opened in Pennsylvania in 1859

1

The saxophone

The safety elevator

The modern petroleum refinery

Pasteurisation

Celluloid

Audio recording

The electrical grid

Steam turbines

Automatic wind turbines for electricity generation

Petrol-powered tractors

1840 ••••• 1850 ••••• 1860 ••••• 1870 ••••• 1880 ••••• 1890 ••••• 1900 ▶

How it works:

We've taken 'greatest inventions in human history' lists - excluding entries from before the Industrial Revolution - from a jury of associations and publications. We've then combined these inventions to create a meta-list of the most-cited breakthroughs and marked them on a timeline

Inventions are colour-coded by category:

○ Agriculture
○ Communication and navigation
○ Electronics and computing
○ Energy
○ Health

○ Home and leisure
○ Manufacturing and industry
○ Military
○ Space exploration and science
○ Transportation

★ **The jury:** The Atlantic, Big Think, Britannica, British Science Association, The History Channel, Inc. magazine, Interesting Engineering, Live Science, National Geographic, Ohio State University department of history, Popular Mechanics

Additional source: Time magazine

AIRPLANES
The Wright brothers tossed a coin to see who would test the Wright Flyer first: Wilbur won but his attempt failed, so it was his younger brother, Orville, who was the first human to fly a plane

What's the best thing ever invented?
(Since the Industrial Revolution)

Penicillin
'I did not invent penicillin. Nature did that. I only discovered it by accident,' said Alexander Fleming of the first true antibiotic

Television
Scottish inventor John Logie Baird broadcast footage of a ventriloquist's dummy called 'Stooky Bill' in his first demonstrations of his television

The nuclear reactor
The first nuclear reactor was built underneath the Stagg Field football stadium at the University of Chicago

ENIAC
The Electronic Numerical Integrator and Calculator was the forerunner of digital computers. It filled an 800-square-foot room

Liquid-fuelled rockets
American Robert Goddard launched the first liquid-fuelled rocket to a height of 41 feet in Auburn, Massachusetts

Nitrogen fixation
The process of converting nitrogen in the air into compounds for use in fertiliser

Air conditioning
Modern AC was invented by engineer Willis Haviland Carrier in 1902

Transistors
The creation of the transistor in 1947 won its three inventors the Nobel Prize in physics in 1956

Satellites
Sputnik became Earth's first artificial satellite on its launch on 4th October 1957

The Ford Model T car

Trainers

The jet engine

The DC-3 plane

The V-2 rocket

Barcodes

Credit cards

TV dinners

Container shipping

1900 • 1910 • 1920 • 1930 • 1940 • 1950 • 1960

What's the best thing since sliced bread?

7th July 1928
The first sale of bread that had been pre-cut with inventor Otto Frederick Rohwedder's automatic slicer. The slices were sold by the Chillicothe Baking Company in Missouri, US

Best things since sliced bread

The two inventions since the launch of sliced bread with the most inclusions on our jury's lists are **penicillin** and **the internet**. Penicillin only narrowly qualified for the title, having been isolated in September 1928, just two months after the advent of sliced bread

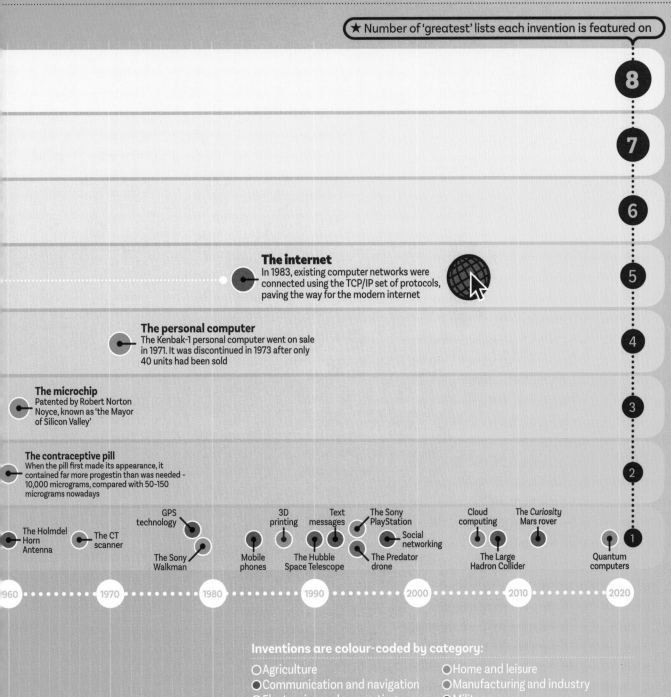

★ Number of 'greatest' lists each invention is featured on

8

7

6

5

The internet
In 1983, existing computer networks were
connected using the TCP/IP set of protocols,
paving the way for the modern internet

The personal computer
The Kenbak-1 personal computer went on sale
in 1971. It was discontinued in 1973 after only
40 units had been sold

4

The microchip
Patented by Robert Norton
Noyce, known as 'the Mayor
of Silicon Valley'

3

The contraceptive pill
When the pill first made its appearance, it
contained far more progestin than was needed –
10,000 micrograms, compared with 50-150
micrograms nowadays

2

GPS
technology

3D
printing

Text
messages

The Sony
PlayStation

Cloud
computing

The *Curiosity*
Mars rover

1

The Holmdel
Horn
Antenna

The CT
scanner

Mobile
phones

Social
networking

The Sony
Walkman

The Hubble
Space Telescope

The Predator
drone

The Large
Hadron Collider

Quantum
computers

1960   1970   1980   1990   2000   2010   2020

Inventions are colour-coded by category:

○ Agriculture
○ Communication and navigation
○ Electronics and computing
○ Energy
○ Health

○ Home and leisure
○ Manufacturing and industry
● Military
● Space exploration and science
○ Transportation

Where do babies come from?

In recent decades, the 'fertility rate' – the average number of children born to each woman during her reproductive years – has fallen dramatically. In many countries it now sits below the average 'replacement level' of 2.1 children per woman needed to keep populations stable

How it works: The map highlights countries and territories with a fertility rate at or above the 'replacement level' of 2.1, the average amount required for 'populations with low mortality' to have a growth rate of zero in the long run according to the UN's 'World Fertility and Family Planning 2020' report

Source: 'Global age-sex-specific fertility, mortality, healthy life expectancy (HALE), and population estimates in 204 countries and territories, 1950-2019: a comprehensive demographic analysis for the Global Burden of Disease Study 2019' published in The Lancet. ■ Grey areas represent countries where no data available

NORTH
AMERICA

SOUTH
AMERICA

Making babies at a sustainable rate
Countries and territories in which average number of children born to each woman is at or above 2.1 – the 'replacement level' at which population numbers remain stable

Not making babies at a sustainable rate
Countries and territories in which average number of children born to each woman is less than 2.1, meaning that in the absence of immigration, population levels will fall

How many babies are being born?
About 385,000 babies are born each day according to the UN. That adds up to more than 140 million a year

EUROPE

ASIA

AFRICA

OCEANIA

TOP FIVE
FERTILITY RATES

Niger 7.44	A	▲ HIGHEST
Chad 6.87	B	
Somalia 6.36	C	
Mali 6.04	D	
Burundi 5.63	E	

BOTTOM FIVE
FERTILITY RATES

V	1.16 Singapore
W	1.14 United Arab Emirates
X	1.13 **Andorra**
Y	1.10 **Puerto Rico**
Z	1.06 **Taiwan**

LOWEST ▼

What's a good innings?

How long can a member of *Homo sapiens* reasonably expect to live – and how does that compare to the longevity of members of the animal kingdom?

How it works: We've researched the oldest known member of different animal species and plotted them out across a 510-year timeline

Oldest cat
38 years, 3 days
Lifespan of **Creme Puff**, the longest-lived cat on record, who lived with a family in Austin, Texas, 1967–2005

40

Oldest spider
43 years
Age of **Number 16**, a wild female trapdoor spider that lived in North Bungulla Reserve, Australia, 1974–2018

Oldest dog
29 years, 5 months
Lifespan of **Bluey**, an Australian cattle dog from Victoria, Australia, the longest-lived dog on record, 1910–1939

Oldest mouse
7 years, 7 months
Fritzy, the longest-lived caged mouse on record, who lived with a family in Edgbaston, UK, 1977–1985

Oldest rabbit
18 years, 10 months
Lifespan of **Flopsy**, the longest-lived rabbit on record, from Tasmania, Australia, caught in 1964

YEARS

20

30

Oldest cow
48 years, 9 months
Lifespan of **Big Bertha**, the longest-lived cow on record, who lived in County Kerry, Ireland, 1945–1993

10

Oldest goat
22 years, 5 months
Lifespan of **McGinty**, the longest-lived goat on record, who lived in Hayling Island, UK, until her death in 2003

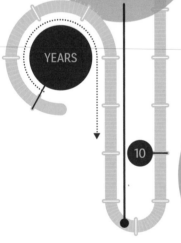

50.75
Current average life expectancy of people born in **Lesotho**, the lowest in the world

50

Sources: Guinness World Records, PRB, RSPCA, UN, WHO

70

Oldest hippopotamus
65 years
Estimated lifespan of **Bertha**, the oldest resident of Manila Zoo, Philippines, 1952–2017

73
Current global average human life expectancy

Oldest Andean condor
79 years
Lifespan of **Thaao**, a condor who died at the Beardsley Zoo in Bridgeport, Connecticut, US, in 2010

How old was the oldest person?
122 years, 164 days
Jeanne Louise Calment, (21st February 1875–4th August 1997) from Arles in France is the oldest human known to have lived

100

110

Oldest horse
62 years
Lifespan of **Old Billy**, a horse bred in Woolston, Lancashire, UK, 1760–1822

60

80

Oldest bird
82 years, 89 days
Lifespan of **Cookie**, a Major Mitchell's cockatoo and officially the longest-lived bird on record, who lived in the US, 1933–2016

120

84.26
Current average life expectancy of people born in **Japan**, the highest in the world

Oldest donkey
54 years
Lifespan of **Suzy**, the longest-lived donkey on record, who lived in New Mexico, US, 1948–2002

Oldest elephant
88 years
Dakshayani, thought to be the world's oldest elephant in captivity, died in 2019 in Kerala, India

90

350

500

Oldest mammal
200 years
Estimated oldest age of a bowhead whale

200

150

300

Oldest crocodile
140 years
Estimated age of **Mr Freshie**, a freshwater crocodile living in Queensland, Australia, 1870–2010

Oldest tortoise
188+ years
Tu'i Malila, a Madagascar radiated tortoise, who lived with the royal family of Tonga from 1777–1965, is the longest-lived chelonian (a family including turtles, terrapins and tortoises) on record

How old was the oldest animal?
507 years
A quahog clam named **'Hafrún'**, living on the seabed off Iceland's north coast, is the oldest animal ever recorded. Believed to have been spawned in 1499, he was reportedly accidentally killed by the scientists who discovered him in 2006

Oldest vertebrate
400 years
Estimated age of oldest known Greenland shark

250

400

450

Do you want to live like common people?

We've tracked some of the most frequently observed characteristics of the planet's 7,860,000,000 humans

What's the commonest age to be?

33.3%

are aged under 20

The next commonest age group is 20-39 (30%), followed by 40-59 (23.2%). Only 1.9% are aged 80-99 and 0.01% are over 100

Which hemisphere are people commonly from?

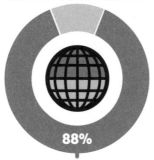

88%

live in the northern hemisphere

A mere 12% of the planet's human population lives in the southern hemisphere

Which continent are people commonly from?

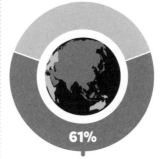

61%

live in Asia

The next most populous continents are Africa (17%), Europe (10%), Latin America and the Caribbean (8%), and North America and Oceania (5%)

Where do people most commonly live?

55.7%

live in towns and cities

The world has become urbanised: just 44.3% of humans live in the countryside

What's the commonest socio-economic group?

49.5%

are 'middle class'

'Middle class' is defined by World Data Lab using criteria including discretionary income. 43.6% of people are 'financially vulnerable', 4.1% are 'poor' and 2.8% are 'rich'

What's the commonest native language?

最近好吗？

12.3%

speak Mandarin Chinese as their first language

Other linguistic big hitters include Spanish (6%), Arabic and English (both at 5.1%), Hindi (3.5%), Bengali (3.3%) and Portuguese (3%)

What's the commonest body mass?

52%

are a healthy weight (with a BMI of 18.5 to 25)

UN research shows that 39.1% of humans are overweight (BMI of 25+), including 13.2% defined as obese (BMI of 30+), and that 8.9% are underweight (BMI of 18.5 or less)

What's the commonest eye colour?

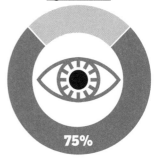

75%

have brown eyes

While brown eyes dominate, human peepers also come in blue (10%), amber (5%), hazel (5%), grey (3%) and green (2%)

How it works: The charts around each illustration show a proportionate representation of the most common response to each question

Sources: CIA World Factbook, UN, Washington Post, World Atlas, World Data Lab

WHO'S THE GREATEST

Questions about sport, cities
and superstructures

Who's the greatest sportsperson of all time?

When it comes to identifying the greatest sportsperson of all time, every fan has an opinion – but who's right? Let's let the data decide

How it works: As our starting point, we took impressionistic 'greatest of all time' lists from sports writers and publications. These ranked athletes from the Olympics and Paralympics as well as cricket, golf, tennis, boxing, Formula 1 and football (the most Googled sports in the UK 2015–2020). If the list was mixed-sex we took the five highest ranked male and female athletes. If not, we took the top five from separate 'best male' and 'best female' lists. We then ranked our shortlisted competitors from 1 to 10 over seven statistical fields. The sportsperson who ranked highest across all fields was judged the greatest and is illustrated on a podium. Press deadlines meant it was not possible to include all of 2021's sporting tournaments including the Tokyo Games, so we took statistics for all sports as of 31st December 2020

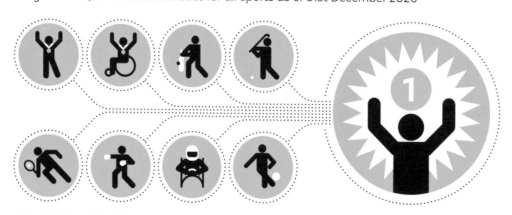

Who's the greatest Olympian of all time?

Over 187,000 athletes have competed at the Olympic Games since 1896;
ten have made their way into this playoff, and only one can be the best of them all

The contenders

NBC's greatest female Olympians of all time
NBC's greatest male Olympians of all time

| 5th | 4th | 3rd | 2nd | 1st | 5th | 4th | 3rd | 2nd | 1st |

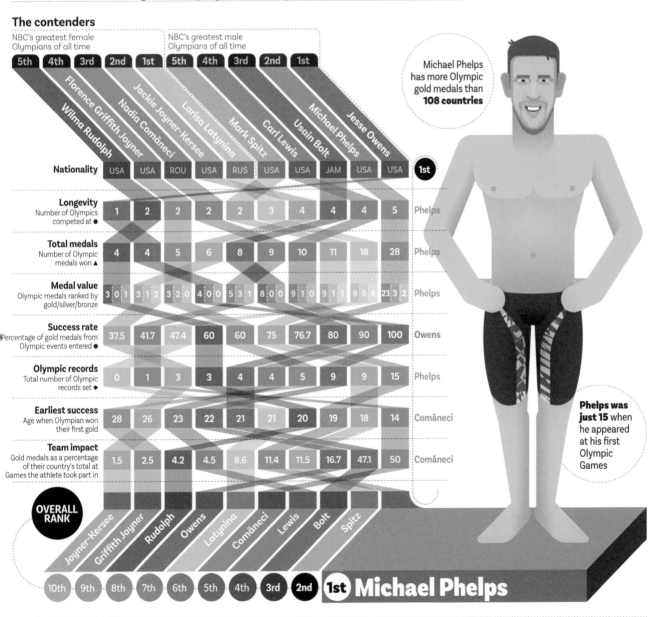

Michael Phelps has more Olympic gold medals than **108 countries**

	Wilma Rudolph	Florence Griffith Joyner	Nadia Comăneci	Jackie Joyner-Kersee	Larisa Latynina	Mark Spitz	Carl Lewis	Usain Bolt	Michael Phelps	Jesse Owens	
Nationality	USA	USA	ROU	USA	RUS	USA	USA	JAM	USA	USA	1st
Longevity Number of Olympics competed at ●	1	2	2	2	2	3	4	4	4	5	Phelps
Total medals Number of Olympic medals won ▲	4	4	5	6	8	9	10	11	18	28	Phelps
Medal value Olympic medals ranked by gold/silver/bronze	3 0 1	3 1 2	3 2 0	4 0 0	5 3 1	8 0 0	9 1 0	9 1 1	9 5 4	23 3 2	Phelps
Success rate Percentage of gold medals from Olympic events entered ●	37.5	41.7	47.4	60	60	75	76.7	80	90	100	Owens
Olympic records Total number of Olympic records set ◆	0	1	3	3	4	4	5	9	9	15	Phelps
Earliest success Age when Olympian won their first gold	28	26	23	22	21	21	20	19	18	14	Comăneci
Team impact Gold medals as a percentage of their country's total at Games the athlete took part in	1.5	2.5	4.2	4.5	8.6	11.4	11.5	16.7	47.1	50	Comăneci

OVERALL RANK

Joyner-Kersee	Griffith Joyner	Rudolph	Owens	Latynina	Comăneci	Lewis	Bolt	Spitz	
10th	9th	8th	7th	6th	5th	4th	3rd	2nd	**1st Michael Phelps**

Phelps was just 15 when he appeared at his first Olympic Games

● In the case of a tie, the Olympian who competed in the most separate events is ranked higher. If there is still a tie then the points are split but the Olympian with the most medals is listed higher for illustration purposes ▲ If total medals are tied then points are split and athlete with more golds is listed higher ◆ If tied, the athlete whose Olympic records were also world records ranks higher. Due to the nature of the sport, Olympic records are not set in gymnastics, but Nadia Comăneci was the first gymnast to receive a perfect score at an Olympic Games, which we've counted as a record

Who's the greatest Paralympian of all time?

The Paralympics started over 60 years ago and have featured some extraordinary athletes. We take a dive into the data to award our own gold medal

The contenders

Pledge Sports' greatest female Paralympians of all time

Pledge Sports' greatest male Paralympians of all time

At the 1988 Seoul Games Trischa Zorn won **ten gold medals** and set eight world records

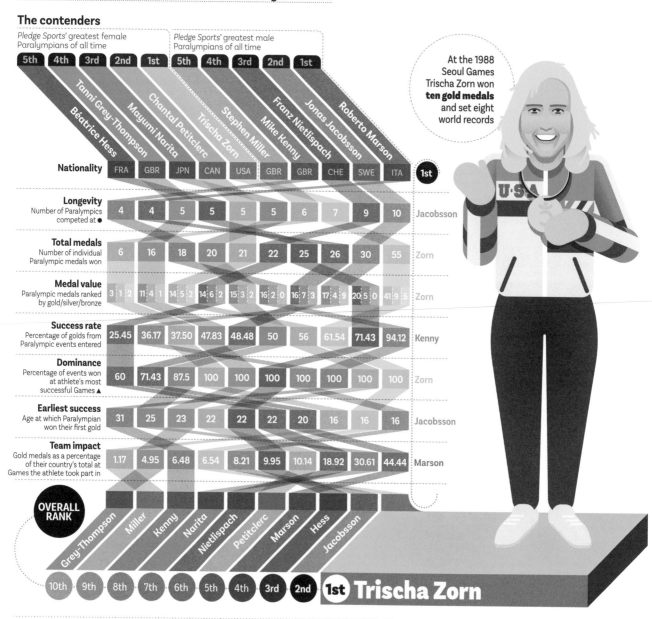

	5th	4th	3rd	2nd	1st	5th	4th	3rd	2nd	1st	1st
	Béatrice Hess	Tanni Grey-Thompson	Mayumi Narita	Chantal Petitclerc	Trischa Zorn	Stephen Miller	Mike Kenny	Franz Nietlispach	Jonas Jacobsson	Roberto Marson	
Nationality	FRA	GBR	JPN	CAN	USA	GBR	GBR	CHE	SWE	ITA	
Longevity Number of Paralympics competed at ●	4	4	5	5	5	5	6	7	9	10	Jacobsson
Total medals Number of individual Paralympic medals won	6	16	18	20	21	22	25	26	30	55	Zorn
Medal value Paralympic medals ranked by gold/silver/bronze	3 1 2	11 4 1	14 5 2	14 6 2	15 3 2	16 2 0	16 7 3	17 4 9	20 5 0	41 9 5	Zorn
Success rate Percentage of golds from Paralympic events entered	25.45	36.17	37.50	47.83	48.48	50	56	61.54	71.43	94.12	Kenny
Dominance Percentage of events won at athlete's most successful Games ▲	60	71.43	87.5	100	100	100	100	100	100	100	Zorn
Earliest success Age at which Paralympian won their first gold	31	25	23	22	22	22	20	16	16	16	Jacobsson
Team impact Gold medals as a percentage of their country's total at Games the athlete took part in	1.17	4.95	6.48	6.54	8.21	9.95	10.14	18.92	30.61	44.44	Marson

OVERALL RANK

Grey-Thompson	Miller	Kenny	Narita	Nietlispach	Petitclerc	Marson	Hess	Jacobsson
10th	9th	8th	7th	6th	5th	4th	3rd	2nd

1st Trischa Zorn

● In the case of a tie the Paralympian who competed in the most separate events is ranked higher. If there is still a tie then the points are split but the Paralympian with the most medals is listed higher for illustration purposes ▲ In the case of a tie the athlete who competed at the most events at their most successful Games ranks higher

Who's the greatest cricketer of all time?

We've picked categories reflecting longevity, success and personal prowess across batting, bowling and fielding to compare titans of cricket and pick a winner

The contenders

GMS's greatest female cricketers of all time

The BBC's greatest male cricketers of all time

Garfield Sobers held the **highest test innings record** for 36 years – 365 not out

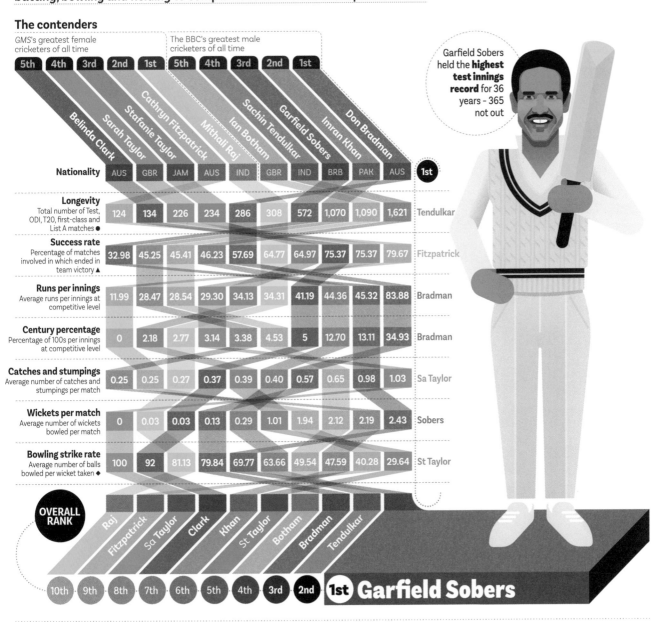

	5th Belinda Clark	**4th** Sarah Taylor	**3rd** Stafanie Taylor	**2nd** Cathryn Fitzpatrick	**1st** Mithali Raj	**5th** Ian Botham	**4th** Sachin Tendulkar	**3rd** Garfield Sobers	**2nd** Imran Khan	**1st** Don Bradman	1st
Nationality	AUS	GBR	JAM	AUS	IND	GBR	IND	BRB	PAK	AUS	
Longevity Total number of Test, ODI, T20, first-class and List A matches ●	124	134	226	234	286	308	572	1,070	1,090	1,621	Tendulkar
Success rate Percentage of matches involved in which ended in team victory ▲	32.98	45.25	45.41	46.23	57.69	64.77	64.97	75.37	75.37	79.67	Fitzpatrick
Runs per innings Average runs per innings at competitive level	11.99	28.47	28.54	29.30	34.13	34.31	41.19	44.36	45.32	83.88	Bradman
Century percentage Percentage of 100s per innings at competitive level	0	2.18	2.77	3.14	3.38	4.53	5	12.70	13.11	34.93	Bradman
Catches and stumpings Average number of catches and stumpings per match	0.25	0.25	0.27	0.37	0.39	0.40	0.57	0.65	0.98	1.03	Sa Taylor
Wickets per match Average number of wickets bowled per match	0	0.03	0.03	0.13	0.29	1.01	1.94	2.12	2.19	2.43	Sobers
Bowling strike rate Average number of balls bowled per wicket taken ◆	100	92	81.13	79.84	69.77	63.66	49.54	47.59	40.28	29.64	St Taylor

OVERALL RANK

Raj	Fitzpatrick	Sa Taylor	Clark	Khan	St Taylor	Botham	Bradman	Tendulkar	
10th	9th	8th	7th	6th	5th	4th	3rd	2nd	**1st** Garfield Sobers

While scores are only shown to two decimal places, rankings reflect the full figures ● We decided to total all matches as not all of the shortlisted cricketers had the same opportunities to play every version (the women's game favours one-day formats, the men's leans towards Tests and T20 cricket wasn't introduced until 2003) ▲ In the case of a tie, the player with the most wins overall ranks higher ◆ Players with fewer than 50 wickets are penalised with 20 points, players with fewer than ten wickets by 50 and players who haven't taken a wicket by 100.

Who's the greatest golfer of all time?

Since the first Open Championship in 1860, golf has produced a torrent of data: we've put it to work to find the best swinger in history

The contenders

Golf Monthly's greatest female golfers of all time

Golf News' greatest male golfers of all time

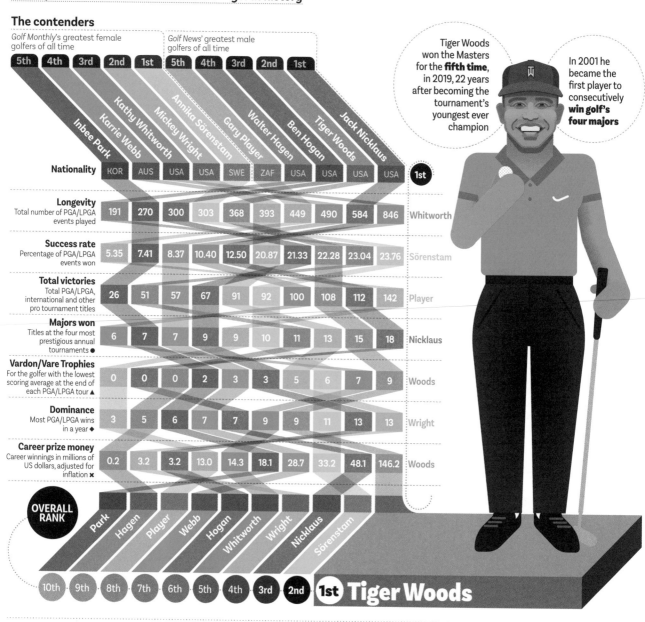

Metric	Inbee Park (5th)	Karrie Webb (4th)	Kathy Whitworth (3rd)	Mickey Wright (2nd)	Annika Sörenstam (1st)	Gary Player (5th)	Walter Hagen (4th)	Ben Hogan (3rd)	Tiger Woods (2nd)	Jack Nicklaus (1st)	Leader
Nationality	KOR	AUS	USA	USA	SWE	ZAF	USA	USA	USA	USA	1st
Longevity — Total number of PGA/LPGA events played	191	270	300	303	368	393	449	490	584	846	Whitworth
Success rate — Percentage of PGA/LPGA events won	5.35	7.41	8.37	10.40	12.50	20.87	21.33	22.28	23.04	23.76	Sörenstam
Total victories — Total PGA/LPGA, international and other pro tournament titles	26	51	57	67	91	92	100	108	112	142	Player
Majors won — Titles at the four most prestigious annual tournaments ●	6	7	7	9	9	10	11	13	15	18	Nicklaus
Vardon/Vare Trophies — For the golfer with the lowest scoring average at the end of each PGA/LPGA tour ▲	0	0	0	2	3	3	5	6	7	9	Woods
Dominance — Most PGA/LPGA wins in a year ◆	3	5	6	7	7	9	9	11	13	13	Wright
Career prize money — Career winnings in millions of US dollars, adjusted for inflation ✖	0.2	3.2	3.2	13.0	14.3	18.1	28.7	33.2	48.1	146.2	Woods

OVERALL RANK

10th	9th	8th	7th	6th	5th	4th	3rd	2nd	1st
Park	Hagen	Player	Webb	Hogan	Whitworth	Wright	Nicklaus	Sörenstam	Tiger Woods

Tiger Woods won the Masters for the **fifth time**, in 2019, 22 years after becoming the tournament's youngest ever champion

In 2001 he became the first player to consecutively **win golf's four majors**

● In the case of a tie, points are split and players are listed by total tournament wins for illustration purposes ▲ In the case of a tie, points are split and the player with the most major wins is listed first ◆ In the case of a tie, the player with the most wins in that year's majors ranks higher ✖ To make comparisons between career prize money fair we took the median year between a player's first and last major, and adjusted it for inflation from that year

Who's the greatest tennis player of all time?

Racket-wielding greats from across the generations face off for the ultimate Grand Slam. Who's smashing it?

The contenders

The Guardian's greatest female tennis players of all time ●

The Guardian's greatest male tennis players of all time ●

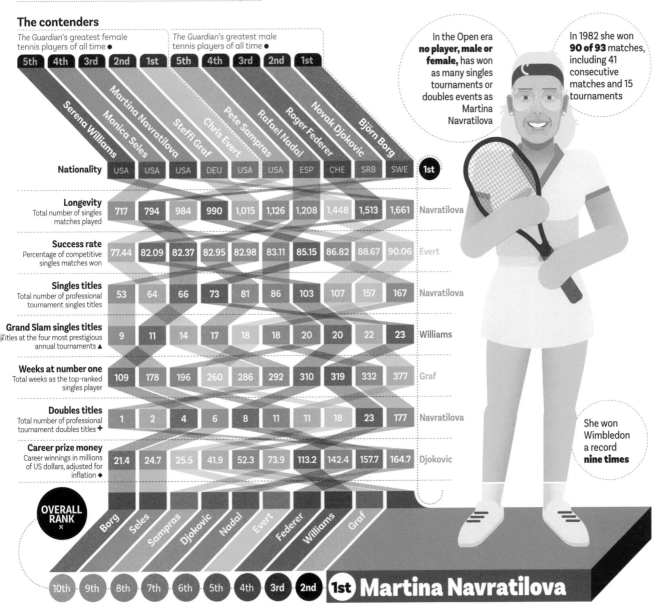

In the Open era **no player, male or female,** has won as many singles tournaments or doubles events as Martina Navratilova

In 1982 she won **90 of 93** matches, including 41 consecutive matches and 15 tournaments

She won Wimbledon a record **nine times**

	Serena Williams	Monica Seles	Martina Navratilova	Steffi Graf	Chris Evert	Pete Sampras	Rafael Nadal	Roger Federer	Novak Djokovic	Björn Borg	1st
	5th	4th	3rd	2nd	1st	5th	4th	3rd	2nd	1st	
Nationality	USA	USA	USA	DEU	USA	USA	ESP	CHE	SRB	SWE	
Longevity Total number of singles matches played	717	794	984	990	1,015	1,126	1,208	1,448	1,513	1,661	Navratilova
Success rate Percentage of competitive singles matches won	77.44	82.09	82.37	82.95	82.98	83.11	85.15	86.82	88.67	90.06	Evert
Singles titles Total number of professional tournament singles titles	53	64	66	73	81	86	103	107	157	167	Navratilova
Grand Slam singles titles Titles at the four most prestigious annual tournaments ▲	9	11	14	17	18	18	20	20	22	23	Williams
Weeks at number one Total weeks as the top-ranked singles player	109	178	196	260	286	292	310	319	332	377	Graf
Doubles titles Total number of professional tournament doubles titles +	1	2	4	6	8	11	11	18	23	177	Navratilova
Career prize money Career winnings in millions of US dollars, adjusted for inflation ◆	21.4	24.7	25.5	41.9	52.3	73.9	113.2	142.4	157.7	164.7	Djokovic

OVERALL RANK ✕

Borg	Seles	Sampras	Djokovic	Nadal	Evert	Federer	Williams	Graf	
10th	9th	8th	7th	6th	5th	4th	3rd	2nd	**1st Martina Navratilova**

● As *The Guardian*'s top five lists are unranked, contenders are ordered alphabetically ▲ If two players have equal numbers of Grand Slam wins, the player with the most Grand Slam finals appearances ranks higher + If number of doubles titles is tied, player with most doubles Grand Slam titles ranks higher ◆ To make comparisons between career prize money fair we took the median year between a player's first and last professional singles match, and adjusted it for inflation from that year ✕ Federer and Evert have the same aggregate score. As the player with the most Grand Slam titles, Federer ranks higher

Who's the greatest boxer of all time?

The finest male and female fighters who ever lived take to the ring and go toe-to-toe over seven rounds of statistics

The contenders

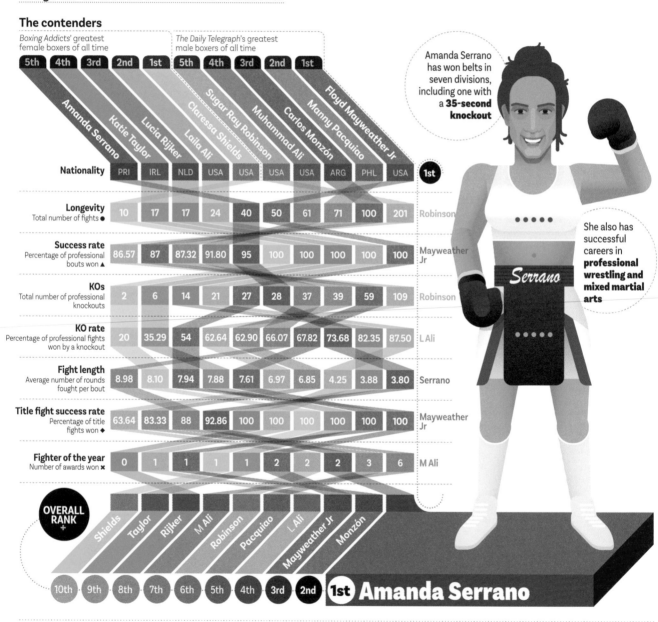

Boxing Addicts' greatest female boxers of all time

The Daily Telegraph's greatest male boxers of all time

	5th	4th	3rd	2nd	1st	5th	4th	3rd	2nd	1st	
	Amanda Serrano	Katie Taylor	Lucia Rijker	Laila Ali	Claressa Shields	Sugar Ray Robinson	Muhammad Ali	Carlos Monzón	Manny Pacquiao	Floyd Mayweather Jr	
Nationality	PRI	IRL	NLD	USA	USA	USA	USA	ARG	PHL	USA	**1st**
Longevity Total number of fights ●	10	17	17	24	40	50	61	71	100	201	Robinson
Success rate Percentage of professional bouts won ▲	86.57	87	87.32	91.80	95	100	100	100	100	100	Mayweather Jr
KOs Total number of professional knockouts	2	6	14	21	27	28	37	39	59	109	Robinson
KO rate Percentage of professional fights won by a knockout	20	35.29	54	62.64	62.90	66.07	67.82	73.68	82.35	87.50	L Ali
Fight length Average number of rounds fought per bout	8.98	8.10	7.94	7.88	7.61	6.97	6.85	4.25	3.88	3.80	Serrano
Title fight success rate Percentage of title fights won ◆	63.64	83.33	88	92.86	100	100	100	100	100	100	Mayweather Jr
Fighter of the year Number of awards won ✖	0	1	1	1	1	2	2	2	3	6	M Ali

OVERALL RANK ✚

Shields	Taylor	Rijker	M Ali	Robinson	Pacquiao	L Ali	Mayweather Jr	Monzón	
10th	9th	8th	7th	6th	5th	4th	3rd	2nd	**1st Amanda Serrano**

Amanda Serrano has won belts in seven divisions, including one with a **35-second knockout**

She also has successful careers in **professional wrestling and mixed martial arts**

● In the case of a tie, points are split. The boxer with the most rounds is listed higher for illustration purposes ▲ If tied, boxers are ranked in order of number of fights
◆ If tied, boxers are ranked in order of their number of title fights ✖ 'Fighter of the Year' is annual awards by *The Ring* (men's boxing) and WBAN (women's boxing).
If tied, boxers are ranked in order of 'Fight of the Year' awards. ✚ Mayweather Jr and Laila Ali have the same aggregate score. As the fighter with the most titles, Mayweather Jr ranks higher

Who's the greatest Formula 1 driver of all time?

The all-male shortlist – despite being a mixed-sex sport, only five female drivers have competed in an F1 race, none of them winning – compete for pole position

The contenders

Top Gear's greatest Formula 1 drivers of all time

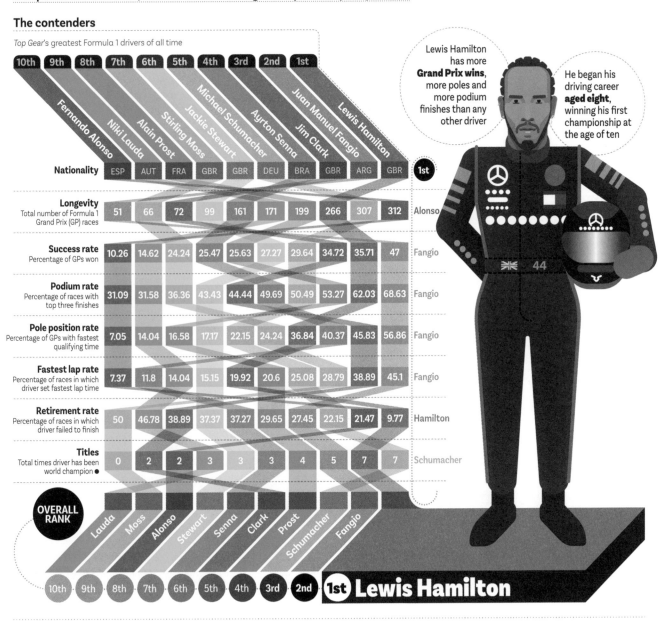

Lewis Hamilton has more **Grand Prix wins**, more poles and more podium finishes than any other driver

He began his driving career **aged eight**, winning his first championship at the age of ten

	10th Fernando Alonso	9th Niki Lauda	8th Alain Prost	7th Stirling Moss	6th Jackie Stewart	5th Michael Schumacher	4th Ayrton Senna	3rd Jim Clark	2nd Juan Manuel Fangio	1st Lewis Hamilton	
Nationality	ESP	AUT	FRA	GBR	GBR	DEU	BRA	GBR	ARG	GBR	1st Alonso
Longevity Total number of Formula 1 Grand Prix (GP) races	51	66	72	99	161	171	199	266	307	312	Alonso
Success rate Percentage of GPs won	10.26	14.62	24.24	25.47	25.63	27.27	29.64	34.72	35.71	47	Fangio
Podium rate Percentage of races with top three finishes	31.09	31.58	36.36	43.43	44.44	49.69	50.49	53.27	62.03	68.63	Fangio
Pole position rate Percentage of GPs with fastest qualifying time	7.05	14.04	16.58	17.17	22.15	24.24	36.84	40.37	45.83	56.86	Fangio
Fastest lap rate Percentage of races in which driver set fastest lap time	7.37	11.8	14.04	15.15	19.92	20.6	25.08	28.79	38.89	45.1	Fangio
Retirement rate Percentage of races in which driver failed to finish	50	46.78	38.89	37.37	37.27	29.65	27.45	22.15	21.47	9.77	Hamilton
Titles Total times driver has been world champion ●	0	2	2	3	3	3	4	5	7	7	Schumacher

OVERALL RANK

Lauda · Moss · Alonso · Stewart · Senna · Clark · Prost · Schumacher · Fangio

10th · 9th · 8th · 7th · 6th · 5th · 4th · 3rd · 2nd · **1st Lewis Hamilton**

● If drivers are tied on the number of championship wins, we rank them in order of the number of times they finished runner-up, in third place, fourth place etc

Who's the greatest football player of all time?

Superstars of the most-watched sport in the world, these players are global icons. But who gets to be crowned history's greatest? It's all about to kick off

The contenders

Bleacher Report's greatest female footballers of all time — 5th, 4th, 3rd, 2nd, 1st

FourFourTwo's greatest male footballers of all time — 5th, 4th, 3rd, 2nd, 1st

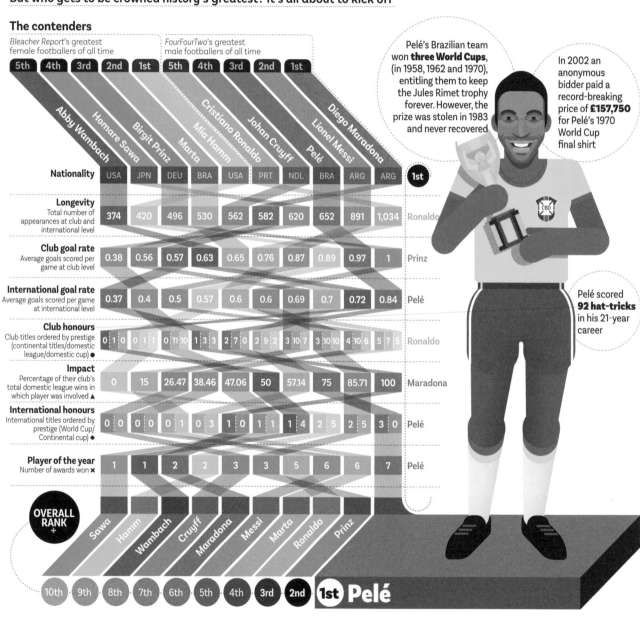

	Abby Wambach	Homare Sawa	Birgit Prinz	Marta	Mia Hamm	Cristiano Ronaldo	Johan Cruyff	Pelé	Lionel Messi	Diego Maradona	1st
Nationality	USA	JPN	DEU	BRA	USA	PRT	NDL	BRA	ARG	ARG	1st
Longevity Total number of appearances at club and international level	374	420	496	530	562	582	620	652	891	1,034	Ronaldo
Club goal rate Average goals scored per game at club level	0.38	0.56	0.57	0.63	0.65	0.76	0.87	0.89	0.97	1	Prinz
International goal rate Average goals scored per game at international level	0.37	0.4	0.5	0.57	0.6	0.6	0.69	0.7	0.72	0.84	Pelé
Club honours Club titles ordered by prestige (continental titles/domestic league/domestic cup) ●	0 1 0	0 1 1	0 1 10	1 3 3	2 7 0	2 9 2	3 10 7	3 10 10	4 10 6	5 7 5	Ronaldo
Impact Percentage of their club's total domestic league wins in which player was involved ▲	0	15	26.47	38.46	47.06	50	57.14	75	85.71	100	Maradona
International honours International titles ordered by prestige (World Cup/Continental cup) ◆	0 0	0 0	0 1	0 3	1 0	1 1	1 4	2 5	2 5	3 0	Pelé
Player of the year Number of awards won ✖	1	1	2	2	3	3	5	6	6	7	Pelé
OVERALL RANK ✚	Sawa	Hamm	Wambach	Cruyff	Maradona	Messi	Marta	Ronaldo	Prinz		
	10th	9th	8th	7th	6th	5th	4th	3rd	2nd	1st Pelé	

Pelé's Brazilian team won **three World Cups**, (in 1958, 1962 and 1970), entitling them to keep the Jules Rimet trophy forever. However, the prize was stolen in 1983 and never recovered

In 2002 an anonymous bidder paid a record-breaking price of **£157,750** for Pelé's 1970 World Cup final shirt

Pelé scored **92 hat-tricks** in his 21-year career

● Ranked by continental titles (eg UEFA Champions League), domestic league titles (eg La Liga) and domestic cup wins (eg Copa del Rey) ▲ With the club at which player won most domestic league titles
◆ Ranked by World Cup and continental cup titles (eg the UEFA European Championship). In the case of a tie, players are ranked in order of number of times as WC runner-up, CC runner-up, etc
✖ Men = Ballon d'Or wins. Although limited to European players until 1995, winners were recalculated in 2016 to retrospectively include non-European players. Women = FIFA World Player of the Year Award winners.
If tied, player with most second place finishes ranks higher ✚ Cruyff and Wambach have same aggregate score. As the player with the most domestic and international titles, Cruyff ranks higher

Who's the greatest of them all?

We pit the athletes with the highest aggregate rating in each sport against one another to find the best of the best (of the best)

1st

Michael Phelps

Born: **30th June 1985, Baltimore, US**

When it comes to the greatest there was one definitive winner – Michael Phelps. His 23 Olympic gold medals over five Games proved both his dominance and longevity at the very highest level – he's a winner that almost everyone can agree on.

2nd

Pelé

Born: **23rd October 1940, Três Corações, Brazil**

The debate around the best footballer ever is fierce, but the data herald a clear winner. Pelé's three World Cup medals and 1,279 goals in 1,363 games (not including his late equaliser in *Escape to Victory*) sees him secure second place on our all-time list.

3rd

Trischa Zorn

Born: **1st June 1964, Orange, US**

Zorn is the most successful Paralympic athlete of all time. The swimmer, who has been blind since birth, competed in seven Paralympics, taking home 12 gold medals from Seoul in 1988 and collecting a total of 55 medals overall.

4th

Martina Navratilova

Born: **18th October 1956, Prague, Czechoslovakia**

Few will ever dominate their sport like Navratilova. During her career she won 344 titles and spent over six years ranked world number one.

5th

Tiger Woods

Born: **30th December 1975, Cypress, US**

From winning the Masters at 21 to wearing the green jacket after his 2019 comeback, Woods' golfing supremacy is likely never to be repeated.

6th

Lewis Hamilton

Born: **7th January 1985, Stevenage, UK**

Hamilton has broken virtually every Formula 1 record going and has time on his side to set the benchmarks unreachably high.

7th

Garfield Sobers

Born: **28th July 1936, Bridgetown, Barbados**

The West Indies captain and all-rounder played with a free-flowing, aggressive style that is still emulated by greats of the modern game.

8th

Amanda Serrano

Born: **9th October 1988, Carolina, Puerto Rico**

The Puerto Rican southpaw is – pound for pound – peerless, setting a record for holding nine world titles from seven different weight classes.

How it works: We scored a sportsperson's finish in every statistical category 1-10, 10 points for first, 9 for second etc. Topping four categories and coming third, fourth and fifth in the others Michael Phelps has a total score of 61

What's so great about Muhammad Ali?

Muhammad Ali christened himself 'the Greatest' and then made good on the claim by becoming the most irresistible and influential sportsperson of the 20th century. We look back at the career of the legendary boxer

How it works: Listed on the right are Ali's 61 career fights with the opponent, year, result and number of rounds fought detailed in the centre. The proportional spikes on either side represent the estimated attendance and amount Ali was reported to have been paid (purse) at the time. The graphic below shows the number of punches thrown in Ali's most famous fight, the Rumble in the Jungle, in 1974

Sources: BoxRec, Greatest of All Time: A Tribute to Muhammad Ali

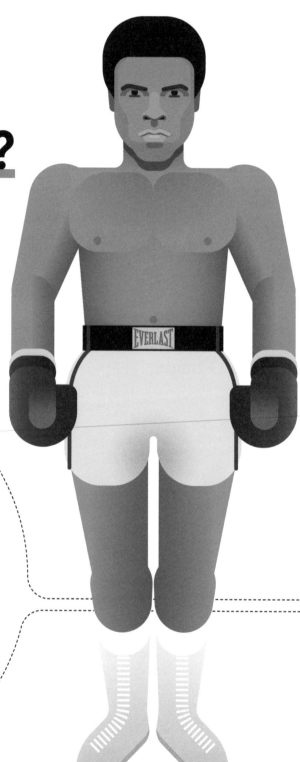

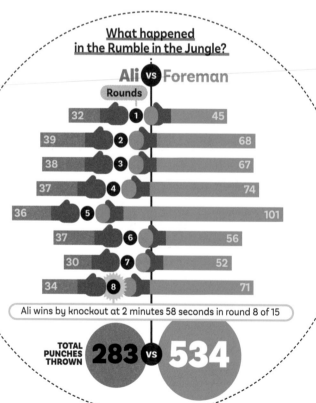

What happened in the Rumble in the Jungle?

Ali vs **Foreman**

Rounds

	Ali	Round	Foreman
	32	1	45
	39	2	68
	38	3	67
	37	4	74
	36	5	101
	37	6	56
	30	7	52
	34	8	71

Ali wins by knockout at 2 minutes 58 seconds in round 8 of 15

TOTAL PUNCHES THROWN **283** vs **534**

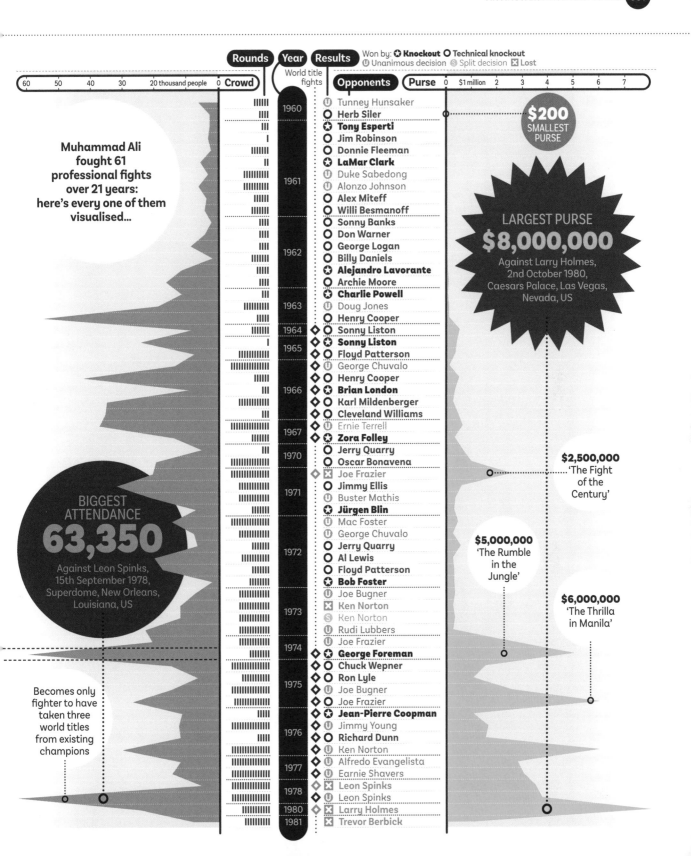

Muhammad Ali
fought 61
professional fights
over 21 years:
here's every one of them
visualised…

Rounds **Year** **Results**
Won by: ✪ **Knockout** ◯ **Technical knockout**
Ⓤ Unanimous decision Ⓢ Split decision ☒ Lost

World title
fights

Crowd **Opponents** **Purse**
60 50 40 30 20 thousand people 0
0 $1 million 2 3 4 5 6 7

$200
SMALLEST
PURSE

LARGEST PURSE
$8,000,000
Against Larry Holmes,
2nd October 1980,
Caesars Palace, Las Vegas,
Nevada, US

BIGGEST
ATTENDANCE
63,350
Against Leon Spinks,
15th September 1978,
Superdome, New Orleans,
Louisiana, US

$2,500,000
'The Fight
of the
Century'

$5,000,000
'The Rumble
in the
Jungle'

$6,000,000
'The Thrilla
in Manila'

Becomes only
fighter to have
taken three
world titles
from existing
champions

Year	Opponent
1960	Ⓤ Tunney Hunsaker
	◯ **Herb Siler**
	✪ **Tony Esperti**
	◯ Jim Robinson
	◯ Donnie Fleeman
	✪ **LaMar Clark**
1961	Ⓤ Duke Sabedong
	Ⓤ Alonzo Johnson
	◯ Alex Miteff
	◯ Willi Besmanoff
	◯ Sonny Banks
	◯ Don Warner
1962	◯ George Logan
	◯ Billy Daniels
	✪ **Alejandro Lavorante**
	◯ Archie Moore
	✪ **Charlie Powell**
1963	Ⓤ Doug Jones
	◯ Henry Cooper
1964	◆ ◯ Sonny Liston
1965	◆ ✪ **Sonny Liston**
	◆ ◯ Floyd Patterson
	◆ Ⓤ George Chuvalo
	◆ ◯ Henry Cooper
1966	◆ ✪ **Brian London**
	◆ ◯ Karl Mildenberger
	◆ ◯ Cleveland Williams
1967	◆ Ⓤ Ernie Terrell
	◆ ✪ **Zora Folley**
1970	◯ Jerry Quarry
	◯ Oscar Bonavena
	◆ ☒ Joe Frazier
1971	◯ Jimmy Ellis
	Ⓤ Buster Mathis
	✪ **Jürgen Blin**
	Ⓤ Mac Foster
	Ⓤ George Chuvalo
1972	◯ Jerry Quarry
	◯ Al Lewis
	◯ Floyd Patterson
	✪ **Bob Foster**
	Ⓤ Joe Bugner
1973	☒ Ken Norton
	Ⓢ Ken Norton
	Ⓤ Rudi Lubbers
1974	Ⓤ Joe Frazier
	◆ ✪ **George Foreman**
	◆ ◯ Chuck Wepner
1975	◆ ◯ Ron Lyle
	◆ Ⓤ Joe Bugner
	◆ ◯ Joe Frazier
	◆ ✪ **Jean-Pierre Coopman**
1976	◆ Ⓤ Jimmy Young
	◆ ◯ Richard Dunn
	◆ Ⓤ Ken Norton
1977	◆ Ⓤ Alfredo Evangelista
	◆ Ⓤ Earnie Shavers
1978	◆ ☒ Leon Spinks
	◆ Ⓤ Leon Spinks
1980	◆ ☒ Larry Holmes
1981	☒ Trevor Berbick

Are athletes getting better?

When Johnny Hayes ran a marathon in under three hours at the 1908 Olympics, it was a landmark achievement. But athletes have come a long way since then. Here's how much faster, higher and further stars of track and field have run, jumped and thrown since records began...

How it works: The bar chart shows the difference between the first official male and female record holder in six athletic events (on white podiums) and the official world record holder on 31st December 2020 (on red podiums). Dates listed are those on which the records were set and nations listed are those athletes were representing.

Source: World Athletics

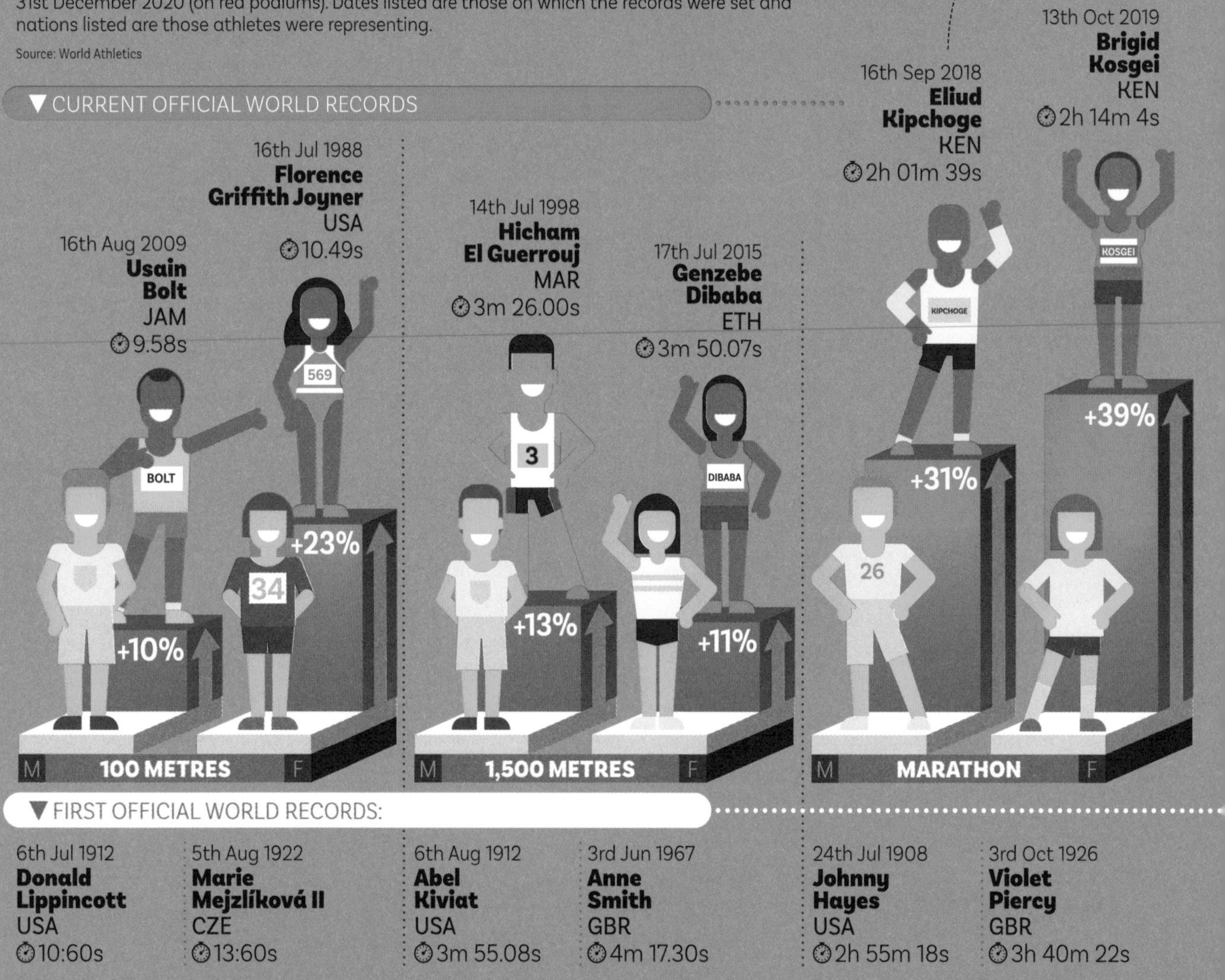

Kipchoge also ran an unofficial time of 01:59:40 in October 2019 which is almost **32% faster** than Hayes's time in 1908

▼ CURRENT OFFICIAL WORLD RECORDS

16th Aug 2009
Usain Bolt
JAM
⏱9.58s

16th Jul 1988
Florence Griffith Joyner
USA
⏱10.49s

14th Jul 1998
Hicham El Guerrouj
MAR
⏱3m 26.00s

17th Jul 2015
Genzebe Dibaba
ETH
⏱3m 50.07s

16th Sep 2018
Eliud Kipchoge
KEN
⏱2h 01m 39s

13th Oct 2019
Brigid Kosgei
KEN
⏱2h 14m 4s

+10% +23%

+13% +11%

+31% +39%

M **100 METRES** F

M **1,500 METRES** F

M **MARATHON** F

▼ FIRST OFFICIAL WORLD RECORDS:

| 6th Jul 1912 **Donald Lippincott** USA ⏱10:60s | 5th Aug 1922 **Marie Mejzlíková II** CZE ⏱13:60s | 6th Aug 1912 **Abel Kiviat** USA ⏱3m 55.08s | 3rd Jun 1967 **Anne Smith** GBR ⏱4m 17.30s | 24th Jul 1908 **Johnny Hayes** USA ⏱2h 55m 18s | 3rd Oct 1926 **Violet Piercy** GBR ⏱3h 40m 22s |

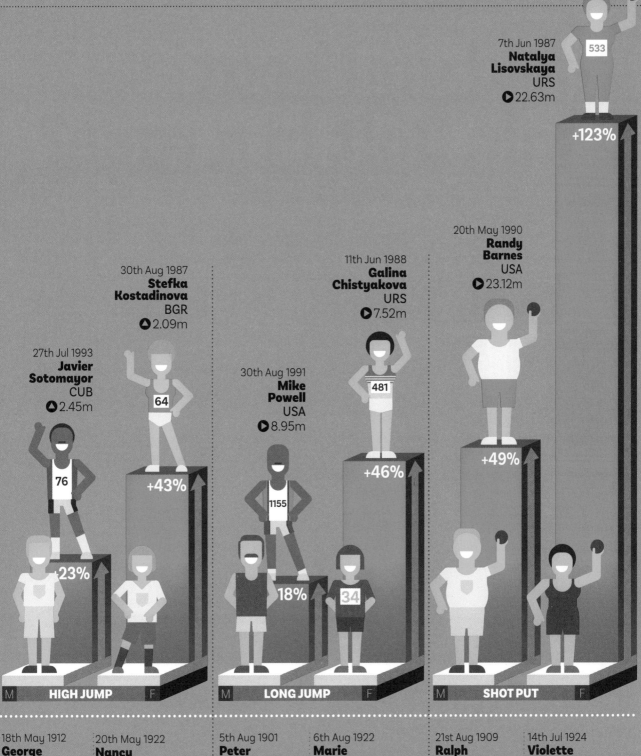

7th Jun 1987
Natalya Lisovskaya
URS
▶22.63m

+123%

20th May 1990
Randy Barnes
USA
▶23.12m

11th Jun 1988
Galina Chistyakova
URS
▶7.52m

30th Aug 1987
Stefka Kostadinova
BGR
▲2.09m

64

+49%

+43%

27th Jul 1993
Javier Sotomayor
CUB
▲2.45m

30th Aug 1991
Mike Powell
USA
▶8.95m

481

76

1155

+46%

+23%

18%

34

M **HIGH JUMP** F

M **LONG JUMP** F

M **SHOT PUT** F

18th May 1912
George Horine
USA
▲2.00m

20th May 1922
Nancy Voorhees
USA
▲1.46m

5th Aug 1901
Peter O'Connor
IRL
▶7.61m

6th Aug 1922
Marie Mejzlíková II
CZE
▶5.16m

21st Aug 1909
Ralph Rose
USA
▶15.54m

14th Jul 1924
Violette Gouraud-Morris
FRA
▶10.15m

Could you beat Usain Bolt in a race?

**Would you be able to cover 100 metres faster than the legendary sprinter?
It depends on how you plan to do it...**

How it works: The bars below proportionally represent the distance you could cover in 9.58 seconds, Usain Bolt's fastest 100 metres time

100 m

16th Aug 2009
Usain Bolt, Olympiastadion, Berlin
▶ 10.44 metres per second

 12.84m

If you were walking
Average walking speed of a healthy adult
▶ 1.34m/s

27.69m

If you were running
Average speed of a participant in a 5km Park Run
▶ 2.89m/s

 56.43m

If you were getting a piggy-back from Rommel Griffith
World record speed for the fastest 100 metres piggy-back race
▶ 5.89m/s

 51.35m

If you were riding a bike
Average cycling speed of a healthy adult
▶ 5.36m/s

 **82.20m**

If you were on a dog sled
World record speed for 100 metres on a sled pulled over sand by four dogs
▶ 8.58m/s

If you were riding a horse
Average speed of Secretariat running the fastest Kentucky Derby of all time **161.42m**
▶ 16.85m/s

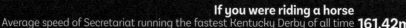

 66.49m

If you were riding an electric scooter
Top speed of a Segway Ninebot KickScooter MAX G30
▶ 6.94m/s

 39.66m

If you were on a bus
Average speed of a London bus
▶ 4.14m/s

Sources: Britannica, Guinness World Records, Newark & Sherwood District Council, ParkRun, Segway, Transport For London, University of Michigan, World Athletics

What's better, men's or women's football?

The men's game may get higher viewing figures, but is that popularity deserved?
We compare the two most recent global soccer showcases to find out

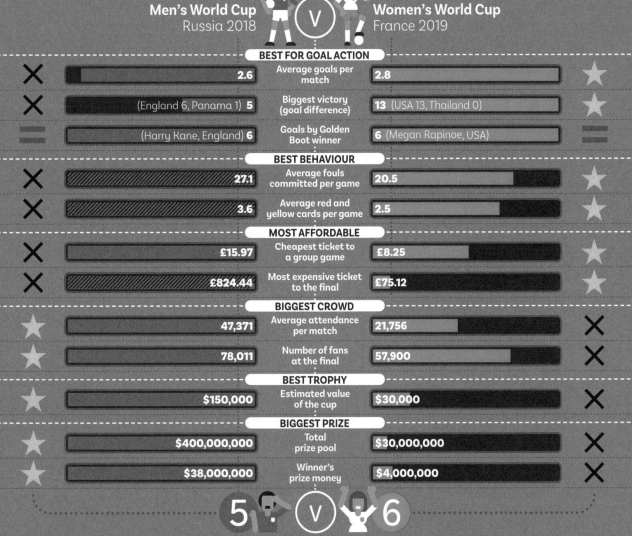

Men's World Cup Russia 2018	V	Women's World Cup France 2019

BEST FOR GOAL ACTION

✗	2.6	Average goals per match	2.8	★
✗	(England 6, Panama 1) 5	Biggest victory (goal difference)	13 (USA 13, Thailand 0)	★
=	(Harry Kane, England) 6	Goals by Golden Boot winner	6 (Megan Rapinoe, USA)	=

BEST BEHAVIOUR

| ✗ | 27.1 | Average fouls committed per game | 20.5 | ★ |
| ✗ | 3.6 | Average red and yellow cards per game | 2.5 | ★ |

MOST AFFORDABLE

| ✗ | £15.97 | Cheapest ticket to a group game | £8.25 | ★ |
| ✗ | £824.44 | Most expensive ticket to the final | £75.12 | ★ |

BIGGEST CROWD

| ★ | 47,371 | Average attendance per match | 21,756 | ✗ |
| ★ | 78,011 | Number of fans at the final | 57,900 | ✗ |

BEST TROPHY

| ★ | $150,000 | Estimated value of the cup | $30,000 | ✗ |

BIGGEST PRIZE

| ★ | $400,000,000 | Total prize pool | $30,000,000 | ✗ |
| ★ | $38,000,000 | Winner's prize money | $4,000,000 | ✗ |

5 V 6

How it works: We've compared figures across 12 categories, awarding a point to the winner of each. The difference between the two is shown proportionally, with the larger number occupying the full bar. If the larger number represents a negative attribute (e.g. ticket price) that bar is striped.

Sources: BBC, fifa.com

Who's the champion of the world?

Nearly every major sport – and a fair few minor ones – has an international tournament to determine global superiority. So which country currently holds the most sporting titles?

How it works: The most prestigious national team knockout tournament in each sport has been charted according to the most recent win. Indoor versions of predominantly outdoor sports and tournaments in which countries are able to send more than one team (eg A and B teams) are excluded. Countries that form the composite team the West Indies are grouped for cricket tournaments only

Sources: BBC, Britannica, CBS, Fifa, Floorball Today, Huffington Post, The ICC, Inside the Games, Japan Times, prokabaddi.com, Sky Sports, The Guardian, worldcurling.org *As of 31st December 2020

Sports involving:
◀ Contact
◀ Hitting
◀ Kicking
◀ Throwing

MEN · WOMEN · MIXED

CURRENT WORLD TITLE HOLDERS*

World Team Squash Championships 21st Dec 2020 — Egypt
World Cup of Darts 8th Nov 2020 — Wales
Cricket World Twenty20 8th Mar 2020 — Australia
Bandy World Championship 22nd Feb 2020 — Sweden
Kabaddi World Cup 16th Feb 2020 — Pakistan
World Handball Championship 15th Dec 2019 — Netherlands
World Floorball Championships 15th Dec 2019 — Sweden
World Ringette Championships 1st Dec 2019 — Finland
Beach Soccer World Cup 1st Dec 2019 — Portugal
Tennis Davis Cup 24th Nov 2019 — Spain
Wrestling World Cup Freestyle 17th Nov 2019 — Japan
Tennis Billie Jean King Cup 10th Nov 2019 — France
Rugby World Cup 2nd Nov 2019 — South Africa
Volleyball World Championship 15th Oct 2019 — Brazil
Basketball World Championship 15th Sep 2019 — Spain
Fistball World Championship 17th Aug 2019 — Germany
World Netball Championships 21st Jul 2019 — New Zealand
Cricket World Cup (one-day international) 14th Jul 2019 — England
Inline Hockey World Championships 13th Jul 2019 — United States
Inline Hockey World Championships 13th Jul 2019 — United States
Football World Cup 7th Jul 2019 — United States
Basketball 3x3 World Championships 23rd Jun 2019 — China
Basketball 3x3 World Championships 23rd Jun 2019 — United States
Softball World Championship 23rd Jun 2019 — Argentina
Water Polo World Cup 23rd Jun 2019 — Serbia
Water Polo World Cup 10th Jun 2019 — United States
Ice Hockey World Championships 26th May 2019 — Finland
Badminton Sudirman Cup 26th May 2019 — China
Wheelchair Tennis World Team Cup 18th May 2019 — Netherlands
Wheelchair Tennis World Team Cup 18th May 2019 — Great Britain
World Curling Championships 27th Apr 2019 — Sweden
Ice Hockey World Championships 14th Apr 2019 — United States
World Curling Championships 7th Apr 2019 — Sweden
World Curling Championships 24th Mar 2019 — Switzerland
Wrestling World Cup Freestyle 17th Mar 2019 — Russia
Bandy World Championship 2nd Feb 2019 — Russia
World Handball Championship 27th Jan 2019 — Denmark

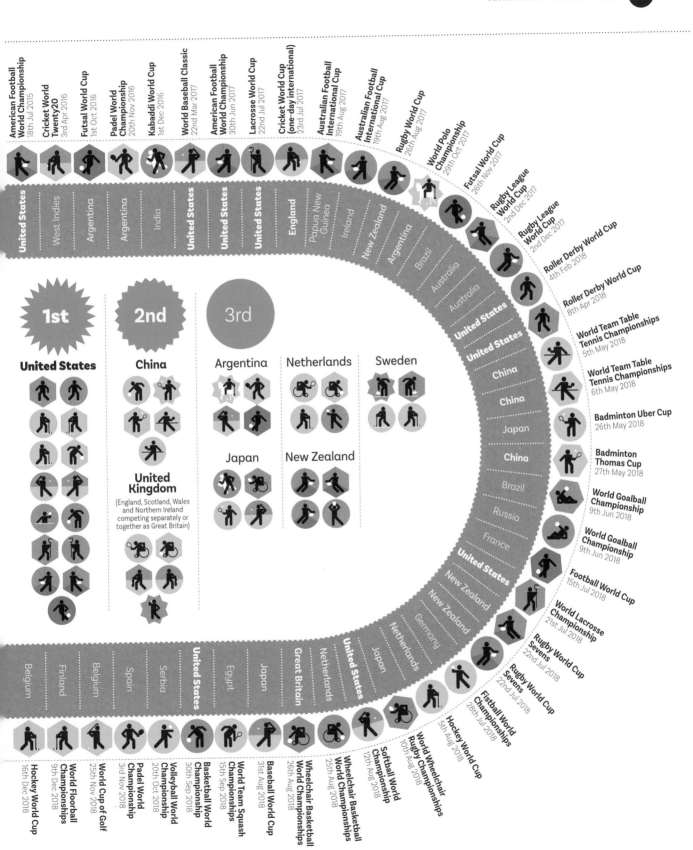

American Football World Championship
18th Jul 2015 — United States

Cricket World Twenty20
3rd Apr 2016 — West Indies

Futsal World Cup
1st Oct 2016 — Argentina

Padel World Championship
20th Nov 2016 — Argentina

Kabaddi World Cup
1st Dec 2016 — India

World Baseball Classic
22nd Mar 2017 — United States

American Football World Championship
30th Jun 2017 — United States

Lacrosse World Cup
22nd Jul 2017 — United States

Cricket World Cup (one-day international)
23rd Jul 2017 — England

Australian Football International Cup
19th Aug 2017 — Papua New Guinea

Australian Football International Cup
19th Aug 2017 — Ireland

Rugby World Cup
26th Aug 2017 — New Zealand

World Polo Championship
29th Oct 2017 — Argentina

Futsal World Cup
26th Nov 2017 — Brazil

Rugby League World Cup
2nd Dec 2017 — Australia

Rugby League World Cup
2nd Dec 2017 — Australia

Roller Derby World Cup
4th Feb 2018 — United States

Roller Derby World Cup
8th Apr 2018 — United States

World Team Table Tennis Championships
5th May 2018 — China

World Team Table Tennis Championships
6th May 2018 — China

Badminton Uber Cup
26th May 2018 — Japan

Badminton Thomas Cup
27th May 2018 — China

World Goalball Championship
9th Jun 2018 — Brazil

World Goalball Championship
9th Jun 2018 — Russia

Football World Cup
15th Jul 2018 — France

World Lacrosse Championship
21st Jul 2018 — United States

Rugby World Cup Sevens
22nd Jul 2018 — New Zealand

Rugby World Cup Sevens
22nd Jul 2018 — New Zealand

Fistball World Championships
26th Jul 2018 — Germany

Hockey World Cup
5th Aug 2018 — Netherlands

World Wheelchair Rugby Championships
10th Aug 2018 — Japan

Softball World Championship
12th Aug 2018 — United States

Wheelchair Basketball World Championships
25th Aug 2018 — Great Britain

Wheelchair Basketball World Championships
26th Aug 2018 — Netherlands

Baseball World Cup
31st Aug 2018 — Japan

World Team Squash Championships
15th Sep 2018 — Egypt

Basketball World Championship
30th Sep 2018 — United States

Volleyball World Championship
20th Oct 2018 — Serbia

Padel World Championship
3rd Nov 2018 — Spain

World Cup of Golf
25th Nov 2018 — Belgium

World Floorball Championships
9th Dec 2018 — Finland

Hockey World Cup
16th Dec 2018 — Belgium

1st United States

2nd China

United Kingdom
(England, Scotland, Wales and Northern Ireland competing separately or together as Great Britain)

3rd Argentina

Netherlands

Sweden

Japan

New Zealand

Who's won an Olympic or Paralympic medal?

NORTH AMERICA

SOUTH AMERICA

The Olympic and Paralympic Games are considered the greatest show on Earth. But which countries are yet to take home a medal? We dive into over 100 years of sporting statistics to find out

How it works: The map highlights countries or territories that have won a gold, silver or bronze medal at a Winter or Summer Olympic or Paralympic Games between 1896 and 2018

Sources: olympic.org, olympedia.org, paralympic.org

Have won a medal
Countries and territories that have won a gold, silver or bronze medal at a Winter or Summer Olympics or Paralympics between 1896 and 2018

Have yet to win a medal
Countries and territories that haven't won any medals at a Winter or Summer Olympics or Paralympics between 1896 and 2018

What about art?
While our map only marks medals won in sporting competitions, art events formed part of the Olympic Games between 1912 and 1948. The only country to win an art medal that hasn't yet won a sporting one is Monaco, which won a bronze for architecture in 1924.

EUROPE

ASIA

AFRICA

OCEANIA

SMALLEST COUNTRY TO WIN A MEDAL:
LIECHTENSTEIN Ⓐ POPULATION: 38,019

With a population a quarter the size of the Isle of Wight,
Liechtenstein is the smallest country to bag an Olympic
or Paralympic medal. Its successes have all come on snow
and ice, winning two gold, two silver and six bronze
medals at the Winter Olympics and a bronze medal at the
Winter Paralympic Games. Seven of its ten Olympic
medals have been won by members of the same family.

LARGEST COUNTRY WITHOUT A MEDAL:
BANGLADESH Ⓑ POPULATION: 163,046,161

Bangladesh is the largest country yet to have an athlete
make an Olympic or Paralympic podium, although prior
to the Tokyo Games it had only sent 38 Olympians and
two Paralympians to compete at any Olympiad. The best
performing of these was Abdullah Hel Baki, who finished
25th of 50 competitors in the 2016 Olympic men's air rifle
shooting competition.

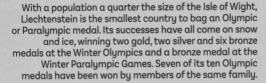

Social Progress Index	Global Gender Gap Report	World Happiness Report	Global Innovation Index	Environmental Performance Index	Global Peace Index
Based on factors including medical care, nutrition, sanitation, education and political freedom	Based on progress towards gender parity in education, health, political participation and the economy	Based on variables underpinning wellbeing such as life expectancy, income, social support and freedom	Based on factors including levels of research and development, venture capital and high-tech production	Based on factors including air quality, fisheries management, CO_2 emissions and biodiversity	Based on ongoing domestic and international conflict, militarisation and the impact of terrorism

Top ten

#	Social Progress Index	Global Gender Gap Report	World Happiness Report	Global Innovation Index	Environmental Performance Index	Global Peace Index
1	Norway	Iceland	Finland	Switzerland	Denmark	Iceland
2	Denmark	Norway	Denmark	Sweden	Luxembourg	New Zealand
3	Finland	Finland	Switzerland	United States	Switzerland	Portugal
4	New Zealand	Sweden	Iceland	United Kingdom	United Kingdom	Austria
5	Sweden	Nicaragua	Norway	Netherlands	France	Denmark
6	Switzerland	New Zealand	Netherlands	Denmark	Austria	Canada
7	Canada	Ireland	Sweden	Finland	Finland	Singapore
8	Australia	Spain	New Zealand	Singapore	Sweden	Czech Republic
9	Iceland	Rwanda	Austria	Germany	Norway	Japan
10	Netherlands	Germany	Luxembourg	South Korea	Germany	Switzerland

NUMBER OF COUNTRIES ON EACH LIST

163	153	153	131	180	163

WORST ▼

Social Progress Index	Global Gender Gap Report	World Happiness Report	Global Innovation Index	Environmental Performance Index	Global Peace Index
Guinea	Oman	India	Zambia	Burundi	Russia
Afghanistan	Lebanon	Malawi	Mali	Chad	CAR
DR Congo	Saudi Arabia	Yemen	Mozambique	Solomon Islands	DR Congo
Niger	Chad	Botswana	Togo	Madagascar	Libya
Burundi	Iran	Tanzania	Benin	Guinea	Somalia
Somalia	DR Congo	CAR	Ethiopia	Côte d'Ivoire	Yemen
Eritrea	Syria	Rwanda	Niger	Sierra Leone	South Sudan
CAR	Pakistan	Zimbabwe	Myanmar	Afghanistan	Iraq
Chad	Iraq	South Sudan	Guinea	Myanmar	Syria
South Sudan	Yemen	Afghanistan	Yemen	Liberia	Afghanistan

● Democratic Republic of the Congo
▲ Central African Republic

What's the best country in the world?

Norway's progressive, Iceland's a peacemaker and New Zealand is blissfully free of corruption. But which nation combines all these traits and more to be the greatest on the planet? And which is currently the worst?

How it works: We gave points to countries ranked in the top and bottom ten of each of ten country indices. The aggregated scores at the end show the countries with the highest and lowest scores overall. Where countries are tied in individual indices, those with the most improved year-on-year position are placed higher in the top ten list while those whose position decreased the most rank lower in the bottom ten. In the case of a tie in aggregated scores, inclusion in the most top or bottom ten lists is the decider. Not every country appeared on every list

Good Country Index

Based on country's contributions to global peace, culture, prosperity, health, climate and equality

World Press Freedom Index

Based on pluralism, media independence, quality of legislative framework and the safety of journalists

Corruption Perception Index

Based on governance, economic quality, business environment, personal freedom and social capital

Democracy Index

Based on 60 indicators in five different categories measuring pluralism, civil liberties and political culture

AGGREGATED TOP TEN COUNTRIES

Good Country Index	World Press Freedom Index	Corruption Perception Index	Democracy Index
Sweden	Norway	New Zealand	Norway
Denmark	Finland	Denmark	Iceland
Germany	Denmark	Finland	Sweden
Canada	Sweden	Switzerland	New Zealand
Netherlands	Netherlands	Singapore	Finland
Finland	Jamaica	Sweden	Ireland
France	Costa Rica	Norway	Canada
United Kingdom	Switzerland	Netherlands	Denmark
Spain	New Zealand	Germany	Australia
Norway	Portugal	Luxembourg	Switzerland

Rank	Aggregated Top Ten
1	Denmark
2	Finland
3	Sweden
4	Norway
5	Switzerland
6	New Zealand
7	Iceland
8	Netherlands
9	Canada
10	United Kingdom

149	180	180	167
Mali	Cuba	DR Congo	Yemen
Bahamas	Laos	North Korea	Tajikistan
Papua New Guinea	Iran	Afghanistan	Saudi Arabia
Gabon	Syria	Sudan	Equatorial Guinea
Burundi	Vietnam	Equatorial Guinea	Turkmenistan
Iraq	Djibouti	Venezuela	Chad
Mauritania	China	Yemen	Syria
Guinea	Eritrea	Syria	CAR
Yemen	Turkmenistan	South Sudan	DR Congo
Libya	North Korea	Somalia	North Korea

AGGREGATED BOTTOM TEN COUNTRIES

WORST ▼

Aggregated Bottom Ten
Chad
North Korea
DR Congo
Iraq
Guinea
CAR
Afghanistan
South Sudan
Syria
Yemen

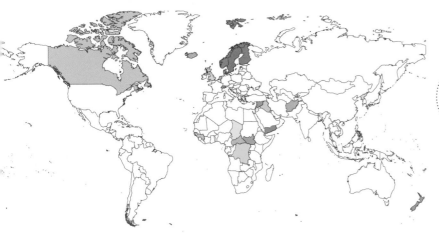

Which city knows how to party?

We compare revellers to residents to analyse the turnout for the biggest festivals in some of the world's capitals of culture

How it works: ● **Average daily attendance** at the city's biggest festival, expressed as a percentage of **the city's population** ●

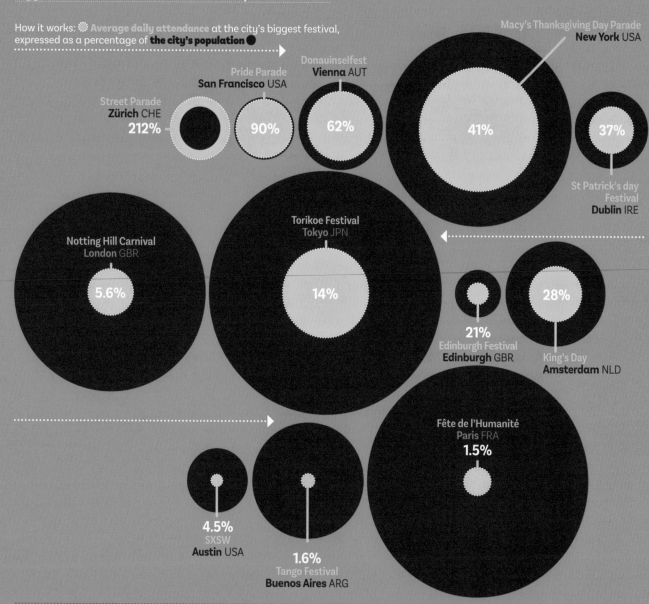

Macy's Thanksgiving Day Parade
New York USA

Donauinselfest
Vienna AUT

Pride Parade
San Francisco USA

Street Parade
Zürich CHE
212%

90%

62%

41%

37%

St Patrick's day Festival
Dublin IRE

Torikoe Festival
Tokyo JPN

Notting Hill Carnival
London GBR

5.6%

14%

21%

Edinburgh Festival
Edinburgh GBR

28%

King's Day
Amsterdam NLD

Fête de l'Humanité
Paris FRA
1.5%

4.5%
SXSW
Austin USA

1.6%
Tango Festival
Buenos Aires ARG

Source: World Cities Culture Forum

Who's ready for a picnic?

Zürich knows how to party, but when it comes to laying out a blanket and unwrapping some nibbles, Dublin's the place to be

How it works: We took the party cities from the page opposite and worked out how much green space they have. Each green square represents one square metre of public parks and gardens per capita

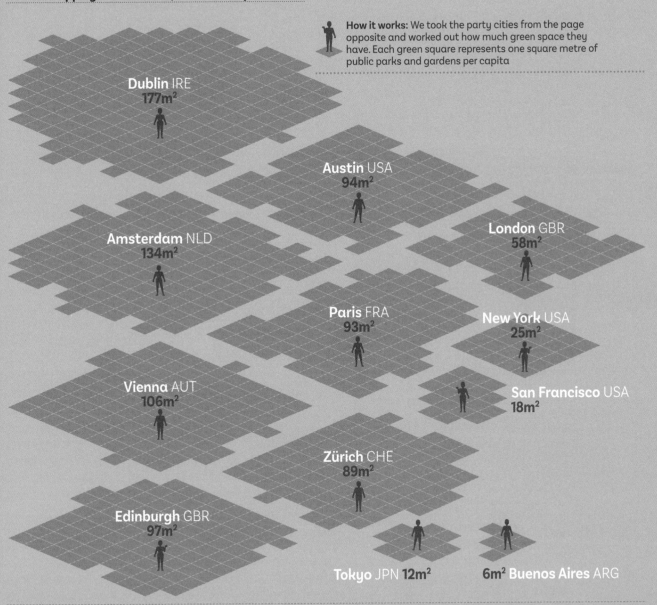

Dublin IRE
177m²

Austin USA
94m²

London GBR
58m²

Amsterdam NLD
134m²

Paris FRA
93m²

New York USA
25m²

Vienna AUT
106m²

San Francisco USA
18m²

Zürich CHE
89m²

Edinburgh GBR
97m²

Tokyo JPN 12m²

6m² **Buenos Aires** ARG

Source: World Cities Culture Forum

What were the tallest towers of their time?

The human urge to build structures that reach to the skies dates back at least five millennia. We've tracked the world's tallest freestanding structures, what they were used for – and how long they held onto the top spot. Nice one, Giza

How it works: The timeline shows the world's tallest recorded freestanding structures since 2560 BC colour-coded by their predominant use:

● Monuments ● Churches and cathedrals
● Commercial buildings ● Communications towers

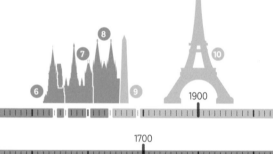

Timeline of the tallest:

1. 2560 BC-1311 AD **Great Pyramid of Giza**, Egypt, △**146m** (eroded to 139m by 1647)
2. 1311-1549   **Lincoln Cathedral**, England, △**160m** (spire collapsed in 1549)
3. 1549-1569   **St Mary's Church**, Stralsund, Germany, △**151m**
4. 1569-1573   **Beauvais Cathedral**, France, △**153m** (spire collapsed in 1573)
3b. 1573-1647   **St Mary's Church**, Stralsund, Germany, △**151m** (spire destroyed by lightning in 1647)
5. 1647-1874   **Strasbourg Cathedral**, France, △**142m**
6. 1874-1876   **St Nikolai**, Hamburg, Germany, △**147m**
7. 1876-1880   **Notre-Dame Cathedral**, Rouen, France, △**151m**
8. 1880-1884   **Cologne Cathedral**, Germany, △**157m**
9. 1884-1889   **Washington Monument**, USA, △**169m**
10. 1889-1930   **Eiffel Tower**, Paris, France, △**300m**
11. 1930-1931   **Chrysler Building**, New York, USA, △**319m**
12. 1931-1967   **Empire State Building**, New York, USA, △**381m**
13. 1967-1975   **Ostankino Tower**, Moscow, Russia, △**540m**
14. 1975-2007   **CN Tower**, Toronto, Canada, △**553m**
15. 2007-   **Burj Khalifa**, Dubai, UAE, △**830m**
16. Scheduled to open 2024 **Jeddah Tower**, Jeddah, Saudi Arabia, △**1,000m**

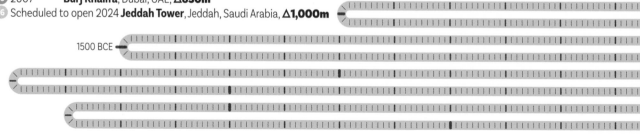

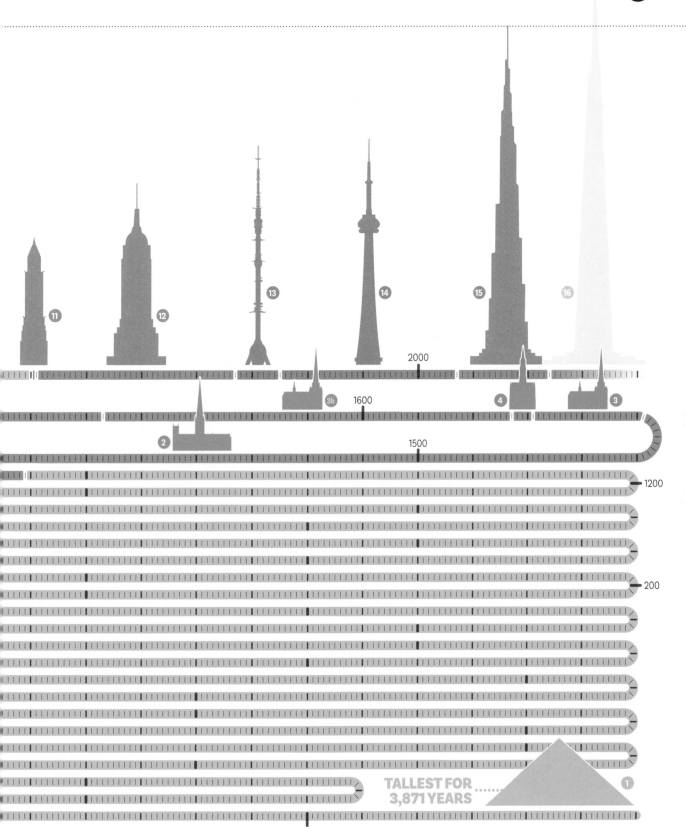

TALLEST FOR
3,871 YEARS

Where are today's tallest buildings?

While the earliest skyscrapers rose from the streets of New York and Chicago, you'll now find more tall buildings in Guangzhou and Shenzhen, with increasing numbers of Chinese cities raising the roof

How it works: Towers are illustrated in proportion to their real world heights which are measured in metres to the tip, including spires or pinnacles. Data correct as of 31st December 2020

The Abraj Al-Bait clockface is the world's biggest, with a diameter of **43 metres** - over six times bigger than the faces of 'Big Ben' (on London's Elizabeth Tower)

1 Burj Khalifa △ **830 m**
Dubai, United Arab Emirates, 2010

2 Shanghai Tower △ **632 m**
Shanghai, China, 2015

3 Abraj Al-Bait Clock Tower △ **601 m**
Mecca, Saudi Arabia, 2012

4 Ping An Finance Centre △ **599 m**
Shenzhen, China, 2017

5 Goldin Finance 117 △ **596 m**
Tianjin, China, 2021

6 Lotte World Tower △ **556 m**
Seoul, South Korea, 2016

7 One World Trade Center △ **546 m**
New York, US, 2014

8 CTF Finance Centre △ **530 m**
Guangzhou, China, 2016

9 Tianjin Finance Centre △ **530m**
Tianjin, China, 2019

10 China Zun △ **528m**
Beijing, China, 2018

600m

400m

200m

Six of the world's ten tallest buildings are in China, which also has more skyscrapers than any other country - almost twice as many as the United States, United Arab Emirates, South Korea and Japan combined

Top five countries with buildings over 200 metres tall:

CHINA 823

UNITED STATES 220

UNITED ARAB EMIRATES 129

SOUTH KOREA 74

JAPAN 44

Source: Council on Tall Buildings and Urban Habitat. Goldin Finance 117 has topped out but has not been completed

What makes an iconic landmark?

We've broken down the ten most photographed landmarks on the planet to find out what makes them so snappable

How it works: The graphic shows a proportional breakdown of attributes shared by the ten landmarks with the most images on Instagram as of June 2020

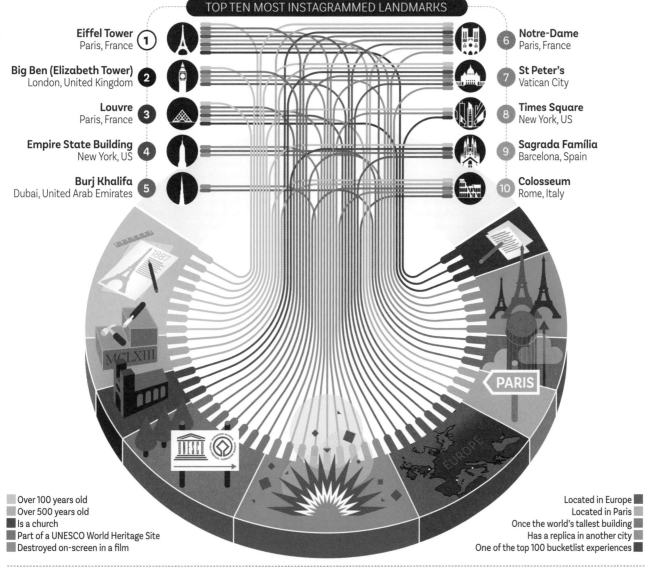

TOP TEN MOST INSTAGRAMMED LANDMARKS

Eiffel Tower
Paris, France
1

Big Ben (Elizabeth Tower)
London, United Kingdom
2

Louvre
Paris, France
3

Empire State Building
New York, US
4

Burj Khalifa
Dubai, United Arab Emirates
5

6 **Notre-Dame**
Paris, France

7 **St Peter's**
Vatican City

8 **Times Square**
New York, US

9 **Sagrada Família**
Barcelona, Spain

10 **Colosseum**
Rome, Italy

- Over 100 years old
- Over 500 years old
- Is a church
- Part of a UNESCO World Heritage Site
- Destroyed on-screen in a film

- Located in Europe
- Located in Paris
- Once the world's tallest building
- Has a replica in another city
- One of the top 100 bucketlist experiences

Sources: bucketlist.org, Condé Nast Traveller ME, USA Today

WHAT DO WE WANT?

Questions about vices,
desires and puggles

916 PAGES

VOGUE

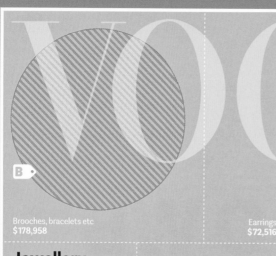

B

Brooches, bracelets etc
$178,958

Earrings
$72,516

Jewellery
and watches
$397,948

Rings
$45,819

Necklaces
$69,070

Watches
$31,585

C

Dresses
$354,195

Skirts and
dresses
$390,872

Skirts
$36,677

Coats and jackets
$263,388

Travel
$200,000

A

Coats
$126,228

D

Jackets and blazers
$115,810

Capes, ponchos and gilets
$21,350

Accessories
$168,482

Bags
$84,525

E

Collars,
ties and scarves
$13,742

Hats
$12,623

Gloves
$47,325

Others
$10,267

Tops etc $62,178

Sweaters,
cardigans
etc
$12,590

T-shirts,
vests and
other tops
$31,081

H

Blouses
and shirts
$18,507

Footwear
$61,870

F

Casual
trousers
$12,321

G

Suits
$11,196

Suits and trousers
$42,919

Smart trousers $19,402

**Miscellaneous
$22,934**

I

Home etc
$12,142

Masks
$10,792

Shoes
$39,686

Boots
$22,184

How much would it cost to buy everything in *Vogue*?

The September issue of *Vogue* is the world's biggest and most influential style publication and has long been a barometer for the health of high fashion, consumerism and the magazine industry. In September 2012 the magazine industry was evidently in excellent health because *Vogue* published the biggest issue in its history to date, at 916 pages. But would your wallet have remained in good health if you had bought every item featured?

How it works: We've added up the cost of buying every priced item featured in the editorial pages of the September 2012 issue of *Vogue US*, the largest issue to date. The graphic opposite represents the total value of all items, broken down proportionally by category and subcategories. The single most expensive items in each category are depicted below, with the circles representing their values proportionally. Advertisements and advertorial pages are excluded from the total values

TOTAL VALUE OF ALL PRODUCTS FEATURED IN THE BIGGEST EVER ISSUE OF *VOGUE*

$1,610,591

Big ticket items: The most expensive single item in each category

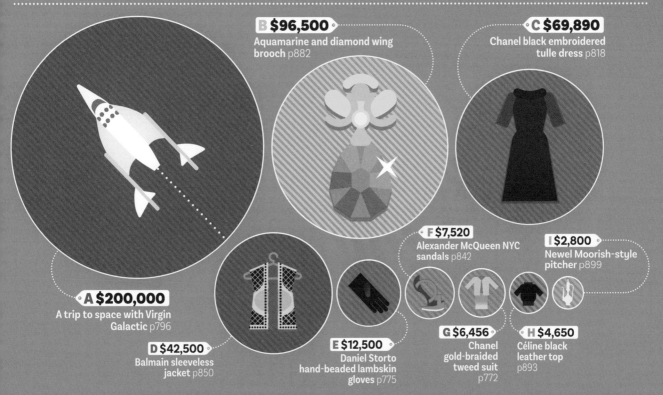

B $96,500
Aquamarine and diamond wing brooch p882

C $69,890
Chanel black embroidered tulle dress p818

F $7,520
Alexander McQueen NYC sandals p842

I $2,800
Newel Moorish-style pitcher p899

A $200,000
A trip to space with Virgin Galactic p796

D $42,500
Balmain sleeveless jacket p850

E $12,500
Daniel Storto hand-beaded lambskin gloves p775

G $6,456
Chanel gold-braided tweed suit p772

H $4,650
Céline black leather top p893

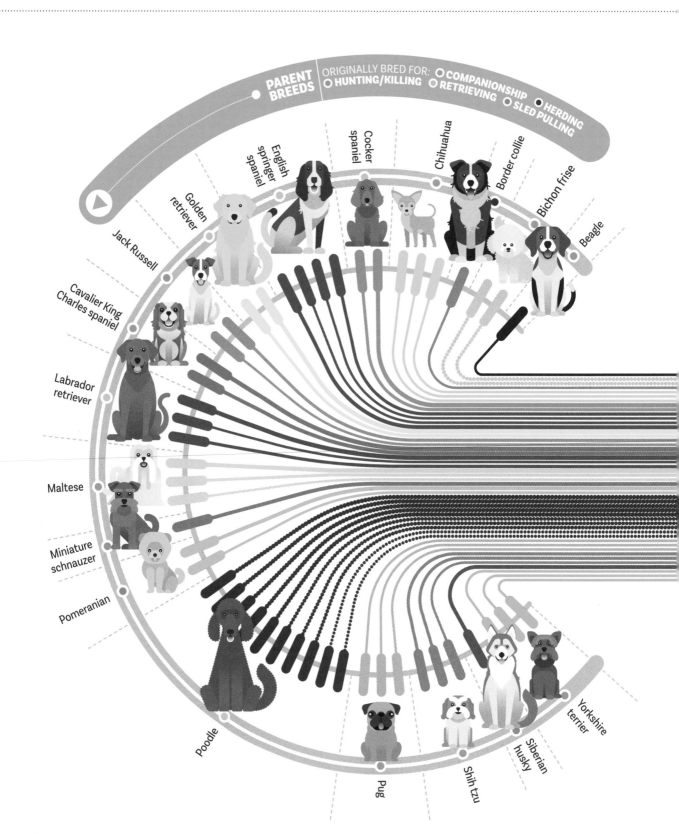

PARENT BREEDS

ORIGINALLY BRED FOR:
○ HUNTING/KILLING ○ COMPANIONSHIP ○ RETRIEVING ● HERDING ○ SLED PULLING

English springer spaniel

Cocker spaniel

Chihuahua

Border collie

Bichon frise

Beagle

Golden retriever

Jack Russell

Cavalier King Charles spaniel

Labrador retriever

Maltese

Miniature schnauzer

Pomeranian

Poodle

Pug

Shih tzu

Siberian husky

Yorkshire terrier

How much is that doggie in the window?

The price of designer dogs in the UK has surged in the last few years, driven in part by Brits looking for furry companions during the coronavirus pandemic. But how big is the rise? And which crossbreed costs the most?

How it works: We've compared the average prices of crossbreed dogs listed for sale in 2019 and 2020 at Pets4Homes.co.uk. Parent breeds are charted on the left, linked with lines to crossbreeds on the right. Dotted lines show hypoallergenic breeds. The coloured circles next to parent breeds and crosses show the original purpose of the parent breeds

Source: Pets4Homes

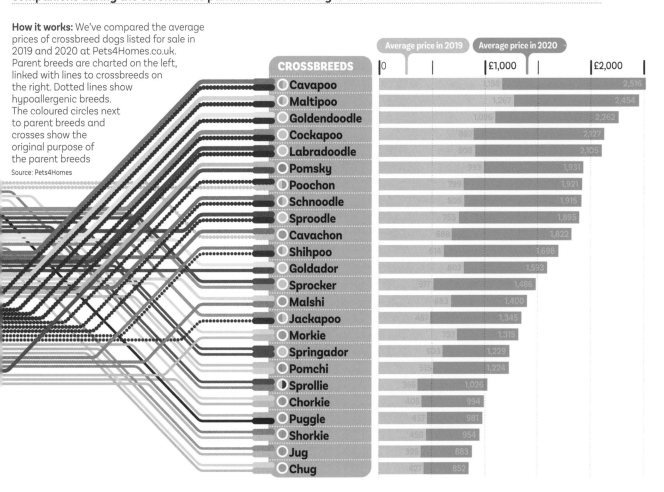

CROSSBREEDS	Average price in 2019	Average price in 2020
Cavapoo	1,158	2,516
Maltipoo	1,267	2,454
Goldendoodle	1,096	2,262
Cockapoo	892	2,127
Labradoodle	908	2,105
Pomsky	993	1,931
Poochon	799	1,921
Schnoodle	805	1,915
Sproodle	755	1,895
Cavachon	688	1,822
Shihpoo	874	1,698
Goldador	802	1,593
Sprocker	517	1,486
Malshi	683	1,400
Jackapoo	467	1,345
Morkie	737	1,315
Springador	603	1,229
Pomchi	515	1,224
Sprollie	366	1,026
Chorkie	405	994
Puggle	457	981
Shorkie	450	954
Jug	399	883
Chug	427	852

What's the most popular parent breed?
Ten of the 24 most popular hybrid dog breeds have a **poodle** as a parent

What's the most popular crossbreed?
Cockapoos, 39,092 of which were sold through Pets4Homes.co.uk in 2020

What's the most expensive crossbreed?
Cavapoos top the list with an average sale price of £2,516 in 2020

Should I liquidise my assets?

The venom of one of the world's deadliest scorpions is reportedly the most expensive liquid in the world. But when you have a spare £7.3 million, should you invest in a litre of the stuff or splash out on some other liquids instead?

How it works: We've listed liquids that can be purchased for the same amount of money as one litre of deathstalker scorpion venom (£7,289,016). The liquids are ordered by highest to lowest cost per litre

1 litre of deathstalker scorpion venom

Each scorpion provides just 0.2 mg of venom per milking. It is used in the identification and treatment of cancer.

COST PER LITRE:
£7,289,016

5 bottles of single malt Scotch whisky

The Macallan Fine and Rare 1926 60-year-old, the most expensive whisky in the world. A bottle sold for £1,452,000 at Sotheby's in 2019.

COST PER LITRE:
£2,074,286

Lots of potential horses

£7,289,016 equates to 8,098 straws of semen from Olympic show-jumping horse Big Star, whose elite ejaculate is highly prized among breeders.

COST PER LITRE:
£884,563

18 bottles of red wine

1945 Romanée-Conti, the world's most expensive wine, a bottle of which sold for the equivalent of £394,517 at Sotheby's in 2018.

COST PER LITRE:
£526,023

40,494 bottles of Chanel No. 5

Given a perfume-industry average of 12 sprays per millilitre, you would be able to spritz yourself with Chanel 7,289,016 times.

COST PER LITRE:
£12,000

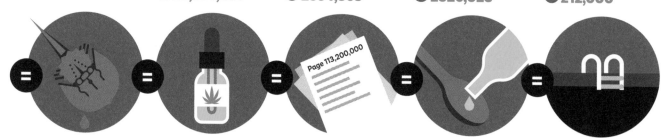

651 litres of lysate

Extracted from the painstakingly harvested blue blood of horseshoe crabs, lysate is used by pharmaceutical companies to detect endotoxin contamination in medicines.

COST PER LITRE:
£11,185.05

363,433 bottles of CBD oil

Much prized for its supposed health benefits, CBD oil is made from hemp and contains flavonoids, terpenes and soothing cannabinoids.

COST PER LITRE:
£1,999

377,473 printer cartridges

You could buy enough Canon Original PG-545XL black ink cartridges to print 113.2 million pages of asset reports.

COST PER LITRE:
£1,287.33

211,582 bottles of olive oil

Enough Lambda, the world's most expensive olive oil, to use in a *BBC Good Food* recipe for moussaka for 158,861 people.

COST PER LITRE:
£344.50

11 swimming pools full of crude oil

Your 173,176 barrels of West Texas Intermediate crude oil would fill those 11 Olympic pools to the brim.

COST PER LITRE:
26p

Sources: Amazon, BBC Good Food, Chanel, Guinness World Records, Modern Farmer, National Geographic, Sotheby's

Do you like what you see?

What we watch has long influenced our buying habits, with items shown onscreen – whether as product placement or simply to further the plot – often mobilising viewers to make a purchase. Here are ten of the most notable telly and film-driven spikes in sales

How it works: We've compiled reported spikes in sales for products that featured prominently in major television series, films or cinematic shorts. ◄ = Year of broadcast/release

▶Stranger Things
▲ Eggo waffles
⊕14%
◄2017

Year-on-year increase in sales of Kellogg's frozen waffles in the US as the second series of the Netflix 1980s-set sci-fi show debuts.

▶Wallace & Gromit: A Close Shave
▲ Wensleydale cheese
⊕15%
◄1995

Year-on-year increase in sales of Wensleydale in the UK.

▶Fleabag
▲ Gin and tonic in a can
⊕24%
◄2019

Week-on-week rise in M&S canned gin and tonic sales after Fleabag and Hot Priest share the drink in the second series.

▶Bridgerton
▲ Needlework kits
⊕30%
◄2020

Month-on-month increase in UK stitching kit sales at Hobbycraft.

▶Popeye the Sailor
▲ Spinach
⊕33%
◄1933

Rise in spinach sales in the US over a five-year period.

▶ET: The Extra-Terrestrial
▲ Reese's Pieces
⊕65%
◄1982

Jump in sales in two weeks after the premiere of the movie, in which ET is tempted out of hiding by the candy.

▶Game of Thrones
▲ Mead
⊕84%
◄2012

Rise in sales of mead in the US over the two years following the broadcast of the second series.

▶The Queen's Gambit
▲ Chess sets
⊕125%
◄2020

Increase in sales of chess sets in the US in month following release.

▶Normal People
▲ Neck chains
⊕130%
◄2020

Month-on-month increase in sales of neck chains by ASOS in the UK.

▶The Great British Bake Off
▲ KitchenAid mixers
⊕150%
◄2014

Increase in UK sales of the high-end device on eBay over the course of the fourth series.

Sources: Business Insider, Forbes, The Independent, Maxim, The Mirror, New York Times, Radio Times, Stylist

Proportion of adult population admitting to the use of cannabis in the year before survey. Countries and territories in alphabetical order:

25%   20%   15%   10%   5%   0%

Do you want to get high?

Cannabis is the most tried illegal drug in the UK – but how many people around the world are actually using it? We've visualised the percentage of adults per country who admitted taking cannabis in the year before they were polled by official national and international surveys

How it works: Countries and territories with available data on cannabis use from the UN Office on Drugs and Crime are listed alphabetically on the inner circle; the percentage of adults admitting to the use of cannabis 12 months before being surveyed is marked on the outer circle

Source: Latest available estimates from the UN Office on Drugs and Crime (UNODC)
*UK figures are England and Wales only

Sierra Leone
Slovakia
Slovenia
South Africa
South Korea
Spain
Sri Lanka
Suriname
Sweden
Switzerland
Taiwan
Thailand
Togo
Trinidad and Tobago
Tunisia
Turkey
Ukraine
United Arab Emirates
United Kingdom*
UNITED STATES
URUGUAY
Uzbekistan
Venezuela
ZAMBIA

Afghanistan
Albania
Algeria
Argentina
Armenia
AUSTRALIA
Austria
Azerbaijan
Bahamas
Bangladesh
Barbados
Belarus
Belgium
Belize
BERMUDA
Bhutan
Bolivia
Bosnia and Herzegovina
Brazil
Bulgaria
Burkina Faso
Cabo Verde
Cambodia
CANADA

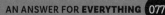

Who are the biggest pot smokers?

Countries with the highest percentages of adults who admitted to using cannabis in the year before survey

1. **Israel** - 27%
2. **United States** - 19.4%
3. **Canada** - 14.7%
4. **Uruguay** - 14.6%
5. **Nigeria** - 14.3%
6. **Chile** - 13.3%
7. **New Zealand** - 11.9%
8. **France** - 11.1%
9. **Bermuda** - 10.9%
10. **Australia** - 10.4%

Who just says no?

Places with the lowest percentages of self-confessed pot smokers

Japan	0.3%
Saudi Arabia	0.3%
Taiwan	0.3%
South Korea	0.3%
Indonesia	0.2%

LOWEST

Saint Lucia
Russia
Romania
Puerto Rico
Portugal
Poland
Philippines
Peru
Paraguay
Panama
Pakistan
Norway
North Macedonia
NIGERIA
Nicaragua
NEW ZEALAND
Netherlands
Myanmar
Morocco
Montenegro
Moldova
Mexico
Mauritius
Malta
Maldives
Malaysia
Madagascar
Macao
Luxembourg
Lithuania
Liberia
Lebanon
Latvia
Laos
Kuwait
Kenya
Kazakhstan
Japan
Jamaica
Italy
ISRAEL
Ireland
Iran
Indonesia
India
Iceland
Hungary
Hong Kong
Honduras
Haiti
Guyana
Guatemala
Greenland
Greece
Germany
Georgia
FRANCE
Finland
Fiji
Estonia
El Salvador
Egypt
Ecuador
Denmark
Czech Republic
Cyprus
Croatia
Costa Rica
Colombia
Dominican Republic

The 20 countries with the biggest per capita cocaine use

1 United Kingdom
1.56 grams for $100

2 United States
1.22 grams for $100

3 Australia
0.38 grams for $100

What does $100 of cocaine look like?

The global manufacture of cocaine is at a record high, with an estimated 1,723 tonnes of the drug in its pure form produced each year. But which countries are consuming the most, how much do users pay for their hits and what are the maximum penalties they face for possession?

How it works: The 20 countries with the highest reported consumption of cocaine per capita according to latest available figures are listed in order. The length of the white line next to each is proportional to the amount of cocaine you could buy in that country for $100 according to latest available figures from the UN Office on Drugs and Crime. The coloured icons represent the maximum custodial sentence issued at a national/federal level for possession of cocaine in each country

$ Fines **🔒** Less than 3 years **Ⅲ** 4-7 years **◉** 8 years or more

Source: UN Office on Drugs and Crime

9 Denmark
1.05 grams for $100

7 Uruguay
5.00 grams for $100

8 Montenegro
1.00 gram for $100

12 Chile
5.50 grams for $100

Canada
4 1.29 grams for $100

Spain
5 1.43 grams for $100

Netherlands
6 1.72 grams for $100

Ireland
11 1.21 grams for $100

France
10 1.21 grams for $100

Italy
14 1.04 grams for $100

Poland
13 1.44 grams for $100

Norway
15 1.01 grams for $100

Iceland
18 0.73 grams for $100

Germany
17 1.20 grams for $100

Sweden
16 0.87 grams for $100

Estonia
19 0.75 grams for $100

North Macedonia
20 1.16 grams for $100

What are you drinking?

Beer, wine or something stronger?
We've analysed the World Health Organization's global alcohol consumption data to find out which country drinks the most of what

How it works: The map shows countries colour-coded by their most consumed alcoholic beverages in terms of litres of pure alcohol consumed. 'Beer' includes malt beers and 'spirits' includes all distilled beverages ▪ Grey areas represent countries where no data available

Sources: International Organisation of Vine and Wine, Kirin via The Daily Telegraph, World Health Organization's Global Health Observatory

NORTH AMERICA

SOUTH AMERICA

Prefer beer
Countries and territories where most alcohol is consumed from beer

Prefer wine
Countries and territories where most alcohol is consumed from wine

Prefer something stronger
Countries and territories where most alcohol is consumed from spirits

Who drinks most overall?

Annual litres of pure alcohol per capita:

Seychelles 20.5
Uganda 15.1
Czech Republic 14.4
Lithuania 13.2
Germany 12.9

Who drinks the most beer?

Annual litres of beer per capita:

Czech Republic 143.3	A
Namibia 108	B
Austria 106	C
Germany 104.2	D
Poland 100.8	E

Who drinks the most wine?

Annual litres of wine per capita:

F	**Luxembourg** 54.2
G	**Portugal** 52.5
H	**France** 51.2
I	Slovenia 45.8
J	Italy 43.6

Think it's better to settle for a partner who is 'more or less okay' rather than waiting for a soulmate
11%

Have a list of people they would class as enemies, either written down or in their head
18%

Say 'maybe' to something despite having no intention of doing it to avoid having to say 'no'
31%

Think their jobs are meaningless
37%

Do not consider the phrase 'If my words caused offence then I apologise' to be a 'proper' apology
56%

Think that nobody deserves to be a billionaire
51%

Talk about the weather at least once a day
41%

Face the shower while showering
44%

Iron their underwear
5%

Would never send a meal back at a restaurant, even if there was something wrong with it
7%

Have told their children that the ice cream van tune means the van has run out of ice cream
12%

Dislike or hate being shown baby photos
21%

Will not leave a group chat online that they don't want to be a part of
33%

Don't like either the Winter Olympics or the Summer Olympics
38%

Do not like pantomimes
42%

Oh yes they do

Believe a dish with a pastry lid but not a full pastry casing can be considered a pie
48%

What are you thinking?

Proportion of adult Britons who...

Opinion polls have long been used to take the temperature of nations on everything from voting intentions to favourite crisp flavours. We've looked at surveys ranging from the serious to the frivolous to find out what the UK really thinks

How it works: The graph represents the percentage of particular responses to questions asked in YouGov opinion polls between 2017 and 2021, with each person icon representing one percentage point

Source: YouGov

Prefer Pancake Day to Valentine's Day
61%

Would rather hear the bad news first, the good news second
67%

Don't eat their five a day
74%

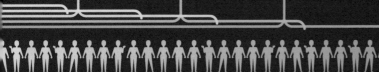

54%
Have bought alcohol when underage

63%
Eat their evening meal before 7pm

70%
Believe golf is boring

81%
Like crumpets

84%
Don't ever greet people with fist bumps

90%
Spend at least some time thinking fondly about the way things used to be

'Ban all Christmas-related advertising until at least 25th November'

'I've seen Sainsbury's selling Xmas puds before 20th September! Implement a law against this and bring the fun back into Xmas.'

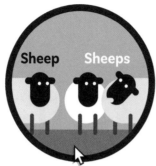

'Change the plural of sheep to sheeps'

'If the letter "s" is good enough for other words it's good enough for sheeps.'

'Common sense should be a legal requirement'

'Teaching people not to drop litter. Good manners. Not ringing 999 for non-emergencies. Putting claims in for stupid things.'

'Film Bad Boys 4 in Mitcham'

'Isn't it time that Mitcham took over cinema screens across the world?'

'Jousting to be included in the Olympics'

'Golf is in the Olympics! Why?! Get it replaced with jousting.'

'Make gingerism part of the discrimination laws'

'Ginger is a race too and they face as much discrimination/derogatory comments as any other person seen as "different" in society.'

'Make Harry Styles and Taylor Swift release a song together'

'I feel it would be incredibly beneficial to society.'

'Put David Attenborough's face on the 20 pound notes!'

'Will settle for a ten-pound note but not a 50 (as I very rarely see them).'

'Recognise Larry the cat with a knighthood'

'Brought into Number 10 as chief mouser, he has since helped the country with his diplomatic skills.'

'Say NO to SO'

'Repeatedly starting a sentence with the word "so" is a poor corruption of the English language.'

'Show us where Frank Ocean is on a map of the world'

'Please tell us. We need to know.'

'Standardise the word for bread roll to the word cob across the EU'

'Barm, baps, breadcake etc... quite obviously wrong. It is a COB. This should be enshrined in law.'

'Get my mate un-barred from the Golden Hind'

'My friend was wrongfully barred from the Golden Hind pub. This is an outrage and must be sorted ASAP.'

'Give British citizenship to Jesus Christ'

'This is in order to recognise the great contribution of Jesus Christ and Christianity in shaping the UK.'

'If a "truth serum" exists, insist all those in office take it'

'We deserve honesty from politicians and senior officials, and would have a stronger country if they were always honest.'

'Increase the standard size bottle of wine to one litre'

'Very often that "extra glass" is needed, and instead of it being in that bottle you have to open a second.'

Who's with me?

In 2011 the UK government launched a revamped e-petitions website. More than half of all petitions submitted since then have been rejected by moderators out of hand: we've delved into some of the pleas that fell on deaf ears

How it works: We've illustrated a selection of the rejected e-petitions submitted since 2011 to the UK government website. They are listed alphabetically and colour-coded by category:

● Arts and entertainment ● Food and drink ● Geography
● Society and politics ● Spelling and grammar ● Sport and leisure

Source: petition.parliament.uk. Figures as of December 2020

○ **141,756 petitions submitted to date**
● **86,026** petitions rejected
● **59,730** petitions accepted
● 194 debated in Parliament

'Stop crisp producers from filling more than 20% of the bag with air'

'As a student, it is forcing me into poverty.'

'Stop improving robots'

'It makes life easier but there is a limit... Please, if you want something to live for and not become a useless pile of flesh and bone, I am begging you to sign this petition.'

'Stop the name change of the pornstar martini'

'My kids deserve to grow up in a society where the name of a drink containing the word pornstar doesn't offend people.'

'Let ice cream vans play melodies after 7pm'

'East Ayrshire council is putting a ban on ice cream vans playing melodies after 7pm and is stopping the public knowing they are in the area.'

HOW DO WE SAVE THE PLANET

?

Questions about flying, energy
and mass veganism

Who's emitting the most CO₂?

The concentration of CO_2 in the atmosphere today is greater than at any time in at least 800,000 years. Nations are scrambling to get their emissions of the key greenhouse gas under control – but which have the furthest to go?

How it works: Map shows per capita CO_2 emissions from fossil fuel combustion and processes only, not from land-use change. It does not show emissions of non-CO_2 greenhouse gases

Sources: EDGAR – Emissions Database for Global Atmospheric Research by the European Commission, National Oceanic and Atmospheric Administration, UN Environment Programme ■ Grey areas represent countries where no data available

NORTH AMERICA

SOUTH AMERICA

Smaller emitters
Countries and territories with CO_2 emissions per person below annual global average of 4.93 tonnes

Bigger emitters
Countries and territories with CO_2 emissions per person above annual global average of 4.93 tonnes

41%

Who's full of hot air?

The G20 group of wealthy industrialised nations (including the EU) produce more than 80 percent of the globe's CO_2 emissions from fossil fuels between them. Fourteen members have increased their CO_2 emissions since 1990 and only six (including the EU) have decreased them. The biggest decrease is from the UK, whose CO_2 emissions have fallen by 41 percent since 1990

EUROPE

ASIA

AFRICA

OCEANIA

LOWEST
CO₂ EMISSIONS
PER PERSON

Burundi Ⓐ

0.03 TONNES PER PERSON

HIGHEST
CO₂ EMISSIONS
PER PERSON

Palau Ⓑ

59.9 TONNES PER PERSON

Highest with a population
of more than a million

Qatar Ⓒ

38.8 TONNES PER PERSON

HIGHEST
CO₂ EMISSIONS
OVERALL

China Ⓓ

11.5BN

TONNES PER YEAR,
30.3% OF THE GLOBAL TOTAL

What causes the UK's emissions?

Since 1990 the UK's greenhouse gas emissions have fallen the fastest of any G20 member. Over the following pages we look at where its remaining emissions come from and how drastic changes could cut them further

How it works: In the infographics on this page and the remainder of this section we've looked at all greenhouse gases emitted by the UK (not just CO_2), expressed in CO_2-equivalent tonnes. Below we've broken down the sources of the UK's emissions, with cloud sizes representing the proportional contributions of each sector. On the right we've looked at how the UK's per capita emissions have changed over time – to work this out we've taken the government's calculation of overall greenhouse gas emissions and added its estimate for aviation and shipping emissions attributable to the UK, which are not included in official totals. In all infographics in this section we've used the latest available figures from credible sources, but these are often estimates and should be taken as giving a broad overview rather than a forensic analysis

Sources: CAIT, Carbon Visuals, Global Carbon Atlas, Global Carbon Project, UK government, Our World in Data, World Bank
*Our calculation of per capita emissions level after 78% reduction from 1990 is based on the UK's projected population in 2035

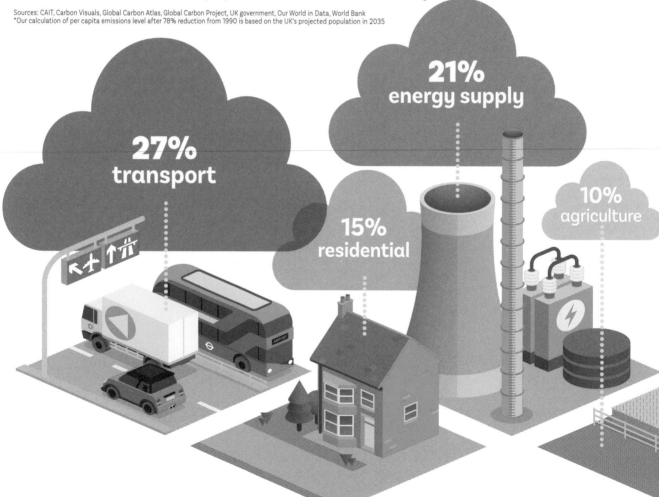

27% transport

21% energy supply

15% residential

10% agriculture

Are emissions rising or falling?

Globally, annual greenhouse gas emissions per person are still on the rise, but the UK is among a small group of countries in which they are falling

How's the UK doing on emissions?

The UK's greenhouse gas emissions have fallen significantly in recent years due to new environmental initiatives and the decline in heavy industry. However, the UK has effectively 'offshored' a lot of emissions to other countries which produce the things it consumes: such emissions are not included in these calculations. And the country's emissions are still greater than its proportion of the global population

UK's share of global population:
0.9%

UK's share of greenhouse gas emissions:
1%

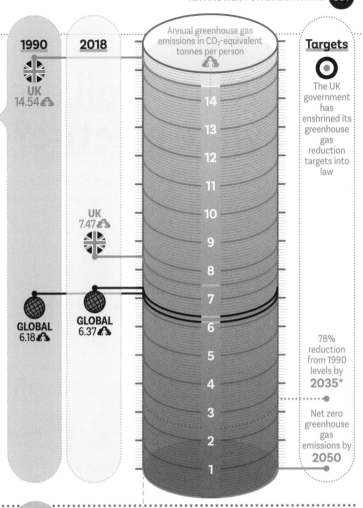

1990

2018

Annual greenhouse gas emissions in CO_2-equivalent tonnes per person

UK
14.54

UK
7.47

GLOBAL
6.18

GLOBAL
6.37

Targets

The UK government has enshrined its greenhouse gas reduction targets into law

78% reduction from 1990 levels by **2035***

Net zero greenhouse gas emissions by **2050**

17%
business

10%
waste management, industrial processes, the public sector and the land-use change and forestry sector

What does a tonne of CO_2 look like?

At normal pressure and 15 degrees Celsius one tonne of carbon dioxide gas occupies 534.8 cubic metres - about the same volume as a swimming pool that is three metres deep and 15 metres wide

1 tonne of CO_2

What if all the UK's cars were electric?

There are a huge number of cars in the UK and the country's residents use them a lot. But what would it cost the planet to move the nation's drivers into fossil fuel-free models? And what would be gained?

How it works: Below we've illustrated a proportional comparison of the numbers of different types of car in the UK, to see how many could be replaced by electric cars. We've then worked out the approximate emissions that would be created by replacing all of them immediately – should this transition take place over a longer period, this increase in emissions would be offset against the emissions cost of producing new internal combustion engine cars as older ones went out of use

Sources: Carbon Brief, Department for Transport, National Grid's Future Energy Scenarios, RAC. *Average emissions from building a mid-sized petrol car: 7 tonnes CO_2-equivalent.
**The mining of the elements needed to produce batteries for electric cars does also have a significant environmental impact beyond the production of greenhouse gases

How many cars are there in the UK?

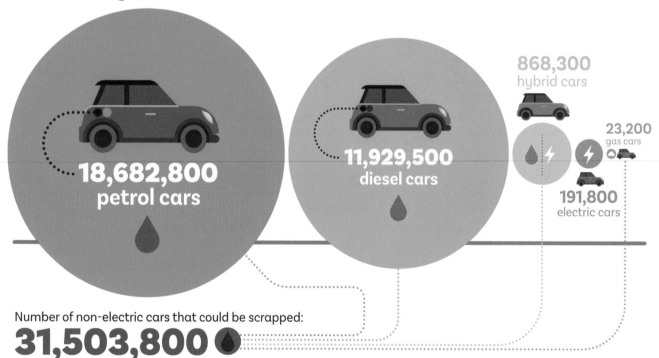

18,682,800
petrol cars

11,929,500
diesel cars

868,300
hybrid cars

23,200
gas cars

191,800
electric cars

Number of non-electric cars that could be scrapped:
31,503,800

Average distance travelled domestically by each UK citizen annually:
6,530 miles

60% by car

27% walking

 7% bus or train

 2% bike

4% air or sea

If all the UK's cars were electric we'd save:

1.02t

Annual greenhouse gas emissions in CO₂-equivalent tonnes per person

Current UK average
7.47

6.45

7
6
5
4
3
2
1

Total saving
68.5 million tonnes
from switching to electric cars

After an initial massive spike in emissions, provided they run on electricity from renewable sources**

Target
Net zero greenhouse gas emissions by **2050**

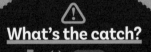

What's the catch?

Average emissions from building an electric car:
10 tonnes of CO₂ equivalent*

Emissions from building 31.5 million electric cars:
315 million
tonnes of CO₂

How's the UK doing?

Sales of electric cars are increasing rapidly, but they still form just a small part of the market

Number of new electric vehicles registered:

15,500 IN 2018
37,850 IN 2019
108,205 IN 2020

6.6% — Percentage of all new vehicles registered in 2020 that are electric cars

What if everyone stopped flying in and out of the UK?

Putting a stop to all flights to, from and within the UK would have major financial and social impacts – but would also save a significant amount of greenhouse gas emissions

How it works: We've visualised the proportional breakdown of the reasons for travel of flights taken to and from the UK's airports. We've then used this breakdown to apportion greenhouse gas emissions in CO_2-equivalent tonnes to each reason for travel

Sources: Department for Transport, UK government. Figures are from before the coronavirus pandemic. *While not reflected in this government figure, the non-greenhouse gas effects of flying – including its impact on cloud formation and ozone generation – significantly increase its contribution to global warming

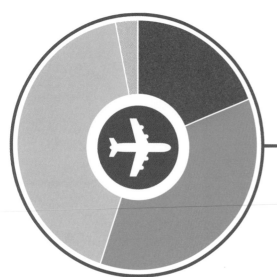

How busy are the UK's airports?

Flights landing at and taking off from UK airports in a normal year:

2,214,000 ✈

Total number of passengers arriving at and departing from UK airports in a normal year:

296,658,000

- ● **Business trips** 19%
- ● **Visiting friends and family** 36%
- ● **Holidays** 42%
- ● **Other** 3%

1.4 million tonnes saved each year
If all UK domestic flights ceased

7 million tonnes saved each year
If everyone stopped flying to or from the UK on business

13.3 million tonnes saved each year
If everyone stopped flying to or from the UK to visit friends and/or family

15.6 million tonnes saved each year
If everyone stopped flying to or from the UK on holiday

Annual greenhouse gas emissions in CO_2-equivalent tonnes per person

 If all the UK's cars were electric we'd save: **1.02t**

 If we all stopped flying in and out of the UK we'd save: **0.57t**

Total saving
38.4 million tonnes
If all flights to, from and within the UK ceased*

Current UK average
7.47

6.45

5.88

7

6

5

4

3

2

1

Target
Net zero greenhouse gas emissions by **2050**

⚠ What's the catch?

Number of people employed in the aviation industry in the UK, including manufacturing, maintenance and air freight:
230,000

Value of the UK aviation industry:
£22 billion

 ## How's the UK doing?

Not very well. The number of people passing through UK airports has almost tripled since 1990

102,418,000 PEOPLE IN 1990

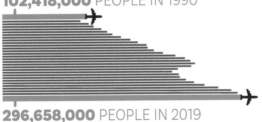

296,658,000 PEOPLE IN 2019

What if the UK closed all its fossil fuel power plants?

Some options for removing oil, coal and gas from electricity production

How it works: We've broken down the sources of the UK's electricity production and made hypothetical estimates of the cost to replace fossil fuels

Sources: Centre for Alternative Technology, BBC, Coire Glas, Department for Business, Ecotricity, Energy and Industrial Strategy, The Eco Experts, EDF, Energy Sage, Inspire Energy, New Statesman, Npower, World Energy

How much does the UK rely on fossil fuels?

Annual electricity produced from the UK's oil, gas and coal power stations:

148,000,000,000kWh

= 148 terawatt hours, enough power to boil 1.5 trillion kettles

●**Oil** + ●**Coal** + ●**Gas** = **45.6%**
● **Renewable energy sources** 37.1%
● **Nuclear energy** 17.3%

Option 1: Swap fossil fuels for home solar panels

3,000kWh
Annual average energy produced by a south-facing 3.5kw domestic solar panel system in the UK

Average system size: 14.6m²

49,333,333
Number of 3.5kw solar panel systems needed to replace energy produced by power stations run on fossil fuels

Total area needed: 720km² (about the size of Anglesey)

£296 billion
Estimated cost of purchasing 49,333,333 3.5kw home solar panel systems at £6,000 each

Building industrial solar power plants to generate the same output would cost an estimated **£71.5 billion**

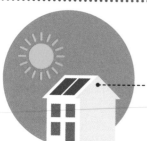

Option 2: Swap fossil fuels for wind turbines

6,000,000kWh
Estimated annual power production of an average onshore wind turbine

12,000,000kWh
Estimated annual power production of an average offshore wind turbine

24,666
Number of onshore wind turbines needed to replace fossil fuel energy production

12,333
Number of offshore wind turbines needed to replace fossil fuel energy production

£72 billion
Estimated cost of building 12,333 3.6 MW offshore turbines, based on UK government estimated pre-development and construction costs

---

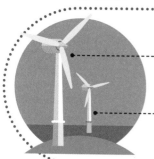

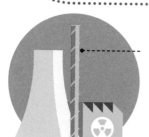

Option 3: Swap fossil fuels for nuclear reactors

 8
Current number of nuclear power plants currently operational in the UK

 14
Number of new nuclear power plants of the generating capacity of Sizewell B, the latest to be completed in the UK, needed to replace current fossil fuel energy production

£77 billion
Estimated cost of building 14 power plants of the same specification as Sizewell B, completed in 1995, based on a cost of £5.5 billion each, adjusted for inflation

If all the UK's cars were electric we'd save: **1.02t**

If we all stopped flying in and out of the UK we'd save: **0.57t**

If the UK closed all its fossil fuel power plants we'd save: **0.88t**

Total saving
58.5 million tonnes
If all emissions from fossil-fuel-burning power plants ceased

Does not factor in the CO_2 costs of construction and installation of new solar, wind or nuclear facilities, or the extra electricity needed if all the country's cars were electric

Annual greenhouse gas emissions in CO_2-equivalent tonnes per person

Current UK average
7.47

6.45

5.88

5.00

7

6

5

4

3

2

1

Target
Net zero greenhouse gas emissions by **2050**

What's the catch?

Though they produce less dangerous waste than nuclear energy, solar and wind energy do fluctuate with the weather. Electricity storage can help even out the supply – at a cost

One such project, Coire Glas in Scotland, will see water pumped uphill during low demand then released to produce hydro-electric power when needed

Estimated capacity: **1,500MW for 24 hours** (would power 3 million homes)
Est efficiency: **75%-85%**
Est completion and cost: **2026, £1 billion+**

 # How's the UK doing?

The country's decarbonisation of its electricity sector has been rapid, particularly when it comes to coal:

Electricity produced from coal-fired power stations:

72% IN 1990

2% IN 2019

 67 days, 22 hours, 55 minutes
The longest stretch so far without producing any coal-fired electricity in the UK, which came to an end on 16th June 2020

What if everyone in the UK went vegan?

Raising livestock produces significant amounts of greenhouse gases. Here's what could happen if the British completely cut out meat and dairy

How it works: We've calculated the potential reduction in greenhouse gases in CO_2-equivalent tonnes if the citizens of the UK switched to a vegan diet. Emissions are calculated based on an average calorie intake of 2,250 per day

Sources: Department for Business, Department for Transport, Department for Environment, Food & Rural Affairs (DEFRA), Finder, OECD-FAO Agricultural Outlook, The Vegan Society, Scarborough, P., Appleby, P.N., Mizdrak, A. et al. Dietary greenhouse gas emissions of meat-eaters, fish-eaters, vegetarians and vegans in the UK, Climatic Change.

How much gas does a vegan emit?

Average annual amount of CO_2 emitted by production, transportation, storage, cooking and wastage of food:

For a British **MEAT-EATER**
2.31 TONNES PER PERSON

65 million tonnes saved each year
If all **57,746,586** of the UK's **meat-eaters** went vegan

For a British **PESCATARIAN**
1.61 TONNES PER PERSON

1.3 million tonnes saved each year
If all **3,141,307** of the UK's **pescatarians** went vegan

For a British **VEGETARIAN**
1.56 TONNES PER PERSON

1.5 million tonnes saved each year
If all **4,010,179** of the UK's **vegetarians** went vegan

For a British **VEGAN**
1.19 TONNES PER PERSON

3.2kg
CO_2 emitted producing one **beef burger***

0.7kg
CO_2 emitted producing one **vegan burger**

*Based on ingredients in BBC Good Food recipes

What about the animals?

If the UK went vegan and didn't increase its food exports to compensate, there would be significant numbers of surplus livestock and, when they died, lots of empty grassland

Current UK livestock populations:

5,055,000 Pigs

9,600,000 Cattle and calves (of which 1,883,000 dairy cows)

32,697,000 Sheep and lambs

181,957,000 Poultry

114,000km^2 UK land used for permanent grassland, rough grazing and outdoor pigs, the same size as Scotland, Wales and Northern Ireland combined

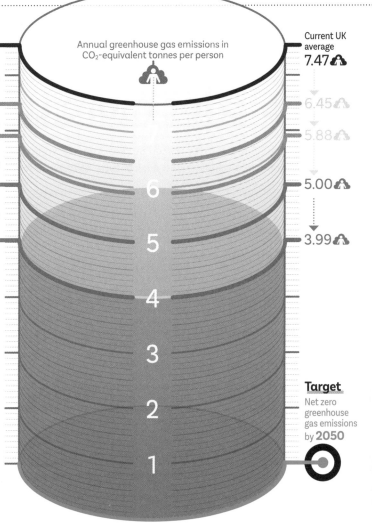

Annual greenhouse gas emissions in CO_2-equivalent tonnes per person

Current UK average
7.47

6.45

5.88

5.00

3.99

  If all the UK's cars were electric we'd save: **1.02t**

 If we all stopped flying in and out of the UK we'd save: **0.57t**

 If the UK closed all its fossil fuel power plants we'd save: **0.88t**

✕ If everyone in the UK went vegan we'd save: **1.01t**

Total saving
67.8 million tonnes
If everyone in the UK went vegan

However, this does include emissions generated by imported meat and dairy products, which are not included in the UK government's calculations or targets

Target
Net zero greenhouse gas emissions by **2050**

What's the catch?

Number of people employed in the UK livestock and dairy industries:
170,000

Value of the UK livestock and dairy industries:
£17 billion

How's the UK doing?

While increasing numbers of Britons are going meat free, overall levels of carnivorous consumption are not falling:

UK annual meat consumption in kilograms per person

IN 2000
TOTAL 59kg
5.9 Lamb/mutton
10.6 Beef/veal
17.1 Pork
25.4 Poultry

IN 2019
TOTAL 61.4kg
3.9
11.4
16
30.1

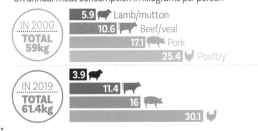

What if the UK planted a lot more trees?

The creation of new forests is seen by many environmental organisations as a key part of getting to net zero, but it will take a lot of trees and a lot of time to register a serious impact on emissions

How it works: We've used Forestry Commission estimates to calculate the CO_2-sequestering potential of different sizes of new forest, which we've represented on the map. Estimates for CO_2 sequestration of trees vary depending on their type, forest location etc

Sources: Climeworks, Forestry Commission, Nature, UK government

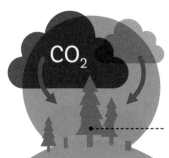

How much CO_2 do trees absorb?

Estimated area of forest needed to offset a million tonnes of CO_2 per year:

1,250km²

Yearly offset of new native woodland in the UK averaged out over 50-year period. The main CO_2 uptake occurs during trees' growing phase. Forest fires can lead to the re-emission of stored CO_2

1.2 million tonnes saved/year

By 2050, if the UK government met its target of planting 50km² of trees every year from 2020:

A total of 1,500km² of trees, about the size of South Yorkshire

9.5 million tonnes saved/year

If the UK planted a new forest the size of the whole of Yorkshire:

11,903km² of trees

62.3 million tonnes saved/year

If the UK planted a new forest the size of Scotland:

77,910km² of trees

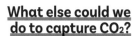

What else could we do to capture CO_2?

Carbon sequestration is an emerging technology which removes carbon dioxide from the air and puts it to agricultural use or otherwise stores it away

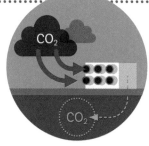

The Climeworks organisation has developed extractors powered by renewable energy which remove carbon dioxide from the air and pump it into underground rock. But how many extractors would be needed to match a forest the size of Scotland?

50 tonnes of CO_2 extracted from the air by each extractor annually

Number of extractors needed to match the CO_2 sequestration of a forest the size of Scotland:

1,246,560

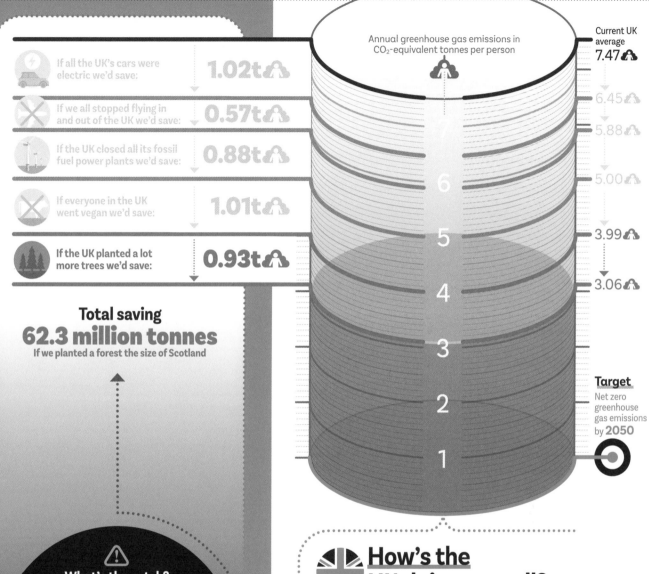

If all the UK's cars were electric we'd save: **1.02t**

If we all stopped flying in and out of the UK we'd save: **0.57t**

If the UK closed all its fossil fuel power plants we'd save: **0.88t**

If everyone in the UK went vegan we'd save: **1.01t**

If the UK planted a lot more trees we'd save: **0.93t**

Annual greenhouse gas emissions in CO_2-equivalent tonnes per person

Current UK average
7.47

6.45
5.88
5.00
3.99
3.06

7
6
5
4
3
2
1

Target
Net zero greenhouse gas emissions by **2050**

Total saving
62.3 million tonnes
If we planted a forest the size of Scotland

What's the catch?

While there is broad scientific agreement that planting trees is a net benefit in terms of climate change, there are some downsides:

Newly planted trees take many years to get up to their full carbon-sequestering capacity

Isoprene, a chemical emitted by some trees, can have warming as well as cooling effects on the planet

Trees with dark leaves can raise temperatures by absorbing more sunlight than bare ground

How's the UK doing overall?

Total greenhouse gas neutrality by 2050 looks ambitious. The UK could decarbonise cars and electricity, go vegan, plant a Scotland-sized forest and still not hit net zero. In addition, the emissions savings from going vegan would not all count towards the UK's targets as they include emissions generated by imported meat and dairy products, which are not included in the UK government's calculations or targets. However, new technologies – like solid-state batteries, low-carbon cement, heat pumps and more energy efficient products – could improve net zero prospects.

Even if the UK hit net zero by 2050, the world might not. If the planet continued on its 1990–2018 trajectory its emissions would have increased by 107 percent from 1990 levels by 2050.

Is there a Planet B?

The most Earth-like planet so far discovered is **Teegarden's Star b**. At a distance of 12 light years away that's a travel time of 324,843 years at humans' current fastest speed.

Proxima Centauri b is our nearest neighbour that is more Earth-like than Mars, and a mere 113,695 years' travel away

Teegarden's Star b
⊕ ESI: **0.95**
▶ 12 light years

TRAPPIST-1 d
⊕ ESI: **0.90**
▶ 41 light years

Proxima Centauri b
⊕ ESI: **0.87**
▶ 4.2 light years

Ross 128 b
⊕ ESI: **0.86**
▶ 11 light years

GJ 1061 c and GJ 1061 d
⊕ ESI: **0.86**
▶ 12 light years

CLOSEST

LESS THAN 100 LIGHT YEARS AWAY ◀

When are we going to Mars?

Elon Musk is planning the launch of a crewed mission to Mars by his SpaceX company in 2026, although he says it might happen two years earlier "if we get lucky". The astronauts will be delivered to the red planet by SpaceX's 'Starship' vehicle, which will be launched by its giant 'Super Heavy' rocket.

GJ 273 b
⊕ ESI: **0.85**
▶ 12 light years

GJ 667 C c
⊕ ESI: **0.80**
▶ 24 light years

TRAPPIST-1 e
⊕ ESI: **0.85**
▶ 41 light years

Wolf 1061 c
⊕ ESI: **0.80**
▶ 14 light years

GJ 667 C f
⊕ ESI: **0.77**
▶ 24 light years

Mars
⊕ ESI: **0.7**
Average distance:
▶ **225 million km**
(12.5 light minutes)

Can we escape to another Earth?

In case humanity's attempts to fix global warming end in failure, we've examined the options for moving to a different planet

How it works: We've used the Habitable Exoplanets Catalog to list all the exoplanets (those outside our solar system) it identifies with an Earth Similarity Index (ESI) rating higher than that of Mars. An ESI score over 0.8 means a planet has a similar size and insolation (exposure to a sun's rays) to Earth. We've ranked the planets by their score as well as their distance from Earth

Sources: Habitable Exoplanets Catalog, Planetary Habitability Laboratory, University of Puerto Rico at Arecibo, The Making of Star Trek by Stephen E Whitfield. *Enterprise travel times based on a maximum safe cruising speed of Warp Factor Six, or 216 times the speed of light, as stated in The Making of Star Trek

TOI-700 d
⊕ESI: **0.93**
▶ 101 light years

K2-72 e
⊕ESI: **0.90**
▶ 217 light years

Kepler-1649 c
⊕ESI: **0.90**
▶ 301 light years

FURTHEST

▶ 100+ ▶ 200+ ▶ 300+ ▶ 400+ ▶ 500+ ▶ 1,000+ ▶

What's a light year?

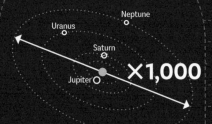

×1,000

According to the laws of physics, the speed of light in a vacuum is the fastest at which conventional matter, energy or any signal carrying information can travel.

One light year is the distance that can be travelled at the speed of light in one Earth year, equivalent to
9,460,528,400,000km
– a distance that is more than 1,000 times the diameter of Neptune's orbit of the sun

Are we nearly there yet?

The fastest that humans have ever travelled in space is 39,897 kilometres per hour – a record set by Apollo 10 in 1969. At that speed it would take us over 27,000 years to travel one light year.

Even *Star Trek*'s fictional *Starship Enterprise* would struggle to reach Kepler-442 b in less than **5.5 years***

Kepler-442 b
⊕ESI: **0.84**
▶ 1,193 light years

Kepler-1229 b
⊕ESI: **0.73**
▶ 865 light years

.95
.9
.85
.8
.75
.7

WHAT'S IN OUR NATURE

Questions about fauna, flora and
the rising tide of chickens

What's that on your wall?

Animal rights activists argue that shooting wild animals is cruel, but that hasn't stopped trophy hunters paying large sums of money to hunt exotic species and send their prizes back home. Here are the 20 most-targeted creatures on the planet

How it works: We've illustrated the species from which the greatest number of legal wild animal trophies were exported from 2015 to 2020 according to the Convention on International Trade in Endangered Species of Wild Fauna and Flora (CITES). Animals are displayed in order from the smallest to the greatest number of trophies exported and displayed alongside information on their natural habitat and their status on the Red List of Threatened Species produced by the International Union for Conservation of Nature (IUCN)

Sources: CITES, IUCN, LionAid

African civet
Civettictis civetta

📍 AFRICA

#20 NUMBER OF TROPHIES:
590

IUCN STATUS:
LEAST CONCERN

Bontebok
Damaliscus pygargus pygargus

📍 AFRICA

#19 NUMBER OF TROPHIES:
649

IUCN STATUS:
LEAST CONCERN

Southern lechwe
Kobus leche

📍 AFRICA

#18 NUMBER OF TROPHIES:
712

IUCN STATUS:
NEAR THREATENED

Bighorn sheep
Ovis canadensis

📍 NORTH AMERICA

#17 NUMBER OF TROPHIES:
715

IUCN STATUS:
LEAST CONCERN

Lion
Panthera leo
📍 AFRICA
#15 NUMBER OF TROPHIES:
817
⚠️ IUCN STATUS:
CRITICALLY ENDANGERED

Siberian ibex
Capra sibirica
📍 CENTRAL ASIA
#14 NUMBER OF TROPHIES:
1,079
◇ IUCN STATUS:
NEAR THREATENED

Vervet monkey
Chlorocebus pygerythrus
📍 AFRICA
#13 NUMBER OF TROPHIES:
1,646
⬤ IUCN STATUS:
LEAST CONCERN

Yellow baboon
Papio cynocephalus
AFRICA 📍
NUMBER OF TROPHIES: #16
720
IUCN STATUS:
LEAST CONCERN ⬤

How many lions are left in Africa?

Estimated African lion population

Countries where
wild lions are
extinct

Countries with
small, scattered
wild lion
populations or
where they may
be extinct

Some wild lion
populations exist

1940s:
450,000

1960s:
100,000

2020:
15,244

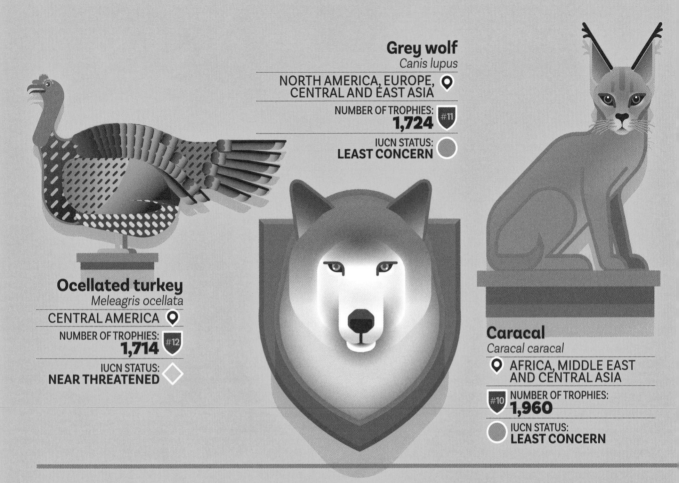

Grey wolf
Canis lupus

NORTH AMERICA, EUROPE, CENTRAL AND EAST ASIA

NUMBER OF TROPHIES:
1,724 #11

IUCN STATUS:
LEAST CONCERN

Ocellated turkey
Meleagris ocellata

CENTRAL AMERICA

NUMBER OF TROPHIES:
1,714 #12

IUCN STATUS:
NEAR THREATENED

Caracal
Caracal caracal

AFRICA, MIDDLE EAST AND CENTRAL ASIA

#10 NUMBER OF TROPHIES:
1,960

IUCN STATUS:
LEAST CONCERN

Where could I buy a bit of a crocodile?

Top five countries with the largest number of legally exported crocodile trophies, 2015-2020

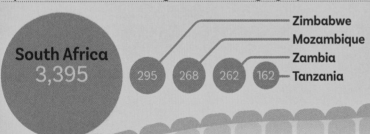

South Africa
3,395

295 — Zimbabwe
268 — Mozambique
262 — Zambia
162 — Tanzania

Brown bear
Ursus arctos

📍 NORTH AMERICA, EUROPE, CENTRAL AND EAST ASIA

#9 NUMBER OF TROPHIES:
2,117

⬤ IUCN STATUS:
LEAST CONCERN

Blackbuck
Antilope cervicapra

📍 CENTRAL ASIA

#8 NUMBER OF TROPHIES:
2,161

⬤ IUCN STATUS:
LEAST CONCERN

Leopard
Panthera pardus

📍 AFRICA AND CENTRAL ASIA

#7 NUMBER OF TROPHIES:
2,980

⬤ IUCN STATUS:
VULNERABLE

Chacma baboon
Papio ursinus

AFRICA 📍

NUMBER OF TROPHIES:
6,191 #5

IUCN STATUS:
LEAST CONCERN ⬤

Nile crocodile
Crocodylus niloticus

AFRICA 📍

NUMBER OF TROPHIES:
4,497 #6

IUCN STATUS:
LEAST CONCERN ⬤

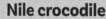

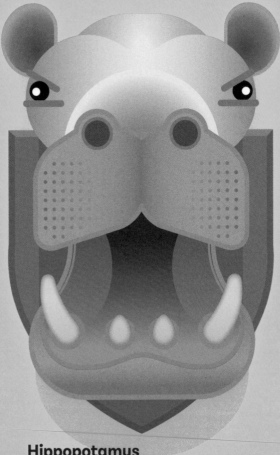

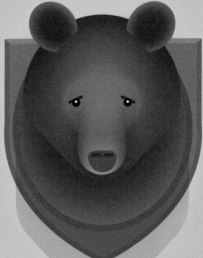

Hartmann's mountain zebra
Equus zebra hartmannae

📍 AFRICA

#3 NUMBER OF TROPHIES:
8,988

⬡ IUCN STATUS:
VULNERABLE

American black bear
Ursus americanus

📍 NORTH AMERICA

#2 NUMBER OF TROPHIES:
13,456

⬤ IUCN STATUS:
LEAST CONCERN

Hippopotamus
Hippopotamus amphibius

📍 AFRICA

#4 NUMBER OF TROPHIES:
6,678

⬡ IUCN STATUS:
VULNERABLE

What's the most prized part of an elephant?

Top five most legally exported African savanna elephant trophies, 2015-2020, by type

405
Feet

702
Bones, skulls and teeth

872
Trunks, ears and tails

7,377
Skins, skin pieces and hair

A further 1,738 unspecified/miscellaneous trophies were reported, plus five pieces of genitalia

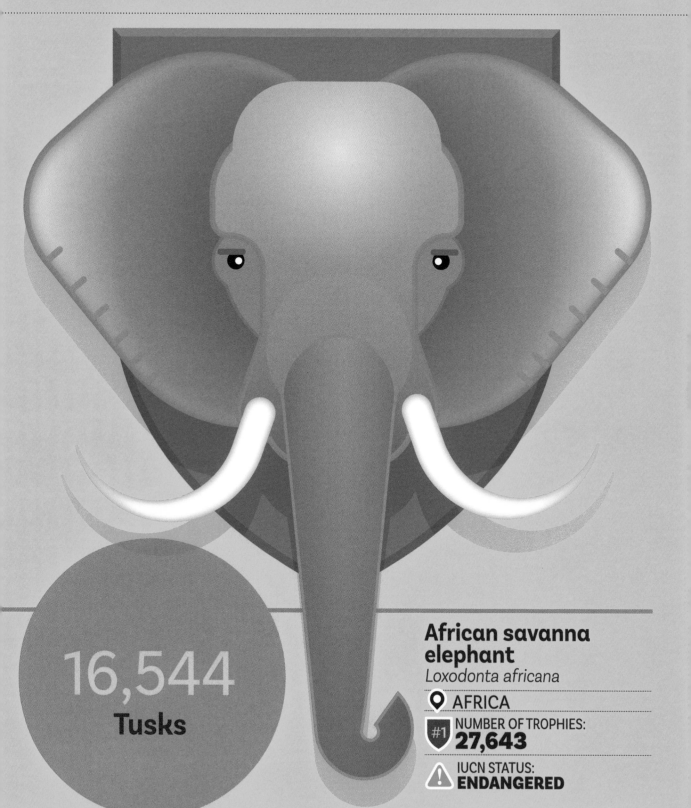

16,544
Tusks

African savanna elephant
Loxodonta africana

◉ AFRICA

#1 NUMBER OF TROPHIES:
27,643

⚠ IUCN STATUS:
ENDANGERED

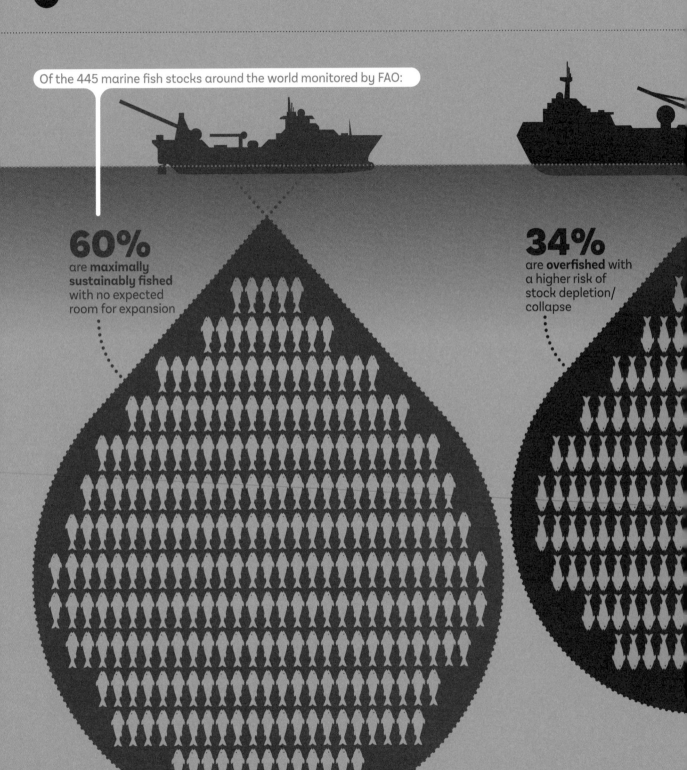

Of the 445 marine fish stocks around the world monitored by FAO:

60%
are **maximally
sustainably fished**
with no expected
room for expansion

34%
are **overfished** with
a higher risk of
stock depletion/
collapse

6%
are **underfished**
and not currently
being exploited

Are there plenty more fish in the sea?

Industrial trawler fishing has had a major impact on global fish stocks
- we take a look at the situation beneath the surface

How it works: Each fish represents one of the 445 aggregated stocks monitored by the Food and Agriculture
Organization of the United Nations, categorised by the level they are being fished at as of 2020

Source: UN Food and Agriculture Organization

Aves
🔍 11,106
Birds, including ostriches, penguins,
sparrows and hummingbirds
⚠✕ 14.8%

⚠ 2,708 **216 ✕**

⚠ 1,459

186 ✕

Insecta
🔍 8,046
Insects, including
mosquitoes,
beetles and bees
⚠✕ 24.7%

Total species with
IUCN status data

Number classified as
under threat by IUCN

Number classified as
extinct by IUCN

Percentage of
species with IUCN
status that are under
threat or already
extinct

Actinopterygii
🔍 16,434
Ray-finned fishes, including cod,
salmon and goldfish
⚠✕ 17.8%

1,851

139 ✕

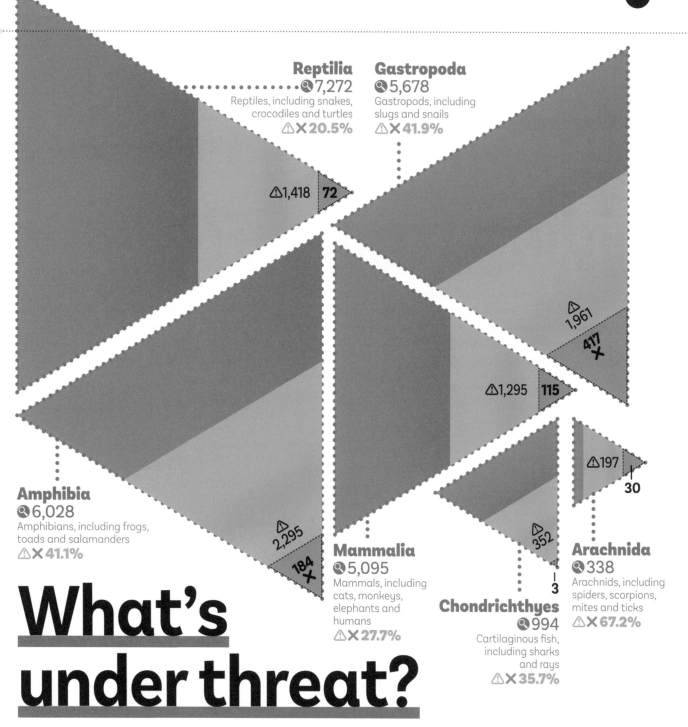

Reptilia
🔍7,272
Reptiles, including snakes,
crocodiles and turtles
⚠✕20.5%

⚠1,418 · 72

Gastropoda
🔍5,678
Gastropods, including
slugs and snails
⚠✕41.9%

⚠1,961

417 ✕

⚠1,295 · 115

⚠197 ·
30

Amphibia
🔍6,028
Amphibians, including frogs,
toads and salamanders
⚠✕41.1%

⚠2,295

184 ✕

Mammalia
🔍5,095
Mammals, including
cats, monkeys,
elephants and
humans
⚠✕27.7%

⚠352

3

Chondrichthyes
🔍994
Cartilaginous fish,
including sharks
and rays
⚠✕35.7%

Arachnida
🔍338
Arachnids, including
spiders, scorpions,
mites and ticks
⚠✕67.2%

What's
under threat?

Driven by land-use changes, pollution and global warming, biodiversity on Earth is in steep decline.
We've used the IUCN Red List to visualise the existential status of key species, from insects to reptiles

How it works: Each triangle represents a class of animals, sized according to the number of species of that class which have status data
available from the International Union for Conservation of Nature (IUCN). Each triangle is colour-coded by the percentage of these species in
each category of the IUCN's 2020 Red List of Threatened Species. Extinct numbers include 'possibly extinct' and 'possibly extinct in the wild'

Source: The International Union for Conservation of Nature's Red List of Threatened Species

Are extinct animals just hiding from us?

In recent years a series of creatures previously believed to have died out have made a dramatic reappearance. Many had been presumed extinct for over a century – particular kudos goes to Bocourt's terrific skink. Great name, great at hiding

How it works: We've charted the years between the last reported sighting of a number of species before they were presumed extinct and the date of their reappearance:

Year of last recorded sighting

Year of rediscovery

Location of rediscovery

Sources: Endangered Species Foundation, Global Wildlife, The Guardian, Gulf News, National Geographic, Scientific American, Shetland News, Surrey Wildlife Trust, Time magazine

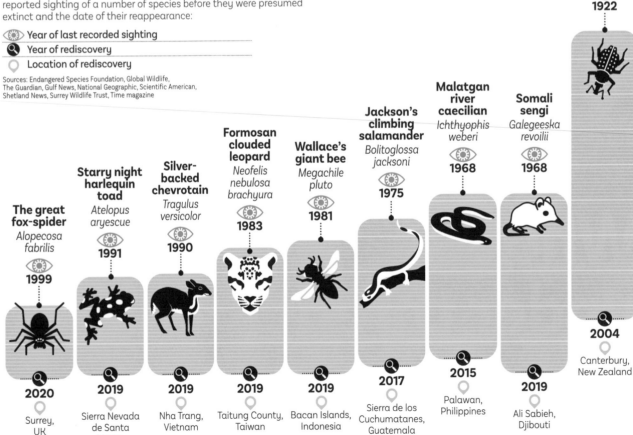

Canterbury knobbled weevil
Hadramphus tuberculatus
1922
2004
Canterbury, New Zealand

Malatgan river caecilian
Ichthyophis weberi
1968
2015
Palawan, Philippines

Somali sengi
Galegeeska revoilii
1968
2019
Ali Sabieh, Djibouti

Jackson's climbing salamander
Bolitoglossa jacksoni
1975
2017
Sierra de los Cuchumatanes, Guatemala

Wallace's giant bee
Megachile pluto
1981
2019
Bacan Islands, Indonesia

Formosan clouded leopard
Neofelis nebulosa brachyura
1983
2019
Taitung County, Taiwan

Silver-backed chevrotain
Tragulus versicolor
1990
2019
Nha Trang, Vietnam

Starry night harlequin toad
Atelopus aryescue
1991
2019
Sierra Nevada de Santa Marta, Colombia

The great fox-spider
Alopecosa fabrilis
1999
2020
Surrey, UK

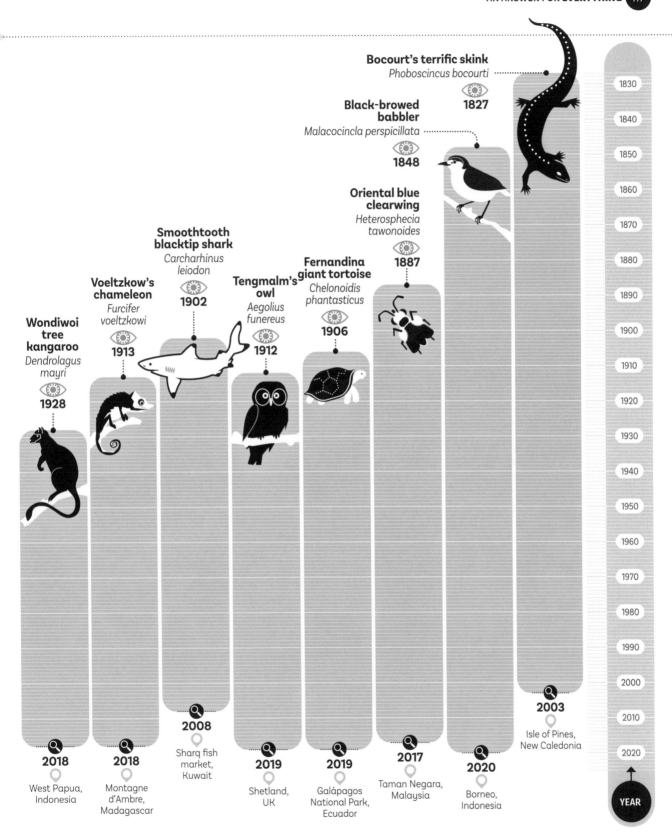

Bocourt's terrific skink
Phoboscincus bocourti
1827

Black-browed babbler
Malacocincla perspicillata
1848

Oriental blue clearwing
Heterosphecia tawonoides
1887

Smoothtooth blacktip shark
Carcharhinus leiodon
1902

Tengmalm's owl
Aegolius funereus
1912

Fernandina giant tortoise
Chelonoidis phantasticus
1906

Voeltzkow's chameleon
Furcifer voeltzkowi
1913

Wondiwoi tree kangaroo
Dendrolagus mayri
1928

2018
West Papua, Indonesia

2018
Montagne d'Ambre, Madagascar

2008
Sharq fish market, Kuwait

2019
Shetland, UK

2019
Galápagos National Park, Ecuador

2017
Taman Negara, Malaysia

2020
Borneo, Indonesia

2003
Isle of Pines, New Caledonia

1830
1840
1850
1860
1870
1880
1890
1900
1910
1920
1930
1940
1950
1960
1970
1980
1990
2000
2010
2020

YEAR

How many chickens are there?

Humans outnumber many of the other animals on the planet – but thanks to our appetites and the invention of industrial farming, even our record high population has been dwarfed by that of chickens

Source: UN Food and Agriculture Organization, numbers as of 2019

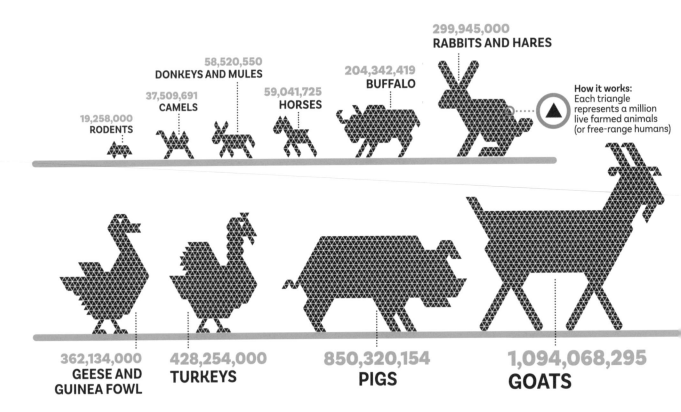

19,258,000
RODENTS

37,509,691
CAMELS

58,520,550
DONKEYS AND MULES

59,041,725
HORSES

204,342,419
BUFFALO

299,945,000
RABBITS AND HARES

How it works:
Each triangle represents a million live farmed animals (or free-range humans)

362,134,000
GEESE AND GUINEA FOWL

428,254,000
TURKEYS

850,320,154
PIGS

1,094,068,295
GOATS

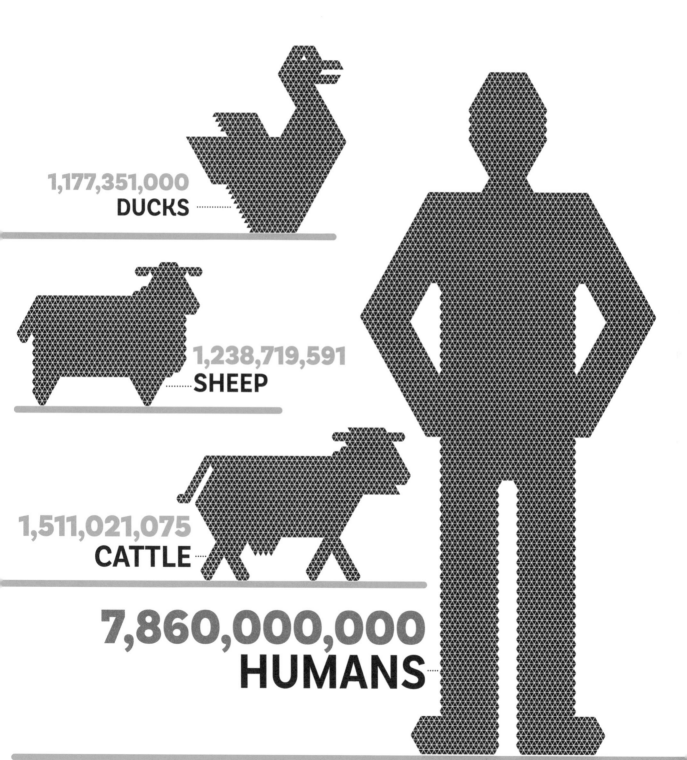

1,177,351,000
DUCKS

1,238,719,591
SHEEP

1,511,021,075
CATTLE

**7,860,000,000
HUMANS**

THERE ARE
25,915,318,000
CHICKENS

Where are all the chickens?

Prior to World War II chickens were widely considered a source of eggs not meat, but with the post-war rationing of pork, lamb and beef, we soon developed a hunger for hen. Since 1961 global consumption of chicken meat has grown by over 500 percent, leading to a world filled with chickens. But where are there more chickens than people?

How it works: The map highlights countries where the stocks of live chickens outnumber people as of 2019. ▪ Grey areas represent countries where no data is available

Sources: UN Food and Agriculture Organisation, Poultry World.
Chicken consumption figures = annual consumption in 2019

NORTH AMERICA

SOUTH AMERICA

Where chickens outnumber people
Countries and territories with more chickens than humans

Where people outnumber chickens
Countries and territories with more humans than chickens

Who eats the most chicken?

Top three countries with the highest average annual chicken consumption per person

63kg	58kg	57kg
Malaysia	USA	Brazil

EUROPE

ASIA

AFRICA

OCEANIA

Ⓐ

TOP FIVE PLACES WITH THE HIGHEST NUMBER
OF CHICKENS PER PERSON

Ⓐ **Brunei** 🐔🐔🐔🐔🐔🐔🐔🐔🐔🐔🐔🐔🐔🐔🐔🐔🐔🐔🐔 39
Ⓑ **Guyana** 🐔🐔🐔🐔🐔🐔🐔🐔🐔🐔🐔🐔🐔🐔🐔🐔🐔🐔 37
Ⓒ **Trinidad and Tobago** 🐔🐔🐔🐔🐔🐔🐔🐔🐔🐔🐔🐔🐔🐔 28
Ⓓ Bolivia 🐔🐔🐔🐔🐔🐔🐔🐔🐔🐔 20
Ⓔ Dominican Republic 🐔🐔🐔🐔🐔🐔🐔🐔🐔 17

What are plants for?

Almost 400,000 plant species have been discovered and catalogued so far around the world, and we've found uses for less than ten percent of them. How exactly does our exploitation of the Earth's flora break down?

How it works: Plants with a catalogued purpose are represented proportionally according to their use. Multi-purpose plants are counted in more than one category

Sources: Kew State of the World's Plants report, World Checklist of Useful Plant Species

Total number of plant species that have a documented use:

40,292

Fuels 2,529

Gene sources 5,212
Including breeding programmes

Environmental 8,983
Including soil improvement, water purification, windbreaks and firebreaks

Food 12,513

Invertebrate food 1,041

Human food 7,039

Animal food 4,433

Materials
13,663

Including fibres, woods
and resins

Pharmaceutical
32,271

Medicines
26,662

Poisons
3,013

Social uses 2,596
Including tobacco
and recreational drugs

ARE YOU NOT ENTERTAINED

?

Questions about films, music
and murderous soap operas

What's your favourite film?

A blockbuster film can unite the world, pulling in crowds from Hollywood to Hull. But what's the secret to making a mega hit? To find out, we've listed the most successful film at the box office every year since the first talkie in 1927

How it works: We've taken The Numbers' list of best-performing films at the global box office every year since 1927 and researched the number of tickets sold, the review score and source material for each. **⊘Tickets data** is the best estimate of tickets sold in the US – the biggest film market in the world over the period and the only one with data going back to 1927 – according to IMDb. Where ticketing data are unavailable we've used the domestic box office in the US divided by the average price of a cinema ticket in the country that year. The **★review score** is the average of a film's critical and audience score out of 100 on Rotten Tomatoes. Films are colour-coded by source material.

FILMS BASED ON:

- An original idea
- Books, short stories, the Bible
- Comic books
- Folk tales
- Historical events
- Songs, plays and musicals
- Television show
- Theme-park rides and toys
- Films that are sequels, prequels or subsequent entries in a franchise

- **!!** Best Picture and Best Director Oscar winners
- **!** Best Picture Oscar winners

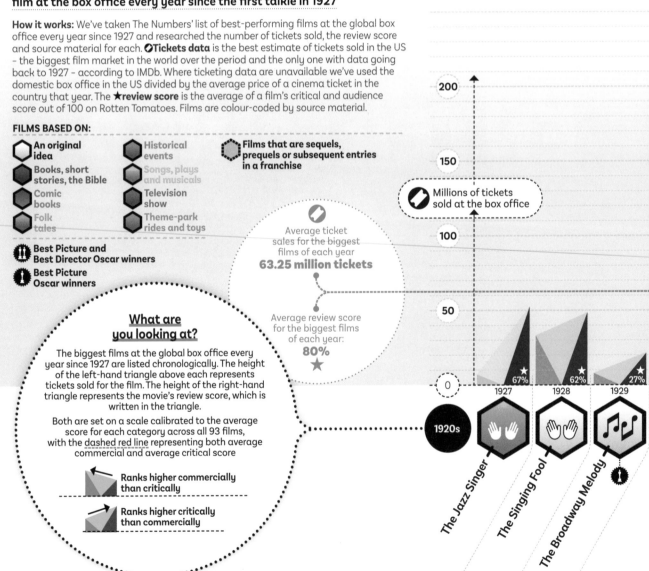

What are you looking at?

The biggest films at the global box office every year since 1927 are listed chronologically. The height of the left-hand triangle above each represents tickets sold for the film. The height of the right-hand triangle represents the movie's review score, which is written in the triangle.

Both are set on a scale calibrated to the average score for each category across all 93 films, with the dashed red line representing both average commercial and average critical score

- ◄ Ranks higher commercially than critically
- ◄ Ranks higher critically than commercially

Average ticket sales for the biggest films of each year
63.25 million tickets

Average review score for the biggest films of each year:
80% ★

Millions of tickets sold at the box office

200

150

100

50

0

1927 ★67% — 1928 ★62% — 1929 ★27%

1920s

The Jazz Singer — The Singing Fool — The Broadway Melody

What's the biggest blockbuster movie of all time?

Gone with the Wind, 1939 ① **202,286,200**

Star Wars, 1977 ② **178,119,500**

The Sound of Music, 1965 ③ **142,485,200**

ET: The Extra-Terrestrial, 1982 ④ **141,854,300**

Titanic, 1997 ⑤ **135,549,800**

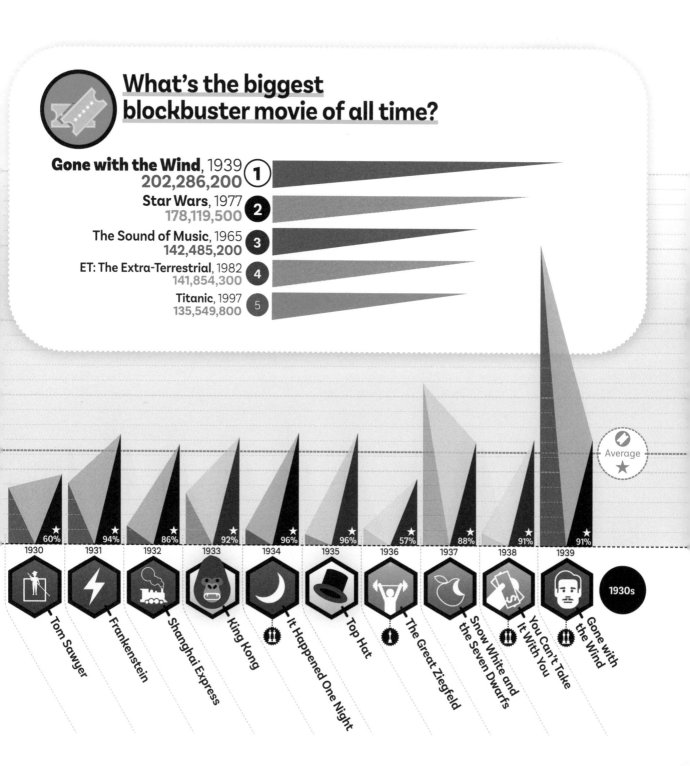

Average ★

1930	1931	1932	1933	1934	1935	1936	1937	1938	1939
60%	94%	86%	92%	96%	96%	57%	88%	91%	91%

Tom Sawyer

Frankenstein

Shanghai Express

King Kong

It Happened One Night

Top Hat

The Great Ziegfeld

Snow White and the Seven Dwarfs

You Can't Take It With You

Gone with the Wind

1930s

What makes a hit Disney film?

A breakdown of the House of Mouse's biggest hits

How it works:
We've taken the 11 Walt Disney Animation Studios films from our list of the biggest blockbusters and analysed them for common attributes. Pixar movies and films that combine live action and animation are excluded

	Royalty	A dead parent	Talking animals	A comic sidekick	Singing about dreams	Love at first sight
Snow White and the Seven Dwarfs, 1937	♛	●	✕	◐	♪	◉
Pinocchio, 1940	✕	✕	!	◐	♪	✕
Bambi, 1942	♛	●	!	◐	✕	◉
Cinderella, 1950	♛	●	!	◐	♪	◉
Peter Pan, 1953	✕	✕	◐	◐	✕	◉
Lady and the Tramp, 1955	✕	◐	!	◐	✕	◉
One Hundred and One Dalmatians, 1961	✕	✕	!	◐	✕	◉
The Jungle Book, 1967	♛	●	!	◐	♪	◉
Aladdin, 1992	♛	●	!	◐	♪	◉
The Lion King, 1994	♛	●	!	◐	♪	✕
Frozen, 2013	♛	●	✕	◐	♪	◉

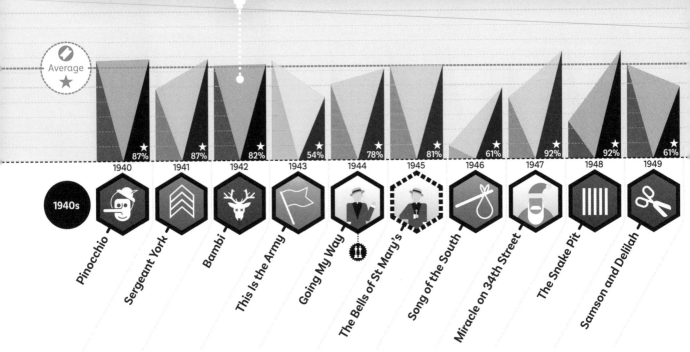

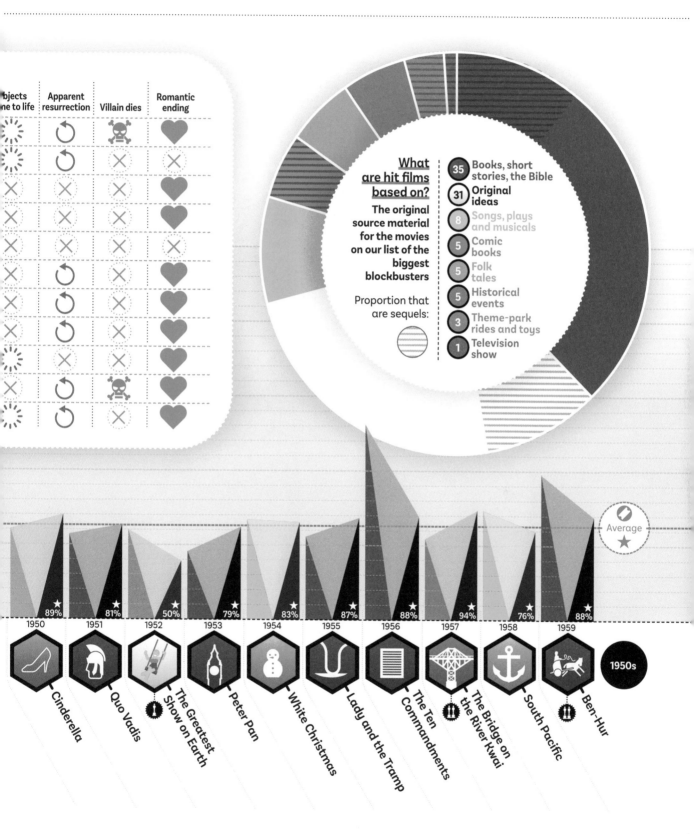

bjects ne to life	Apparent resurrection	Villain dies	Romantic ending

What are hit films based on?

The original source material for the movies on our list of the biggest blockbusters

Proportion that are sequels:

35	Books, short stories, the Bible
31	Original ideas
8	Songs, plays and musicals
5	Comic books
5	Folk tales
5	Historical events
3	Theme-park rides and toys
1	Television show

Average ★

1950	1951	1952	1953	1954	1955	1956	1957	1958	1959	
89%	81%	50%	79%	83%	87%	88%	94%	76%	88%	
Cinderella	Quo Vadis	The Greatest Show on Earth	Peter Pan	White Christmas	Lady and the Tramp	The Ten Commandments	The Bridge on the River Kwai	South Pacific	Ben-Hur	1950s

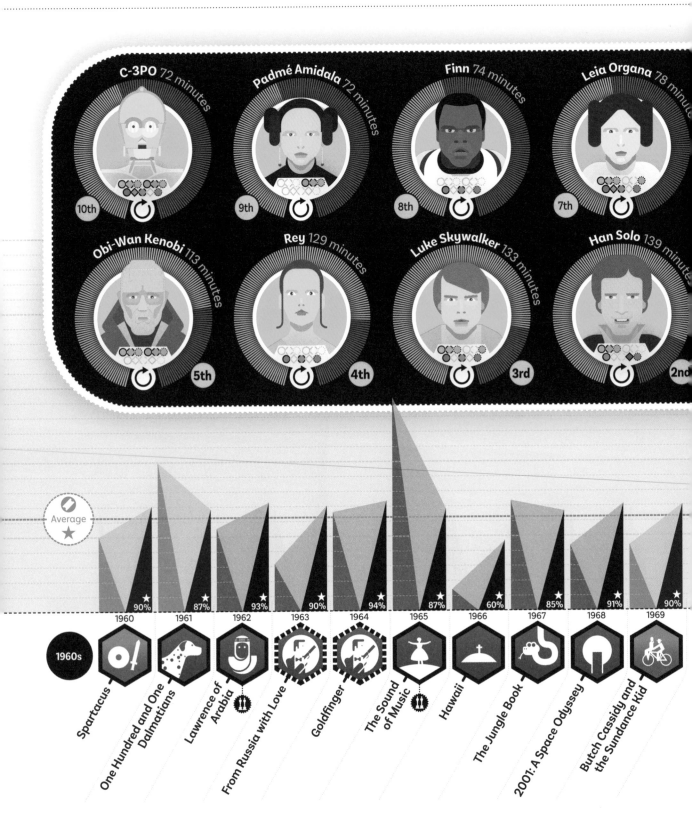

C-3PO 72 minutes
10th

Padmé Amidala 72 minutes
9th

Finn 74 minutes
8th

Leia Organa 78 minutes
7th

Obi-Wan Kenobi 113 minutes
5th

Rey 129 minutes
4th

Luke Skywalker 133 minutes
3rd

Han Solo 139 minutes
2nd

Average
★

1960 90%
1961 87%
1962 93%
1963 90%
1964 94%
1965 87%
1966 60%
1967 85%
1968 91%
1969 90%

1960s

Spartacus

One Hundred and One Dalmatians

Lawrence of Arabia

From Russia with Love

Goldfinger

The Sound of Music

Hawaii

The Jungle Book

2001: A Space Odyssey

Butch Cassidy and the Sundance Kid

Chewbacca 80 minutes

6th

Anakin Skywalker/Darth Vader 165 minutes

1st

Who rules a galaxy far, far away?

The top ten Star Wars characters ranked by screen time

How it works:
We've listed the ten characters that have been seen most on screen across all Star Wars films to date (including as ghosts, dreams and visions). Each character's total screentime is shown proportionally, rounded to the nearest minute. The films they appeared in are indicated with a colour-coded symbol
Source: Screen Rant

- Episode IV – A New Hope 1977
- Episode V – The Empire Strikes Back 1980
- Episode VI – Return of the Jedi 1983
- Episode I – The Phantom Menace 1999
- Episode II – Attack of the Clones 2002
- Episode III – Revenge of the Sith 2005
- Episode VII – The Force Awakens 2015
- ◇ Rogue One 2016
- Episode VIII – The Last Jedi 2017
- ◇ Solo: A Star Wars Story 2018
- Episode IX – The Rise of Skywalker 2019

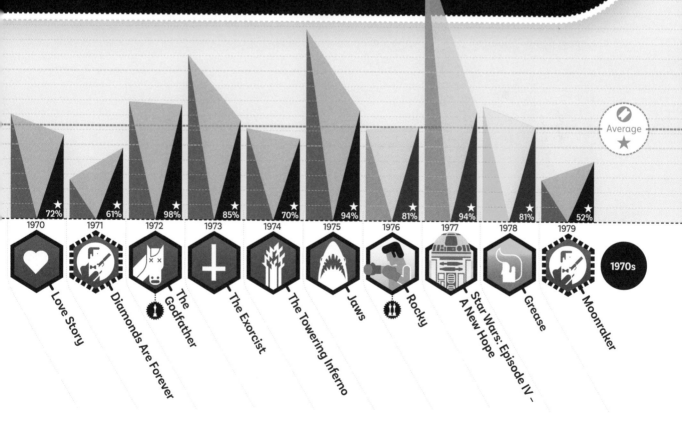

Average ★

1970	1971	1972	1973	1974	1975	1976	1977	1978	1979	1970s
★ 72%	★ 61%	★ 98%	★ 85%	★ 70%	★ 94%	★ 81%	★ 94%	★ 81%	★ 52%	

Love Story

Diamonds Are Forever

The Godfather

The Exorcist

The Towering Inferno

Jaws

Rocky

Star Wars: Episode IV – A New Hope

Grease

Moonraker

Who's directed the biggest films?

Directors behind the most films on our list of the biggest blockbusters

How it works: All co-directors – such as Disney's Hamilton Luske, Clyde Geronimi and Wilfred Jackson – receive a point for every film they worked on

Steven Spielberg

Hamilton Luske

Clyde Geronimi

Wilfred Jackson

James Cameron

Cecil B DeMille

Anthony Russo

Joe Russo

Who's the most popular movie star of all time?

Actors who star in the most films on our list of the biggest blockbusters

How it works: For lead actors we've analysed the lists of actors with top billing (first three names listed in credits) only. For supporting actor we've included all credited actors

Sources: Rotten Tomatoes, IMDb

Harrison Ford

Carrie Fisher

Mark Hamill

Robert Downey Jr

Sean Connery

Who's the most popular supporting actor?

Warwick Davis

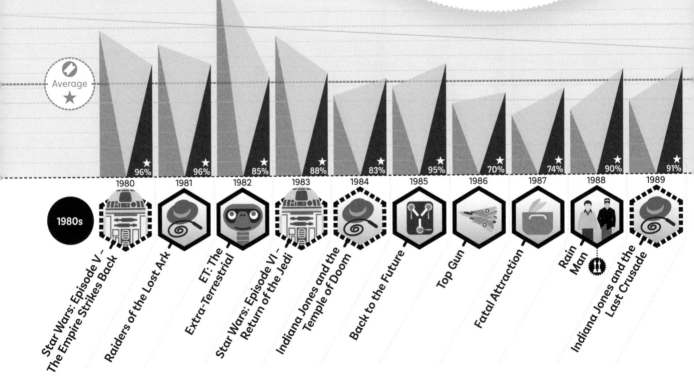

Average ★

1980s	1980	1981	1982	1983	1984	1985	1986	1987	1988	1989
	96%	96%	85%	88%	83%	95%	70%	74%	90%	91%

- Star Wars: Episode V – The Empire Strikes Back
- Raiders of the Lost Ark
- ET: The Extra-Terrestrial
- Star Wars: Episode VI – Return of the Jedi
- Indiana Jones and the Temple of Doom
- Back to the Future
- Top Gun
- Fatal Attraction
- Rain Man
- Indiana Jones and the Last Crusade

When was the golden age of blockbusters?

We've taken our list of the biggest films of every year to find which decades had...

	The biggest blockbusters Average number of tickets sold in the US	The best blockbusters Average review score for each film decade	The most Oscar-winning blockbusters Academy Award for Best Picture recipients per decade	The most blockbusters based on an original idea Films that are not sequels or based on a book, comic, historical event, toy, theme-park ride etc
1st	**1970s** 82,023,390	**1960s** 86.6%	**1930s** ●●●●	**1980s** ⬡⬡⬡⬡⬡⬡
2nd	**1980s** 71,593,750	**1980s** 86.6%	**1950s** ●●●	**1990s** ⬡⬡⬡⬡
3rd	**1950s** 70,197,714	**1930s** 84.9%	**1960s** ●●	**1920s** ⬡⬡
4th	**1990s** 69,472,880	**2010s** 82.4%	**1970s** ●●	**1930s** ⬡⬡
5th	**2010s** 64,802,070	**1950s** 81.2%	1920s ●	**1940s** ⬡⬡
6th	**1960s** 64,789,844	**1970s** 78.6%	1940s ●	**1970s** ⬡⬡
7th	**2000s** 62,722,390	**1990s** 78%	1980s ●	1950s ⬡
8th	**1940s** 49,775,933	**1940s** 77.3%	1990s ●	2000s ⬡
9th	**1930s** 47,703,905	**2000s** 77.2%	2000s ●	1960s 0
10th	**1920s** 17,111,111	**1920s** 51.8%	2010s 0	2010s 0

Sources: The Academy of Motion Picture Arts and Sciences, IMDb, The Numbers, Rotten Tomatoes

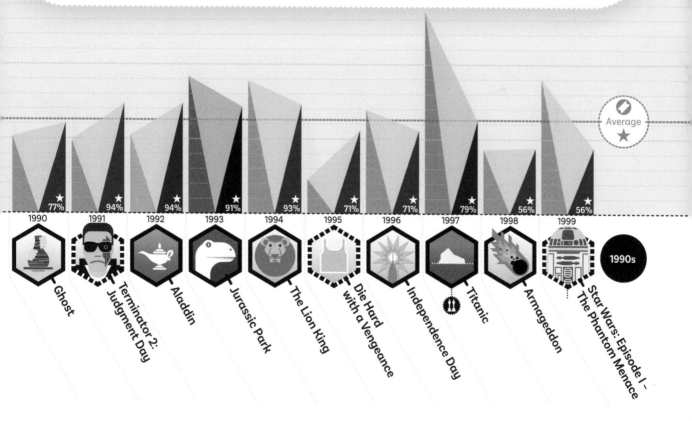

Average ★

1990	1991	1992	1993	1994	1995	1996	1997	1998	1999
77%	94%	94%	91%	93%	71%	71%	79%	56%	56%
Ghost	Terminator 2: Judgment Day	Aladdin	Jurassic Park	The Lion King	Die Hard with a Vengeance	Independence Day	Titanic	Armageddon	Star Wars: Episode I – The Phantom Menace

1990s

What are the biggest and best mega-franchises?

Five franchises comprising eight or more movies have films on our list: we've compared their average box office takings and review scores

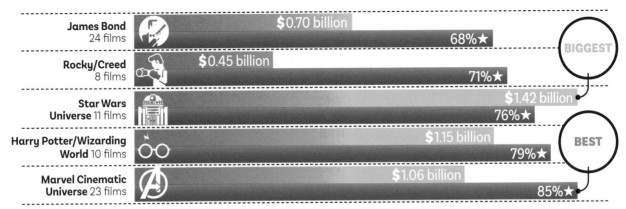

Franchise		Box office	Review
James Bond 24 films		$0.70 billion	68%★ — BIGGEST
Rocky/Creed 8 films		$0.45 billion	71%★
Star Wars Universe 11 films		$1.42 billion	76%★
Harry Potter/Wizarding World 10 films		$1.15 billion	79%★ — BEST
Marvel Cinematic Universe 23 films		$1.06 billion	85%★

How it works: Box office figures are adjusted for inflation. The box office takings of the Star Wars special editions released in 1997 are adjusted at a different rate to the original versions released in the '70s and '80s. The **review score** is the average of a film's critical and audience score out of 100 on Rotten Tomatoes. Only official films are counted. Franchises are listed in order of the release of their first instalment. Christopher Nolan's Batman films are treated as their own trilogy rather than part of the DC Extended Universe, which doesn't have a film on our list of blockbusters

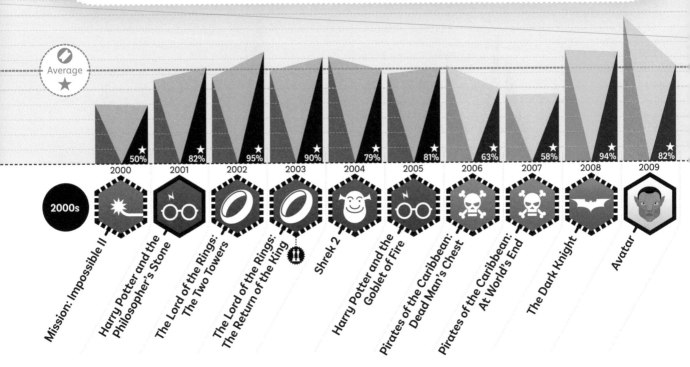

Average ★

2000s

Year	Film	Score
2000	Mission: Impossible II	50%
2001	Harry Potter and the Philosopher's Stone	82%
2002	The Lord of the Rings: The Two Towers	95%
2003	The Lord of the Rings: The Return of the King	90%
2004	Shrek 2	79%
2005	Harry Potter and the Goblet of Fire	81%
2006	Pirates of the Caribbean: Dead Man's Chest	63%
2007	Pirates of the Caribbean: At World's End	58%
2008	The Dark Knight	94%
2009	Avatar	82%

What are the best and worst blockbusters?

The films on our list of the biggest blockbusters which have the highest and lowest review scores

▲ BEST

The Godfather 98%
It Happened One Night 96%
Top Hat 96%
Raiders of the Lost Ark 96%
The Empire Strikes Back 96%

WORST ▼

Moonraker 52%
Mission: Impossible II 50%
The Greatest Show on Earth 50%
Transformers: Age of Extinction 34%
The Broadway Melody 27%

Average review score 80%

What happened next?

The Covid-19 pandemic saw many cinemas closed and studios postponing their blockbusters-in-waiting. The result was a surprising box office champion for 2020

Box office takings for Avengers: Endgame, the highest-grossing film of 2019: **$2,825,778,570**

Box office takings for Japanese anime movie Demon Slayer: Mugen Train, the highest-grossing film of 2020: **$479,495,948**

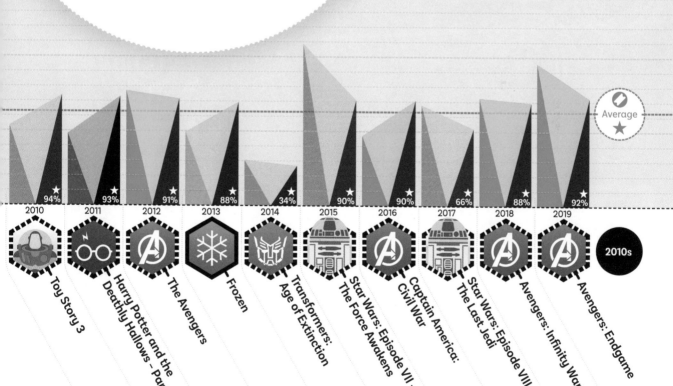

Average ★

2010	2011	2012	2013	2014	2015	2016	2017	2018	2019
★ 94%	★ 93%	★ 91%	★ 88%	★ 34%	★ 90%	★ 90%	★ 66%	★ 88%	★ 92%

2010s

Toy Story 3
Harry Potter and the Deathly Hallows – Part 2
The Avengers
Frozen
Transformers: Age of Extinction
Star Wars: Episode VII – The Force Awakens
Captain America: Civil War
Star Wars: Episode VIII – The Last Jedi
Avengers: Infinity War
Avengers: Endgame

How many heroes does it take to make $24 billion?

Between 2008 and 2019 the box office was dominated by the 23 highly lucrative films of the Marvel Cinematic Universe which between them grossed $24,291,435,246. We've charted their intricate web of characters and crossovers to see how the superheroes came together

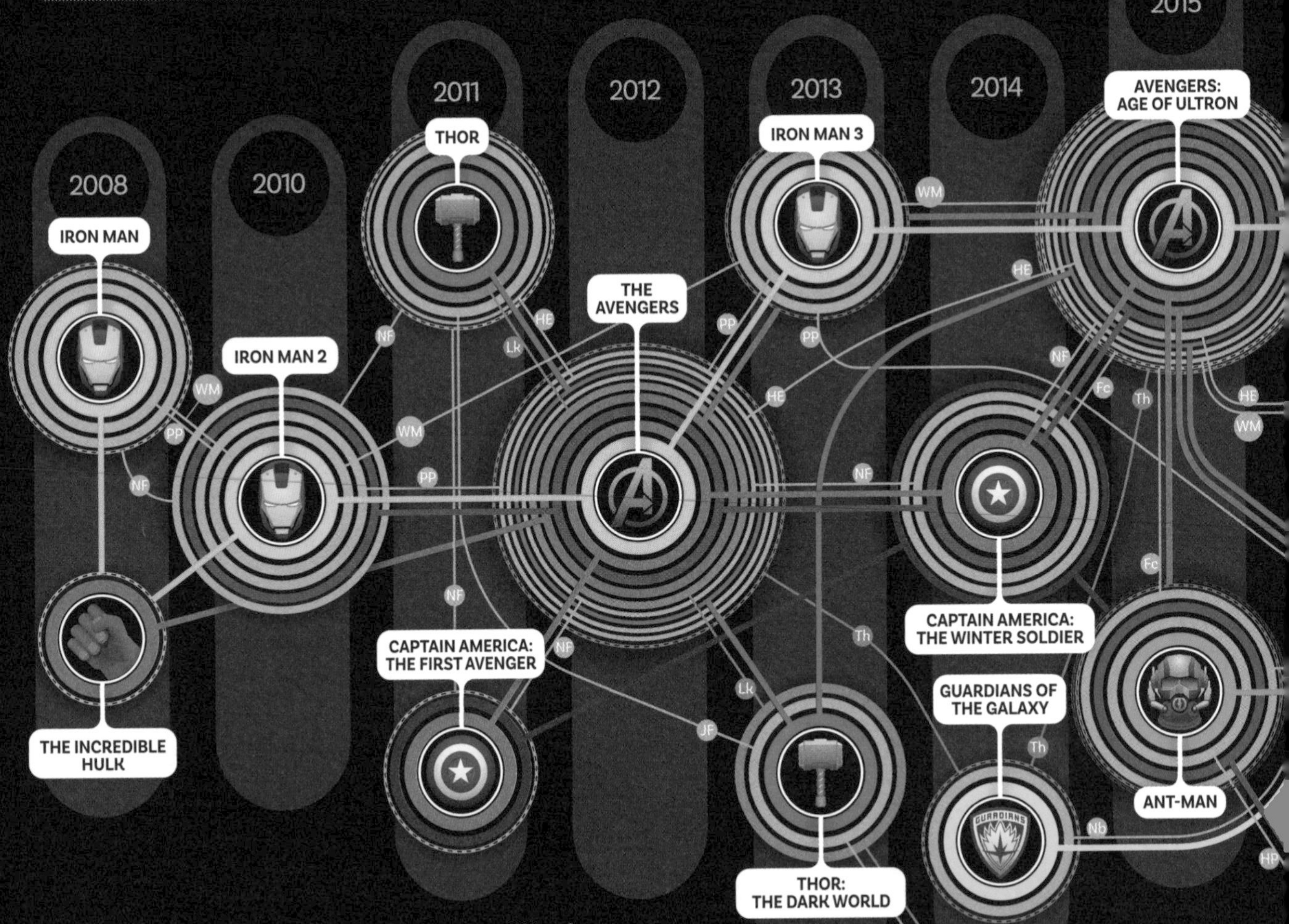

2015

2011   2012   2013   2014

AVENGERS:
AGE OF ULTRON

THOR

IRON MAN 3

2008   2010

IRON MAN

THE
AVENGERS

IRON MAN 2

THE INCREDIBLE
HULK

CAPTAIN AMERICA:
THE FIRST AVENGER

CAPTAIN AMERICA:
THE WINTER SOLDIER

GUARDIANS OF
THE GALAXY

ANT-MAN

THOR:
THE DARK WORLD

How it works: The timeline above shows the 23 Marvel films from 2008 to 2019 (Marvel's 'phases' 1-3) grouped by year of release. The rings around each film icon show which characters featured in the film. Those whose names appear in the titles of films (including Black Widow from phase 4) are represented by coloured lines and the ten supporting characters with the most screen time are represented with grey lines.
The Guardians of the Galaxy (Rocket, Gamora, Peter Quill, Drax, Mantis and Groot) are represented by a single yellow line. Character lines are arranged in concentric circles with the innermost showing the character with the most screen time – dashed circles denote a cameo or post-credits appearance. The bar chart on the right shows characters' average screen time per film to the nearest minute.

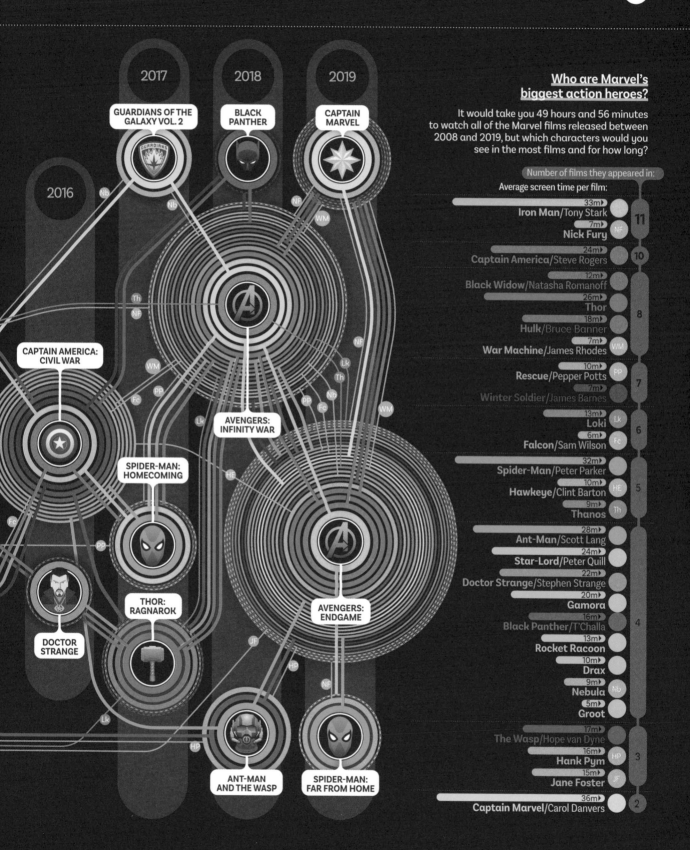

2017

GUARDIANS OF THE GALAXY VOL. 2

2018

BLACK PANTHER

2019

CAPTAIN MARVEL

2016

CAPTAIN AMERICA: CIVIL WAR

AVENGERS: INFINITY WAR

SPIDER-MAN: HOMECOMING

DOCTOR STRANGE

THOR: RAGNAROK

AVENGERS: ENDGAME

ANT-MAN AND THE WASP

SPIDER-MAN: FAR FROM HOME

Who are Marvel's biggest action heroes?

It would take you 49 hours and 56 minutes to watch all of the Marvel films released between 2008 and 2019, but which characters would you see in the most films and for how long?

Number of films they appeared in:
Average screen time per film:

	33m▶		
Iron Man/Tony Stark			**11**
7m▶			
Nick Fury	NF		
24m▶			**10**
Captain America/Steve Rogers			
12m▶			
Black Widow/Natasha Romanoff			
26m▶			
Thor			**8**
18m▶			
Hulk/Bruce Banner			
7m▶			
War Machine/James Rhodes	WM		
10m▶			
Rescue/Pepper Potts	PP		**7**
7m▶			
Winter Soldier/James Barnes			
13m▶			
Loki	Lk		**6**
6m▶			
Falcon/Sam Wilson	Fc		
32m▶			
Spider-Man/Peter Parker			
10m▶			
Hawkeye/Clint Barton	HE		**5**
9m▶			
Thanos	Th		
28m▶			
Ant-Man/Scott Lang			
24m▶			
Star-Lord/Peter Quill			
22m▶			
Doctor Strange/Stephen Strange			
20m▶			
Gamora			
16m▶			**4**
Black Panther/T'Challa			
13m▶			
Rocket Racoon			
10m▶			
Drax			
9m▶			
Nebula	Nb		
5m▶			
Groot			
17m▶			
The Wasp/Hope van Dyne			
16m▶			
Hank Pym	HP		**3**
15m▶			
Jane Foster	JF		
36m▶			
Captain Marvel/Carol Danvers			**2**

Who's the best James Bond?

It's a debate that's been raging for years – who's the best actor to don James Bond's bow tie and shoulder holster? We pit the six actors who have so far played the super-spy against one another

How it works: We've rated the six actors to have played James Bond in official Eon films over eight categories:

- How many Bond films have they been in? ◯
- What's the average critical score of their Bond films? ●
- What's the average box office of their Bond films? ◑
- What's their best reviewed Bond film? ◯
- What's their biggest box office hit as Bond? ◯
- How many martinis do they drink per Bond film? ◯
- How many kisses do they have per Bond film? ◯
- How many people do they kill per Bond film? ◯

The stacked bar charts under each Bond are composed of proportionally sized coloured blocks, with each coloured set representing a category. The text in the block representing the largest number in each category is appears in bold; the other blocks in that category are sized proportionally in relation to that winning number. Box office figures are adjusted for inflation at US dollar rate. Unofficial Bond films are excluded

*Daniel Craig's total and average-per-film figures do not include No Time to Die, which was yet to be released at time of going to press

Sources: BBC, IMDb, MI6 Headquarters, The Numbers, Rotten Tomatoes, US Bureau of Labor Statistics

Sean Connery 1962–1971

- 6
- **85.3%**
- $834m
- **99%** Goldfinger
- $1.17bn Thunderball
- 0.5
- **3**
- 13.7

George Lazenbu 1969

- 1
- 81%
- $581m
- 81% On Her Majesty's Secret Service
- $0.58bn OHMSS
- 1
- **3**
- 8

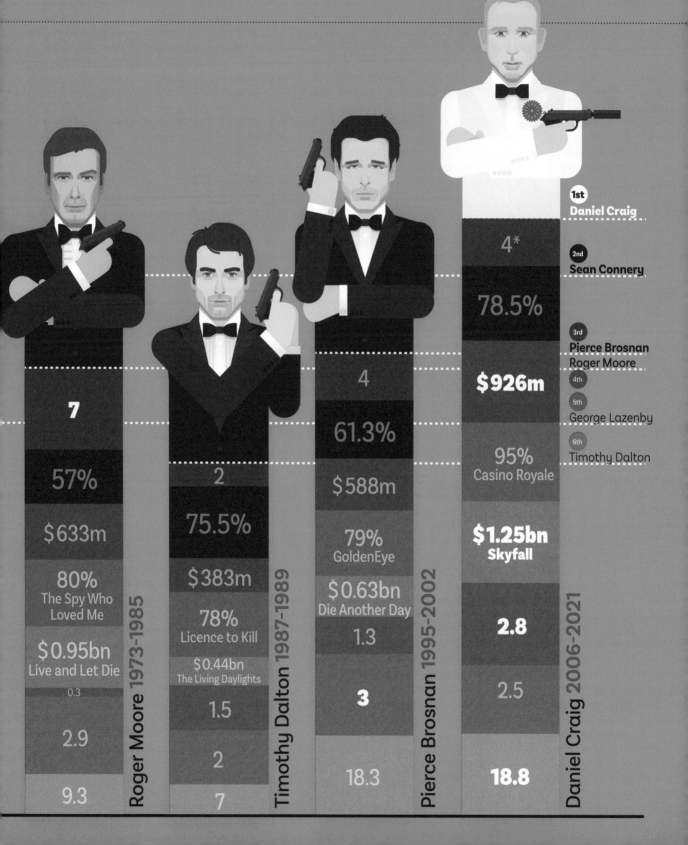

1st
Daniel Craig

4*

2nd
Sean Connery

78.5%

3rd
Pierce Brosnan
Roger Moore

4th

$926m

5th

George Lazenby

95%
Casino Royale

6th

Timothy Dalton

Roger Moore 1973-1985

7

57%

$633m

80%
The Spy Who
Loved Me

$0.95bn
Live and Let Die

0.3

2.9

9.3

Timothy Dalton 1987-1989

2

75.5%

$383m

78%
Licence to Kill

$0.44bn
The Living Daylights

1.5

2

7

Pierce Brosnan 1995-2002

4

61.3%

$588m

79%
GoldenEye

$0.63bn
Die Another Day

1.3

3

18.3

Daniel Craig 2006-2021

$926m

$1.25bn
Skyfall

2.8

2.5

18.8

Where have you been, Mr Bond?

James Bond may well be the best-travelled spy in film and literary history, clocking up air miles at an impressive rate. We've mapped every place 007 is known to have visited on Her Majesty's secret service

How it works: The map shows every identified country or territory visited by James Bond in official films, novels and short stories. Former countries and areas visited, such as the Soviet Union, are marked with the modern equivalent (Russia, Ukraine, etc). Film locations doubling for other countries are discounted

Sources: Empire, Fandom, The New Zealand Herald, Vox

NORTH AMERICA

D

SOUTH AMERICA

On Her Majesty's secret service

Countries and territories 007 has visited

I've been expecting you, Mr Bond

Countries and territories 007 has yet to visit

Who's been a double agent?

UK places that have passed as more exotic locales in Bond films

Aldershot, Hampshire, doubles as **North Korea** in *Die Another Day*, 2002

Swindon, Wiltshire, doubles as **Kazakhstan** in *The World is Not Enough*, 1999

Epsom, Surrey doubles as **St Petersburg** in *GoldenEye*, 1995

Pinewood Studios, Buckinghamshire doubles as **space** in *Moonraker*, 1979

EUROPE

ASIA

AFRICA

OCEANIA

Where's Bond been on screen?

Cities that 007 has visited the most
in the official Bond films, excluding London

Hong Kong 3 trips **A**

Istanbul 3 trips **B**

Venice 3 trips **C**

Where's Bond been in the books?

Cities that 007 has visited the most
in the official Bond books, excluding London

D **New York City** 7 trips

E Hong Kong 4 trips

F Paris 4 trips

How do you win an Oscar?

Which movie roles are linked with glory at the Academy Awards? We analysed 93 years of Best Actress and Best Actor awards to identify the character types most closely associated with winning the most prestigious film gong going

How it works: Winners of the Academy Awards for Best Actress and Best Actor are listed in order of the year of the ceremony at which they won their award. The most commonly shared attributes of the winning roles are represented proportionally in the central section

Sources: The Academy of Motion Picture Arts and Sciences, IMDb

BEST ACTOR WINNERS

Emil Jannings as Grand Duke Sergius Alexander	1929
Emil Jannings as August Schilling	1929
Warner Baxter as the Cisco Kid	1930
George Arliss as Benjamin Disraeli	1930
Lionel Barrymore as Stephen Ashe	1931
Wallace Beery as Andy 'Champ' Purcell	1932
Fredric March as Dr Jekyll and Mr Hyde	1932
Charles Laughton as King Henry VIII of England	1934
Clark Gable as Peter Warner	1935
Victor McLaglen as 'Gypo' Nolan	1936
Paul Muni as Louis Pasteur	1937
Spencer Tracy as Manuel Fidello	1938
Spencer Tracy as Father Flanagan	1939
Robert Donat as Charles Edward Chipping	1940
James Stewart as Macaulay 'Mike' Connor	1941
Gary Cooper as Alvin C York	1942
James Cagney as George M Cohan	1943
Paul Lukas as Kurt Muller	1944
Bing Crosby as Father Chuck O'Malley	1945
Ray Milland as Don Birnam	1946
Fredric March as Al Stephenson	1947
Ronald Colman as Anthony John	1948
Laurence Olivier as Hamlet, Prince of Denmark	1949
Broderick Crawford as Willie Stark	1950
*****José Ferrer** as Cyrano de Bergerac	1951
Humphrey Bogart as Charlie Allnut	1952
Gary Cooper as Marshal Will Kane	1953
★ **William Holden** as Sergeant JJ Sefton	1954
Marlon Brando as Terry Malloy	1955
Ernest Borgnine as Marty Piletti	1956
Yul Brynner as King Mongkut of Siam	1957
Alec Guinness as Colonel Nicholson	1958
David Niven as Major Angus Pollock	1959
Charlton Heston as Judah Ben-Hur	1960
Burt Lancaster as Elmer Gantry	1961
Maximilian Schell as Hans Rolfe	1962
★ **Gregory Peck** as Atticus Finch	1963
Sidney Poitier as Homer Smith	1964
Rex Harrison as Professor Henry Higgins	1965
Lee Marvin as Kid Shelleen and Tim Strawn	1966
Paul Scofield as Sir Thomas More	1967
Rod Steiger as Police Chief Bill Gillespie	1968
Cliff Robertson as Charly Gordon	1969
John Wayne as Rooster Cogburn	1970
George C Scott as General George S Patton, Jr	1971
Gene Hackman as Jimmy 'Popeye' Doyle	1972
Marlon Brando as Vito Corleone	1973
Jack Lemmon as Harry Stoner	1974
Art Carney as Harry Coombes	1975
Jack Nicholson as Randle Patrick 'Mac' McMurphy	1976
Peter Finch as Howard Beale	1977
Richard Dreyfuss as Elliot Garfield	1978
Jon Voight as Luke Martin	1979
Dustin Hoffman as Ted Kramer	1980
Robert De Niro as Jake LaMotta	1981
Henry Fonda as Norman Thayer, Jr	1982
Ben Kingsley as Mohandas Karamchand Gandhi	1983
Robert Duvall as Mac Sledge	1984
F Murray Abraham as Antonio Salieri	1985
William Hurt as Luis Molina	1986
Paul Newman as 'Fast' Eddie Felson	1987
Michael Douglas as Gordon Gekko	1988
Dustin Hoffman as Raymond Babbitt	1989
Daniel Day-Lewis as Christy Brown	1990
Jeremy Irons as Claus von Bülow	1991
Anthony Hopkins as Hannibal Lecter	1992
★ **Al Pacino** as Lieutenant Colonel Frank Slade	1993
Tom Hanks as Andrew Beckett	1994
Tom Hanks as Forrest Gump	1995
Nicolas Cage as Ben Sanderson	1996
Geoffrey Rush as David Helfgott	1997
Jack Nicholson as Melvin Udall	1998
Roberto Benigni as Guido Orefice	1999
Kevin Spacey as Lester Burnham	2000
Russell Crowe as Maximus Decimus Meridius	2001
Denzel Washington as Detective Alonzo Harris	2002
Adrien Brody as Władysław Szpilman	2003
Sean Penn as Jimmy Markum	2004
Jamie Foxx as Ray Charles	2005
Philip Seymour Hoffman as Truman Capote	2006
Forest Whitaker as Idi Amin	2007
Daniel Day-Lewis as Daniel Plainview	2008
Sean Penn as Harvey Milk	2009
Jeff Bridges as Otis 'Bad' Blake	2010
Colin Firth as King George VI	2011
Jean Dujardin as George Valentin	2012
Daniel Day-Lewis as Abraham Lincoln	2013
Matthew McConaughey as Ron Woodroof	2014
Eddie Redmayne as Stephen Hawking	2015
Leonardo DiCaprio as Hugh Glass	2016
Casey Affleck as Lee Chandler	2017
Gary Oldman as Winston Churchill	2018
*****Rami Malek** as Freddie Mercury	2019
Joaquin Phoenix as Arthur Fleck	2020
Anthony Hopkins as Anthony	2021

FIC
CHA

HISTORI

N
AM

BRIT
FROM ELS

T
PRESE
D

RECENT P

D

WHC

SOLDI
LAWM
MONAR
POLITI
CREATIVE/MEDIA
PERFO
BUSINESS
CRI

WHO P

S
SC

SE

AND W

DO
D
SC

DIE

★
Dead certs:
Winning roles
which
match all top
categories

1929 Janet Gaynor as Diane/Angela/The Wife - Indre ★
1930 **Mary Pickford** as Norma Besant
1930 **Norma Shearer** as Jerry Bernard Martin
1931 **Marie Dressler** as Min Divot
1932 **Helen Hayes** as Madelon Claudet
1934 Katharine Hepburn as Eva Lovelace ★
1935 **Claudette Colbert** as Ellie Andrews
1936 Bette Davis as Joyce Heath ★
1937 **Luise Rainer** as Anna Held
1938 **Luise Rainer** as O-Lan
1939 **Bette Davis** as Julie Marsden
1940 **Vivien Leigh** as Scarlett O'Hara
1941 **Ginger Rogers** as Kitty Foyle
1942 **Joan Fontaine** as Lina McLaidlaw Aysgarth
1943 **Greer Garson** as Kay Miniver
1944 **Jennifer Jones** as Bernadette Soubirous
1945 **Ingrid Bergman** as Paula Alquist Anton
1946 **Joan Crawford** as Mildred Pierce
1947 **Olivia de Havilland** as Josephine 'Jody' Norris
1948 **Loretta Young** as Katie Holstrom
1949 **Jane Wyman** as Belinda McDonald
1950 **Olivia de Havilland** as Catherine Sloper
1951 **Judy Holliday** as Emma 'Billie' Dawn
1952 **Vivien Leigh** as Blanche DuBois
1953 **Shirley Booth** as Lola Delaney
1954 **Audrey Hepburn** as Princess Ann
1955 **Grace Kelly** as Georgie Elgin
1956 **Anna Magnani** as Serafina Delle Rose
1957 **Ingrid Bergman** as Anna Koreff/Anastasia
1958 **Joanne Woodward** as Eve White/Eve Black/Jane
1959 **Susan Hayward** as Barbara Graham
1960 **Simone Signoret** as Alice Aisgill
1961 **Elizabeth Taylor** as Gloria Wandrous
1962 **Sophia Loren** as Cesira
1963 **Anne Bancroft** as Annie Sullivan
1964 **Patricia Neal** as Alma Brown
1965 **Julie Andrews** as Mary Poppins
1966 **Julie Christie** as Diana Scott
1967 **Elizabeth Taylor** as Martha
1968 **Katharine Hepburn** as Christina Drayton
1969 **Katharine Hepburn** as Eleanor of Aquitaine
1969 **Barbra Streisand** as Fanny Brice
1970 **Maggie Smith** as Jean Brodie
1971 **Glenda Jackson** as Gudrun Brangwen
1972 **Jane Fonda** as Bree Daniels
1973 **Liza Minnelli** as Sally Bowles
1974 **Glenda Jackson** as Vicki Allessio
1975 Ellen Burstyn as Alice Hyatt ★
1976 **Louise Fletcher** as Nurse Mildred Ratched
1977 **Faye Dunaway** as Diana Christensen
1978 Diane Keaton as Annie Hall ★
1979 **Jane Fonda** as Sally Hyde
1980 **Sally Field** as Norma Rae Webster
1981 **Sissy Spacek** as Loretta Lynn
1982 **Katharine Hepburn** as Ethel Thayer
1983 **Meryl Streep** as Sophie Zawistowska
1984 **Shirley MacLaine** as Aurora Greenway
1985 **Sally Field** as Edna Spalding
1986 **Geraldine Page** as Carrie Watts
1987 **Marlee Matlin** as Sarah Norman
1988 **Cher** as Loretta Castorini
1989 **Jodie Foster** as Sarah Tobias
1990 **Jessica Tandy** as Daisy Werthan
1991 **Kathy Bates** as Annie Wilkes
1992 **Jodie Foster** as Clarice Starling
1993 **Emma Thompson** as Margaret Schlegel
1994 **Holly Hunter** as Ada McGrath
1995 **Jessica Lange** as Carly Marshall
1996 **Susan Sarandon** as Sister Helen Prejean
1997 **Frances McDormand** as Marge Gunderson
1998 **Helen Hunt** as Carol Connelly
1999 **Gwyneth Paltrow** as Viola De Lesseps
2000 Hilary Swank as Brandon Teena*
2001 **Julia Roberts** as Erin Brockovich
2002 **Halle Berry** as Leticia Musgrove
2003 Nicole Kidman as Virginia Woolf*
2004 **Charlize Theron** as Aileen Wuornos
2005 **Hilary Swank** as Maggie Fitzgerald
2006 **Reese Witherspoon** as June Carter
2007 **Helen Mirren** as Queen Elizabeth II
2008 **Marion Cotillard** as Édith Piaf
2009 Kate Winslet as Hanna Schmitz*
2010 **Sandra Bullock** as Leigh Anne Tuohy
2011 **Natalie Portman** as Nina Sayers
2012 **Meryl Streep** as Margaret Thatcher
2013 **Jennifer Lawrence** as Tiffany Maxwell
2014 **Cate Blanchett** as Jeanette 'Jasmine' Francis
2015 **Julianne Moore** as Alice Howland
2016 **Brie Larson** as Joy Newsome
2017 **Emma Stone** as Mia Dolan
2018 **Frances McDormand** as Mildred Hayes
2019 **Olivia Colman** as Queen Anne
2020 **Renée Zellweger** as Judy Garland
2021 **Frances McDormand** as Fern

∗
Long shots:
Winning roles which match only one of the top categories – every winner matches at least one of the top categories

BEST ACTRESS WINNERS

Who's in the lead?

Multiple winners of the Academy Awards for Best Actor or Best Actress in a leading role:

Katharine Hepburn
Morning Glory, 1934
Guess Who's Coming to Dinner, 1968
The Lion in Winter, 1969
On Golden Pond, 1982

Daniel Day-Lewis
My Left Foot, 1990
There Will Be Blood, 2008
Lincoln, 2013

Frances McDormand
Fargo, 1997
Three Billboards Outside Ebbing, Missouri, 2018,
Nomadland, 2021

BEST OF THE REST:
Double Best Actor/Actress award winners:

Ingrid Bergman, Marlon Brando, Gary Cooper, Bette Davis, Olivia de Havilland, Tom Hanks, Dustin Hoffman, Anthony Hopkins, Sally Field, Jane Fonda, Jodie Foster, Glenda Jackson, Vivien Leigh, Fredric March, Jack Nicholson, Sean Penn, Luise Rainer, Meryl Streep, Hilary Swank, Elizabeth Taylor, Spencer Tracy

SHOULD YOU GROW A BEARD?

36% of Best Actor winners have won wearing some kind of facial hair

BEST DECADE FOR FACE FUZZ:
1970s

SHOULD YOU PLAY A SPORTSPERSON?

No! There's zero chance of winning as a sportsperson – unless you play a boxer:

WALLACE BEERY
in *The Champ*, 1932

ROBERT DE NIRO
in *Raging Bull*, 1981

HILARY SWANK
in *Million Dollar Baby*, 2005

SHOULD YOU DYE YOUR HAIR?

Best Actress winners by hair colour

● **BLONDE/ LIGHT BROWN**
● **BRUNETTE**
● **BLACK**
● **RED/AUBURN**
● **GREY**

What's so great about Meryl Streep?

When it comes to Oscar nominations for acting, nobody beats Meryl Streep. Of her 61 roles to date, over a third have resulted in Academy Award nominations. Here's how her record compares to other thespian big-hitters, with her critical and box office highs and lows visualised

How it works: Listed on the right are all of Streep's dramatic roles in feature films to date along with a proportional representation of their critical score on Rotten Tomatoes and total global box office takings. Box office numbers are adjusted for inflation

Sources: The Academy of Motion Picture Arts and Sciences, IMDb, The Numbers, Rotten Tomatoes

700   600

Who's been nominated for the most acting Oscars?

Performers who have been nominated eight or more times for the Academy Awards for Best Actor, Best Actress, Best Supporting Actor or Best Supporting Actress

⬤ **Nominations** ★ **Wins**

Meryl Streep
Katharine Hepburn
Jack Nicholson
Bette Davis
Laurence Olivier
Spencer Tracy
Paul Newman
Al Pacino
Marlon Brando
Jack Lemmon
Denzel Washington
Geraldine Page
Glenn Close
Peter O'Toole

BIGGEST
BOX OFFICE
$748,469,052
Mamma Mia!

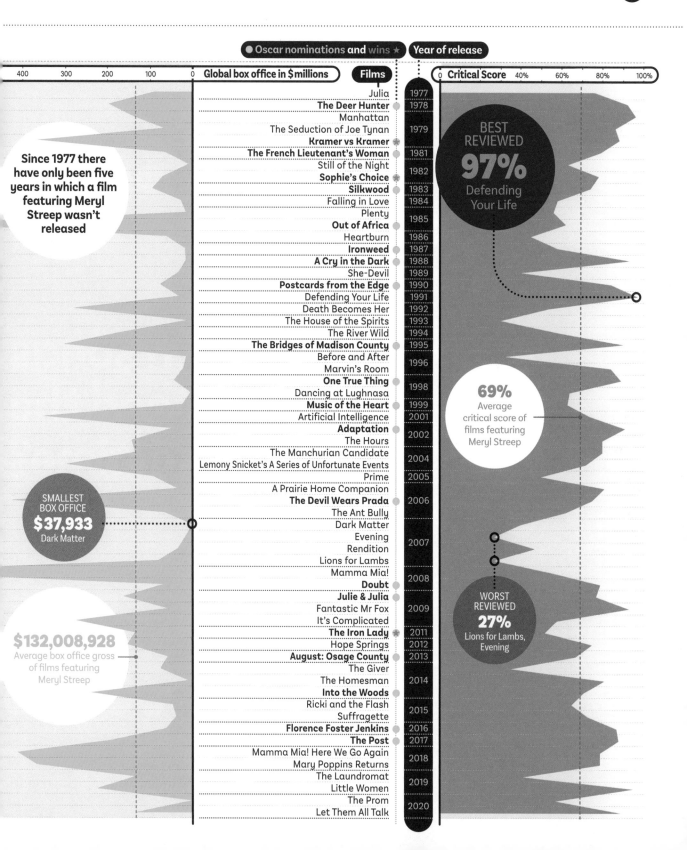

● Oscar nominations **and** wins ★   Year of release

Global box office in $millions   Films   **Critical Score**

| 400 | 300 | 200 | 100 | 0 |

| 0 | 40% | 60% | 80% | 100% |

Since 1977 there have only been five years in which a film featuring Meryl Streep wasn't released

BEST REVIEWED **97%** Defending Your Life

Julia	1977
The Deer Hunter	1978
Manhattan	
The Seduction of Joe Tynan	1979
Kramer vs Kramer ★	
The French Lieutenant's Woman ●	1981
Still of the Night	1982
Sophie's Choice ★	
Silkwood ●	1983
Falling in Love	1984
Plenty	1985
Out of Africa ●	
Heartburn	1986
Ironweed ●	1987
A Cry in the Dark ●	1988
She-Devil	1989
Postcards from the Edge ●	1990
Defending Your Life	1991
Death Becomes Her	1992
The House of the Spirits	1993
The River Wild	1994
The Bridges of Madison County ●	1995
Before and After	1996
Marvin's Room	
One True Thing ●	1998
Dancing at Lughnasa	
Music of the Heart ●	1999
Artificial Intelligence	2001
Adaptation ●	2002
The Hours	
The Manchurian Candidate	2004
Lemony Snicket's A Series of Unfortunate Events	
Prime	2005
A Prairie Home Companion	
The Devil Wears Prada ●	2006
The Ant Bully	
Dark Matter	
Evening	2007
Rendition	
Lions for Lambs	
Mamma Mia!	2008
Doubt ●	
Julie & Julia ●	2009
Fantastic Mr Fox	
It's Complicated	
The Iron Lady ★	2011
Hope Springs	2012
August: Osage County ●	2013
The Giver	
The Homesman	2014
Into the Woods ●	
Ricki and the Flash	2015
Suffragette	
Florence Foster Jenkins ●	2016
The Post ●	2017
Mamma Mia! Here We Go Again	2018
Mary Poppins Returns	
The Laundromat	2019
Little Women	
The Prom	2020
Let Them All Talk	

69% Average critical score of films featuring Meryl Streep

SMALLEST BOX OFFICE **$37,933** Dark Matter

$132,008,928 Average box office gross of films featuring Meryl Streep

WORST REVIEWED **27%** Lions for Lambs, Evening

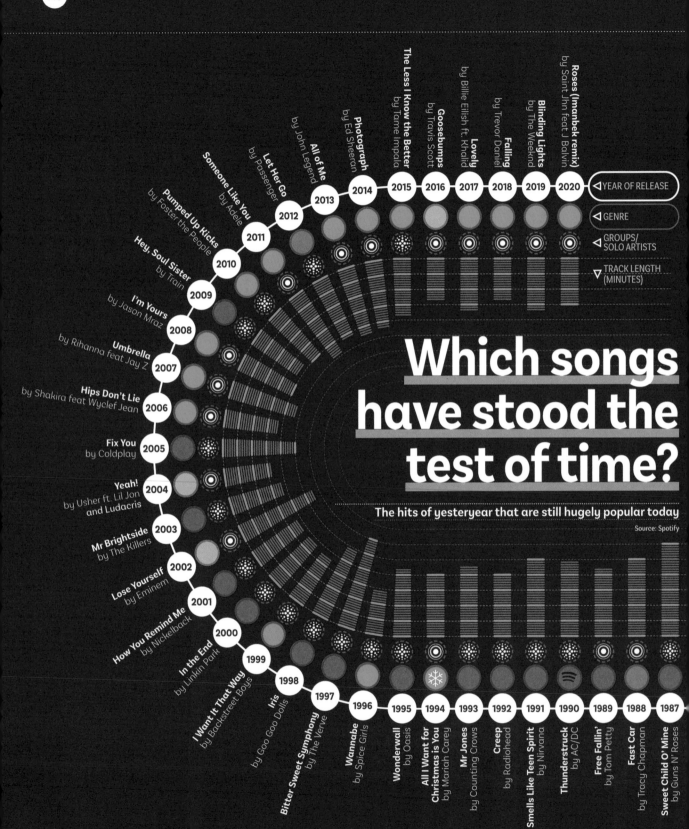

Which songs have stood the test of time?

The hits of yesteryear that are still hugely popular today

Source: Spotify

YEAR OF RELEASE

GENRE

GROUPS/ SOLO ARTISTS

TRACK LENGTH (MINUTES)

Roses (Imanbek remix) by Saint Jhn feat J Balvin — 2020

Blinding Lights by The Weeknd — 2019

Falling by Trevor Daniel — 2018

Lovely by Billie Eilish ft. Khalid — 2017

Goosebumps by Travis Scott — 2016

The Less I Know the Better by Tame Impala — 2015

2014

Photograph by Ed Sheeran — 2013

All of Me by John Legend — 2012

Let Her Go by Passenger — 2011

Someone Like You by Adele — 2010

Pumped Up Kicks by Foster the People — 2010

Hey, Soul Sister by Train — 2009

I'm Yours by Jason Mraz — 2008

Umbrella by Rihanna feat Jay Z — 2007

Hips Don't Lie by Shakira feat Wyclef Jean — 2006

Fix You by Coldplay — 2005

Yeah! by Usher ft. Lil Jon and Ludacris — 2004

Mr Brightside by The Killers — 2003

Lose Yourself by Eminem — 2002

How You Remind Me by Nickelback — 2001

In the End by Linkin Park — 2000

I Want It That Way by Backstreet Boys — 1999

Iris by Goo Goo Dolls — 1998

Bitter Sweet Symphony by The Verve — 1997

Wannabe by Spice Girls — 1996

Wonderwall by Oasis — 1995

All I Want for Christmas is You by Mariah Carey — 1994

Mr Jones by Counting Crows — 1993

Creep by Radiohead — 1992

Smells Like Teen Spirit by Nirvana — 1991

Thunderstruck by AC/DC — 1990

Free Fallin' by Tom Petty — 1989

Fast Car by Tracy Chapman — 1988

Sweet Child O' Mine by Guns N' Roses — 1987

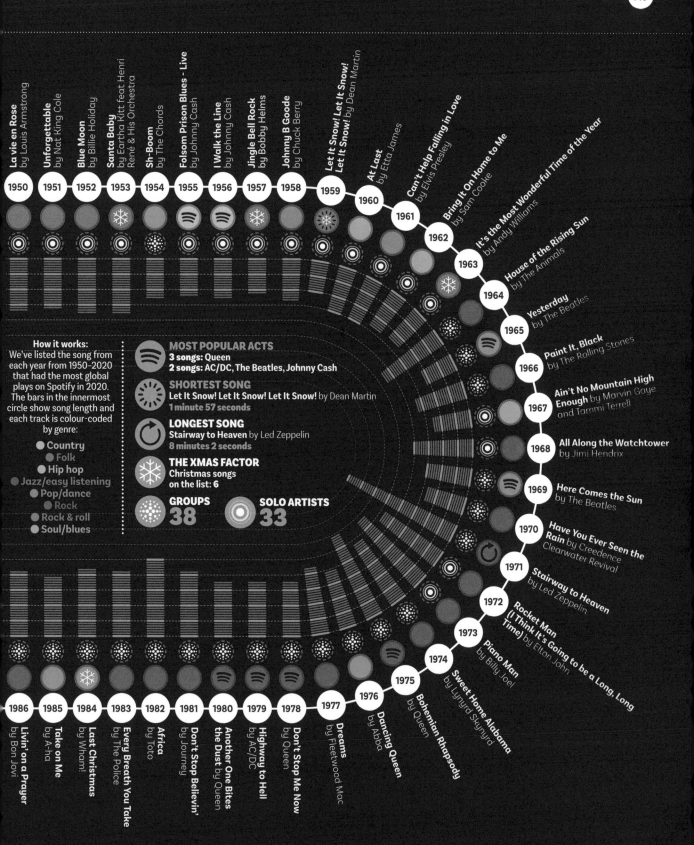

How it works:
We've listed the song from each year from 1950–2020 that had the most global plays on Spotify in 2020. The bars in the innermost circle show song length and each track is colour-coded by genre:

- Country
- Folk
- Hip hop
- Jazz/easy listening
- Pop/dance
- Rock
- Rock & roll
- Soul/blues

MOST POPULAR ACTS
3 songs: Queen
2 songs: AC/DC, The Beatles, Johnny Cash

SHORTEST SONG
Let It Snow! Let It Snow! Let It Snow! by Dean Martin
1 minute 57 seconds

LONGEST SONG
Stairway to Heaven by Led Zeppelin
8 minutes 2 seconds

THE XMAS FACTOR
Christmas songs on the list: 6

GROUPS 38   **SOLO ARTISTS** 33

La vie en Rose by Louis Armstrong — 1950
Unforgettable by Nat King Cole — 1951
Blue Moon by Billie Holiday — 1952
Santa Baby by Eartha Kitt feat Henri René & His Orchestra — 1953
Sh-Boom by The Chords — 1954
Folsom Prison Blues – Live by Johnny Cash — 1955
I Walk the Line by Johnny Cash — 1956
Jingle Bell Rock by Bobby Helms — 1957
Johnny B Goode by Chuck Berry — 1958
Let It Snow! Let It Snow! Let It Snow! by Dean Martin — 1959
At Last by Etta James — 1960
Can't Help Falling in Love by Elvis Presley — 1961
Bring It On Home to Me by Sam Cooke — 1962
It's the Most Wonderful Time of the Year by Andy Williams — 1963
House of the Rising Sun by The Animals — 1964
Yesterday by The Beatles — 1965
Paint It, Black by The Rolling Stones — 1966
Ain't No Mountain High Enough by Marvin Gaye and Tammi Terrell — 1967
All Along the Watchtower by Jimi Hendrix — 1968
Here Comes the Sun by The Beatles — 1969
Have You Ever Seen the Rain by Creedence Clearwater Revival — 1970
Stairway to Heaven by Led Zeppelin — 1971
Rocket Man (I Think It's Going to be a Long, Long Time) by Elton John — 1972
Piano Man by Billy Joel — 1973
Sweet Home Alabama by Lynyrd Skynyrd — 1974
Bohemian Rhapsody by Queen — 1975
Dancing Queen by Abba — 1976
Dreams by Fleetwood Mac — 1977
Don't Stop Me Now by Queen — 1978
Highway to Hell by AC/DC — 1979
Another One Bites the Dust by Queen — 1980
Don't Stop Believin' by Journey — 1981
Africa by Toto — 1982
Every Breath You Take by The Police — 1983
Last Christmas by Wham! — 1984
Take on Me by A-ha — 1985
Livin' on a Prayer by Bon Jovi — 1986

Who's the biggest musical act of all time?

Is Madonna or Mariah getting listened to the most? And who's the bigger hit machine, Barbra Streisand or Drake? We've pitched Billboard's 20 'Greatest Artists of All Time' against each other in key chart and streaming achievements to see who tops the bill

How it works: We took Billboard's 20 greatest artists and assessed their careers across six categories. The concentric coloured bars in each circle represent the artists' rank in each category: the greater the number of bars, the higher the ranking. We then gave each artist an overall score based on their combined rankings and used this to count them down from the 20th to the number one biggest musical act of all time.

In the case of ties: in number one singles, the artist with the song on the chart for the most weeks ranks higher; in Hot 100 entries and songs with most weeks on the chart, the act with the most number one singles ranks higher; in top 10 albums, the act with the album with the most weeks on the chart ranks higher; in album with most weeks on the chart, the act with the most top 10 albums overall ranks higher. Monthly listeners = average number of people streaming act's songs across June 2020 and June 2021.

Categories in which the artist ranks first are marked with a star ★ and a white line on the outermost ring. Hot 100 entries include collaborations featuring the artist. Paul McCartney statistics include recordings with the band Wings

Sources: Billboard, Spotify

#20

Garth Brooks

Number 1 singles: **0**

Hot 100 entries: **9**

Song with most weeks in chart: **Wrapped Up in You, 20**

Top 10 albums: **19**

Album with most weeks in chart: **No Fences, 224**

Monthly listeners: **730,620**

#16

Elvis Presley

Number 1 singles: **7**

Hot 100 entries: **109**

Song with most weeks in chart: **Way Down, 21**

Top 10 albums: **12**

Album with most weeks in chart: **It's Christmas Time, 76**

Monthly listeners: **12,335,501**

#19

Chicago

Number 1 singles: **3**

Hot 100 entries: **46**

Song with most weeks in chart:
Hard Habit to Break, 25

Top 10 albums: **12**

Album with most weeks in chart:
Chicago Transit Authority, 171

Monthly listeners: **6,786,147**

#18

Rod Stewart

Number 1 singles: **4**

Hot 100 entries: **52**

Song with most weeks in chart:
My Heart Can't Tell You No, 25

Top 10 albums: **17**

Album with most weeks in chart:
**It Had to Be You:
The Great American Songbook, 86**

Monthly listeners: **9,330,157**

#17

Barbra Streisand

Number 1 singles: **5**

Hot 100 entries: **41**

Song with most weeks in chart:
Evergreen, 25

Top 10 albums: **34**

Album with most weeks in chart:
Funny Girl OST, 108

Monthly listeners: **4,049,903**

#15

Janet Jackson

Number 1 singles: **10**

Hot 100 entries: **41**

Song with most weeks in chart:
Together Again, 46

Top 10 albums: **10**

Album with most weeks in chart:
**Janet Jackson's
Rhythm Nation 1814, 108**

Monthly listeners: **5,472,281**

#14

Billy Joel

Number 1 singles: **3**

Hot 100 entries: **42**

Song with most weeks in chart:
The River of Dreams, 27

Top 10 albums: **13**

Album with most weeks in chart:
The Stranger, 137

Monthly listeners: **15,428,594**

#13

Paul McCartney

Number 1 singles: **9**

Hot 100 entries: **47**

Song with most weeks in chart:
Say Say Say, 22

Top 10 albums: **21**

Album with most weeks in chart:
Band on the Run, 120

Monthly listeners: **12,660,566**

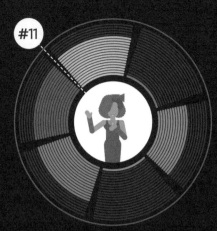

Prince

Number 1 singles: **5**

Hot 100 entries: **47**

Song with most weeks in chart:
1999, 30

Top 10 albums: **19**

Album with most weeks in chart:
1999, 163

Monthly listeners: **9,799,561**

Whitney Houston

Number 1 singles: **11**

Hot 100 entries: **40**

Song with most weeks in chart:
I Will Always Love You, 29

Top 10 albums: **8**

Album with most weeks in chart:
Whitney Houston, 176

Monthly listeners: **20,740,081**

Stevie Wonder

Number 1 singles: **10**

Hot 100 entries: **63**

Song with most weeks in chart:
I Just Called to Say I Love You, 26

Top 10 albums: **11**

Album with most weeks in chart:
Talking Book, 109

Monthly listeners: **15,370,614**

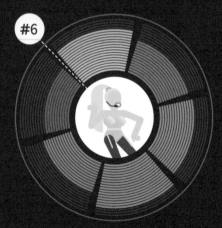

Madonna

Number 1 singles: **12**

Hot 100 entries: **57**

Song with most weeks in chart:
Borderline, 30

Top 10 albums: **22**

Album with most weeks in chart:
Madonna, 168

Monthly listeners: **14,913,025**

Elton John

Number 1 singles: **9**

Hot 100 entries: **67**

Song with most weeks in chart:
Candle in the Wind 1997, 42

Top 10 albums: **20**

Album with most weeks in chart:
Goodbye Yellow Brick Road, 111

Monthly listeners: **26,844,544**

Rihanna

Number 1 singles: **14**

Hot 100 entries: **62**

Song with most weeks in chart:
Needed Me, 45

Top 10 albums: **8**

Album with most weeks in chart:
Anti, 270

Monthly listeners: **42,840,899**

The Rolling Stones

Number 1 singles: **8**

Hot 100 entries: **57**

Song with most weeks in chart:
Start Me Up, 24

★ Top 10 albums: **37**

Album with most weeks in chart:
Some Girls, 88

Monthly listeners: **20,321,839**

Michael Jackson

Number 1 singles: **13**

Hot 100 entries: **51**

Song with most weeks in chart:
Billie Jean, 25

Top 10 albums: **10**

Album with most weeks in chart:
Thriller, 472

Monthly listeners: **24,775,140**

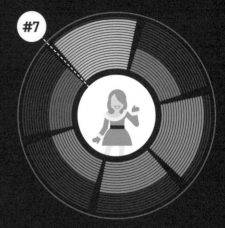

Mariah Carey

Number 1 singles: **19**

Hot 100 entries: **49**

Song with most weeks in chart:
All I Want for Christmas Is You, 44

Top 10 albums: **18**

Album with most weeks in chart:
Music Box, 128

Monthly listeners: **13,767,091**

Taylor Swift

Number 1 singles: **7**

Hot 100 entries: **136**

★ Song with most weeks in chart:
You Belong with Me, 50

Top 10 albums: **11**

Album with most weeks in chart:
1989, 337

Monthly listeners: **38,255,013**

Drake

Number 1 singles: **8**

★ Hot 100 entries: **233**

Song with most weeks in chart:
God's Plan, 36

Top 10 albums: **12**

Album with most weeks in chart:
Take Care, 430

★ Monthly listeners: **56,365,043**

The Beatles

★ Number 1 singles: **20**

Hot 100 entries: **71**

Song with most weeks in chart:
Twist and Shout, 26

Top 10 albums: **32**

★ Album with most weeks in chart:
Abbey Road, 474

Monthly listeners: **23,756,744**

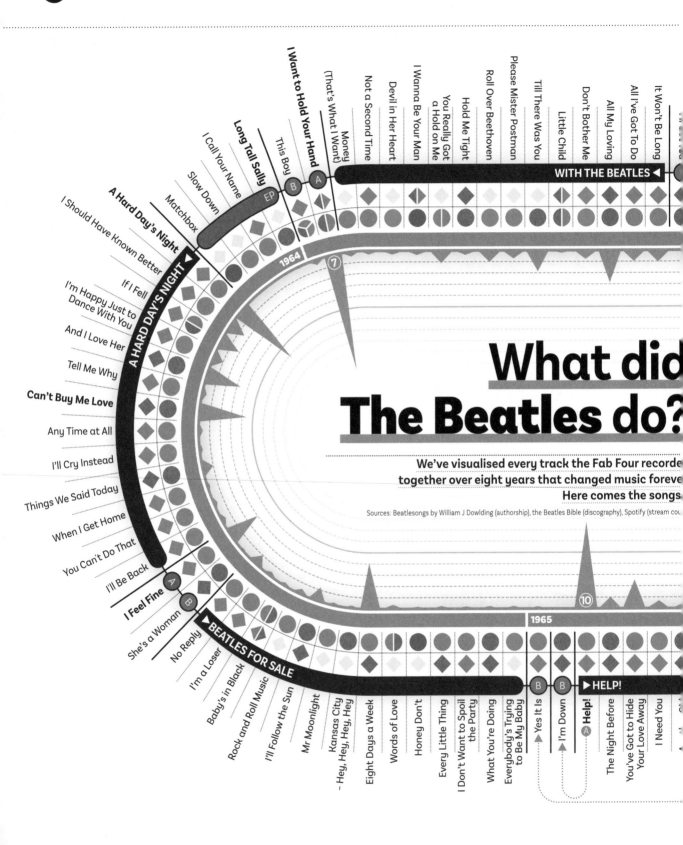

What did The Beatles do?

We've visualised every track the Fab Four recorded together over eight years that changed music forever. Here comes the songs

Sources: Beatlesongs by William J Dowlding (authorship), the Beatles Bible (discography), Spotify (stream cou...

WITH THE BEATLES ◄

I Want to Hold Your Hand

Money (That's What I Want)
This Boy
I Call Your Name
Slow Down
Matchbox
Long Tall Sally
A Hard Day's Night
I Should Have Known Better
If I Fell
I'm Happy Just to Dance With You
And I Love Her
Tell Me Why
Can't Buy Me Love
Any Time at All
I'll Cry Instead
Things We Said Today
When I Get Home
You Can't Do That
I'll Be Back
I Feel Fine
She's a Woman
No Reply

A HARD DAY'S NIGHT

Not a Second Time
Devil in Her Heart
I Wanna Be Your Man
You Really Got a Hold on Me
Hold Me Tight
Roll Over Beethoven
Please Mister Postman
Till There Was You
Little Child
Don't Bother Me
All My Loving
All I've Got To Do
It Won't Be Long

BEATLES FOR SALE

I'm a Loser
Baby's in Black
Rock and Roll Music
I'll Follow the Sun
Mr Moonlight
Kansas City – Hey, Hey, Hey, Hey
Eight Days a Week
Words of Love
Honey Don't
Every Little Thing
I Don't Want to Spoil the Party
What You're Doing
Everybody's Trying to Be My Baby
Yes It Is
I'm Down
Help!
The Night Before
You've Got to Hide Your Love Away
I Need You

► HELP!

1964
1965
EP
⑦
⑩

FIRST TWO RECORDS PREVIOUSLY RELEASED AS SINGLES

Every Beatles song released in the UK
Album tracks and **singles** 1963-1970

Average number of streams for each song per day on Spotify

Albums, EPs, singles (A-sides/B-sides)

She Loves You · Thank You Girl · From Me to You · Twist and Shout · There's a Place · A Taste of Honey · Do You Want to Know a Secret · Baby It's You · PS I Love You · **Love Me Do** · **Please Please Me** · Ask Me Why · Boys · Chains · Anna (Go to Him) · Misery · I Saw Her Standing There

A · B · A

PLEASE PLEASE ME ◄

◄ EP · A · B

◆ **Writer**

● **Lead vocals**

1963 Year of release

⑥

50,000

How it works:
We've listed every song released by The Beatles between 1963 and 1970 and illustrated the average daily plays of each one on Spotify. Each track is colour-coded (see key, right) to denote who wrote it and who performed lead vocals

100,000

John Lennon

Paul McCartney

George Harrison

Ringo Starr

100,000

50,000

⑤

⑨

1966 ►

You're Going to Lose That Girl · **Ticket to Ride** · Act Naturally · It's Only Love · You Like Me Too Much · Tell Me What You See · I've Just Seen a Face · Yesterday · Dizzy Miss Lizzy · Drive My Car · Norwegian Wood (This Bird Has Flown) · You Won't See Me · Nowhere Man · Think for Yourself · The Word · Michelle · What Goes On · Girl · I'm Looking Through You · In My Life · Wait · If I Needed Someone · Run for Your Life · **We Can Work It Out** · **Day Tripper** · **Paperback Writer** · Rain

A

► **RUBBER SOUL**

A · A · A · B

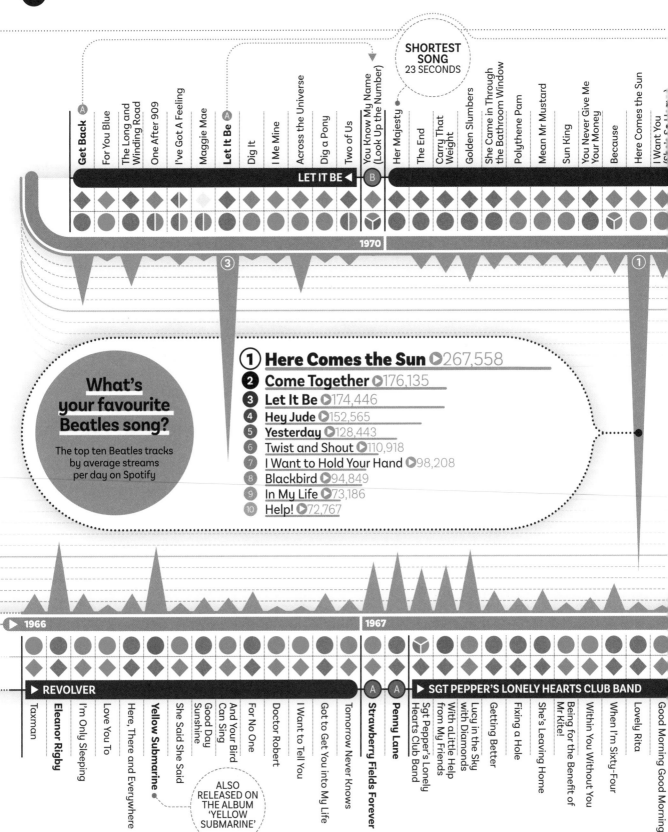

SHORTEST SONG
23 SECONDS

Get Back · For You Blue · The Long and Winding Road · One After 909 · I've Got A Feeling · Maggie Mae · Let It Be · Dig It · I Me Mine · Across the Universe · Dig a Pony · Two of Us · You Know My Name (Look Up the Number) · Her Majesty · The End · Carry That Weight · Golden Slumbers · She Came in Through the Bathroom Window · Polythene Pam · Mean Mr Mustard · Sun King · You Never Give Me Your Money · Because · Here Comes the Sun · I Want You (She's So...)

LET IT BE ◀

1970

What's your favourite Beatles song?

The top ten Beatles tracks by average streams per day on Spotify

1 **Here Comes the Sun** ▶267,558
2 **Come Together** ▶176,135
3 **Let It Be** ▶174,446
4 **Hey Jude** ▶152,565
5 **Yesterday** ▶128,443
6 Twist and Shout ▶110,918
7 I Want to Hold Your Hand ▶98,208
8 Blackbird ▶94,849
9 In My Life ▶73,186
10 Help! ▶72,767

1966

▶ REVOLVER

Taxman · Eleanor Rigby · I'm Only Sleeping · Love You To · Here, There and Everywhere · Yellow Submarine · She Said She Said · Good Day Sunshine · And Your Bird Can Sing · For No One · Doctor Robert · I Want to Tell You · Got to Get You into My Life · Tomorrow Never Knows · Strawberry Fields Forever · Penny Lane

1967

▶ SGT PEPPER'S LONELY HEARTS CLUB BAND

Sgt Pepper's Lonely Hearts Club Band · With a Little Help from My Friends · Lucy in the Sky with Diamonds · Getting Better · Fixing a Hole · She's Leaving Home · Being for the Benefit of Mr Kite! · Within You Without You · When I'm Sixty-Four · Lovely Rita · Good Morning Good Morning

ALSO RELEASED ON THE ALBUM 'YELLOW SUBMARINE'

LONGEST SONG
8 MINUTES
15 SECONDS
Ⓐ

Octopus's Garden
Oh! Darling
Maxwell's Silver Hammer
Something
Come Together
Old Brown Shoe
The Ballad of John and Yoko
Don't Let Me Down
All You Need Is Love
It's All Too Much
Hey Bulldog
All Together Now
Only a Northern Song
Good Night
Revolution 9
Cry Baby Cry
Savoy Truffle
Honey Pie
Revolution 1
Long, Long, Long
Helter Skelter
Sexy Sadie
Everybody's Got Something to Hide Except Me and My Monkey
Mother Nature's Son
Yer Blues
Birthday
Julia
I Will
Why Don't We Do It in the Road?
Don't Pass Me By
Rocky Raccoon
Piggies
Blackbird
I'm So Tired
Martha My Dear
Happiness Is a Warm Gun
While My Guitar Gently Weeps
The Continuing Story of Bungalow Bill
Wild Honey Pie
Ob-La-Di, Ob-La-Da
Glass Onion
Dear Prudence
Back in the USSR

ABBEY ROAD ◀ Ⓑ Ⓐ Ⓑ **YELLOW SUBMARINE** ◀

▶ THE BEATLES (WHITE ALBUM)

1969

50,000

100,000

Average number of streams for each song per day on Spotify

100,000

50,000

1968

② ⑧ ④

Sgt Pepper's Lonely Hearts Club Band (reprise)
A Day in the Life
Baby You're a Rich Man
Hello Goodbye
Magical Mystery Tour
Your Mother Should Know
I Am the Walrus
The Fool on the Hill
Flying
Blue Jay Way
Lady Madonna
The Inner Light
Hey Jude
Revolution

Ⓑ Ⓐ DOUBLE EP Ⓐ Ⓑ Ⓐ Ⓑ

What's your favourite Beatles album?

How have The Beatles' albums stood the test of time – and who wrote the songs on them? We can work it out

How it works: The pie charts below represent the band's 12 original studio albums. The size of each represents the combined total daily plays of each album's tracks and the colour-coded segments show the proportional songwriting credits. Albums are in chronological order, rank in terms of combined daily plays is shown above each album title

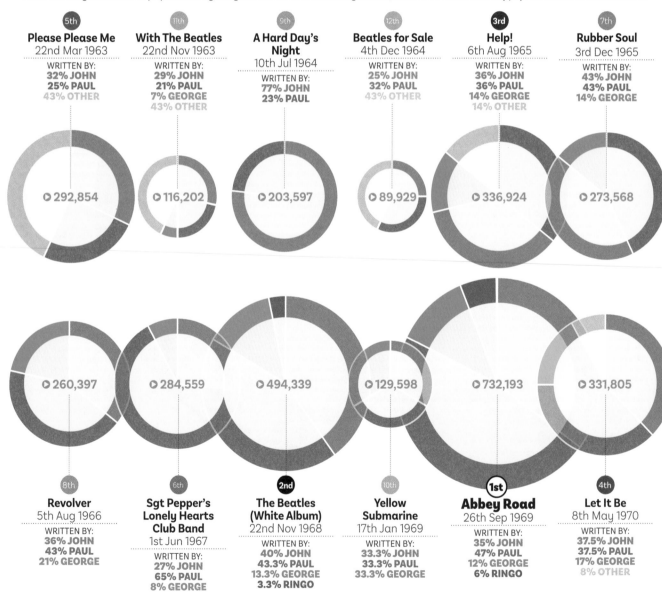

5th
Please Please Me
22nd Mar 1963
WRITTEN BY:
32% JOHN
25% PAUL
43% OTHER

▶ 292,854

11th
With The Beatles
22nd Nov 1963
WRITTEN BY:
29% JOHN
21% PAUL
7% GEORGE
43% OTHER

▶ 116,202

9th
A Hard Day's Night
10th Jul 1964
WRITTEN BY:
77% JOHN
23% PAUL

▶ 203,597

12th
Beatles for Sale
4th Dec 1964
WRITTEN BY:
25% JOHN
32% PAUL
43% OTHER

▶ 89,929

3rd
Help!
6th Aug 1965
WRITTEN BY:
36% JOHN
36% PAUL
14% GEORGE
14% OTHER

▶ 336,924

7th
Rubber Soul
3rd Dec 1965
WRITTEN BY:
43% JOHN
43% PAUL
14% GEORGE

▶ 273,568

▶ 260,397

▶ 284,559

▶ 494,339

▶ 129,598

▶ 732,193

▶ 331,805

8th
Revolver
5th Aug 1966
WRITTEN BY:
36% JOHN
43% PAUL
21% GEORGE

6th
Sgt Pepper's Lonely Hearts Club Band
1st Jun 1967
WRITTEN BY:
27% JOHN
65% PAUL
8% GEORGE

2nd
The Beatles (White Album)
22nd Nov 1968
WRITTEN BY:
40% JOHN
43.3% PAUL
13.3% GEORGE
3.3% RINGO

10th
Yellow Submarine
17th Jan 1969
WRITTEN BY:
33.3% JOHN
33.3% PAUL
33.3% GEORGE

1st
Abbey Road
26th Sep 1969
WRITTEN BY:
35% JOHN
47% PAUL
12% GEORGE
6% RINGO

4th
Let It Be
8th May 1970
WRITTEN BY:
37.5% JOHN
37.5% PAUL
17% GEORGE
8% OTHER

Who's the best Beatle?

Pitting the Fab Four against each other in terms of work rate and popularity

◆ Who wrote most of The Beatles' songs?

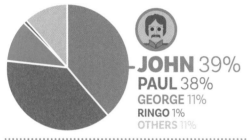

JOHN 39%
PAUL 38%
GEORGE 11%
RINGO 1%
OTHERS 11%

◆ Who wrote the most popular Beatles songs?

Total average daily Spotify streams for all songs written by each artist:

JOHN ▶ 1,458,141
PAUL ▶ 2,038,854
GEORGE ▶ 522,414
RINGO ▶ 30,600

● Who sang lead vocals on most of The Beatles' songs?

JOHN 42%
PAUL 38%
GEORGE 14%
RINGO 6%

● Who sang lead vocals on the most popular Beatles songs?

Total average daily Spotify streams for all songs sung by each artist:

JOHN ▶ 1,698,840
PAUL ▶ 1,841,416
GEORGE ▶ 576,489
RINGO ▶ 150,138

Who gave a little help to their friends?

Let It Be did not mark the last time The Beatles appeared on a record together, with the former bandmates often popping up on each other's solo albums. But who was the most collaborative?

Coloured segments represent appearances by pictured Beatle on solo albums by **JOHN**, **PAUL**, **GEORGE** and **RINGO**

How it works: The graph on pages 154-157 shows average global daily plays of Beatles songs over a four-year period since the band's back catalogue was made available on Spotify on 24th December 2015. All Beatles songs released between 1963 and 1970 are included and ordered chronologically by date of release and in album running order (original UK release). A-sides of singles are marked in bold. If a song was released as both a single and as an album track it is ordered according to its place on the album. Tracks released after the final studio album, Let It Be, are excluded (so no 'Free as a Bird' or 'Real Love' from the Anthology albums). Only EPs featuring songs not released as singles or on an original album are included. The second side of the album Yellow Submarine, which was written by George Martin and didn't feature The Beatles as performers, is also excluded. Alternative versions such as live performances and demos are excluded, but different mixes and remastered versions of the originals are added together to form the total count. For authorship and singing performance popularity, if a song has more than one writer or lead singer then the streams are divided between them equally. For the album rankings, plays of the song 'Yellow Submarine', which appeared on both Revolver and Yellow Submarine, are counted on both albums. The Magical Mystery Tour release is not counted as an album as it was classed as a double EP in the UK

Who gets into the Rock & Roll Hall of Fame?

In 1983 the Rock & Roll Hall of Fame was set up to celebrate the pioneers of popular music. Every year its jury inducts more members, but who gets in? For the moment it's still something of a boys' club

How it works: We've proportionally represented musicians inducted into the Rock & Roll Hall of Fame categories 'Musical Excellence', 'Early Influences' and 'Performers'. Numbers are correct as of May 2021. Band members are illustrated separately. If an inductee is a member of more than one inducted group, they are only illustrated once

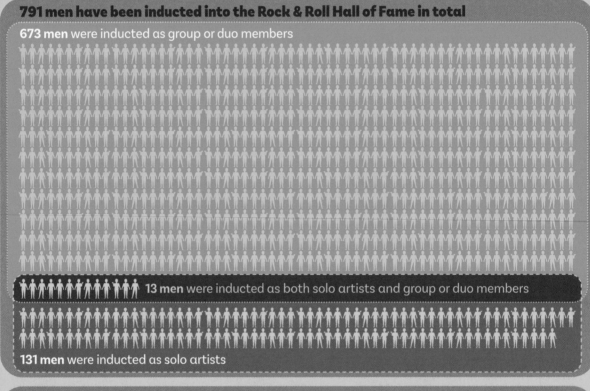

791 men have been inducted into the Rock & Roll Hall of Fame in total

673 men were inducted as group or duo members

13 men were inducted as both solo artists and group or duo members

131 men were inducted as solo artists

71 women have been inducted into the Rock & Roll Hall of Fame in total

44 women were inducted as group or duo members

Stevie Nicks and **Tina Turner** were inducted as both solo artists and group or duo members

29 women were inducted as group members

Source: The Rock & Roll Hall of Fame

What's better, Broadway or the West End?

The world's two great anglophone theatre districts go head to head: which pulls in the most punters, earns the most cash and dishes out the most munificent treatment to stage managers?

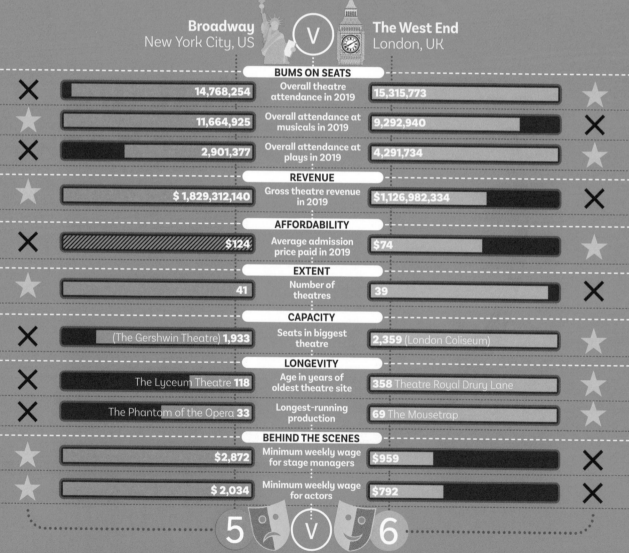

	Broadway New York City, US	V	The West End London, UK	
	BUMS ON SEATS			
✕	14,768,254	Overall theatre attendance in 2019	15,315,773	★
★	11,664,925	Overall attendance at musicals in 2019	9,292,940	✕
✕	2,901,377	Overall attendance at plays in 2019	4,291,734	★
	REVENUE			
★	$ 1,829,312,140	Gross theatre revenue in 2019	$1,126,982,334	✕
	AFFORDABILITY			
✕	$124	Average admission price paid in 2019	$74	★
	EXTENT			
★	41	Number of theatres	39	✕
	CAPACITY			
✕	(The Gershwin Theatre) 1,933	Seats in biggest theatre	2,359 (London Coliseum)	★
	LONGEVITY			
✕	The Lyceum Theatre 118	Age in years of oldest theatre site	358 Theatre Royal Drury Lane	★
✕	The Phantom of the Opera 33	Longest-running production	69 The Mousetrap	★
	BEHIND THE SCENES			
★	$2,872	Minimum weekly wage for stage managers	$959	✕
★	$ 2,034	Minimum weekly wage for actors	$792	✕

5 V 6

How it works: We've compared the latest available figures across 11 categories, awarding a point to the winner of each. The difference between the two is shown proportionally, with the larger number occupying the full bar. If the larger number represents a negative attribute (eg higher admission price) that bar is striped

Sources: Broadway Direct, the Broadway League, Encore Tickets, London Coliseum, Playbill, Society of London Theatre, The Daily Telegraph, What's on Stage

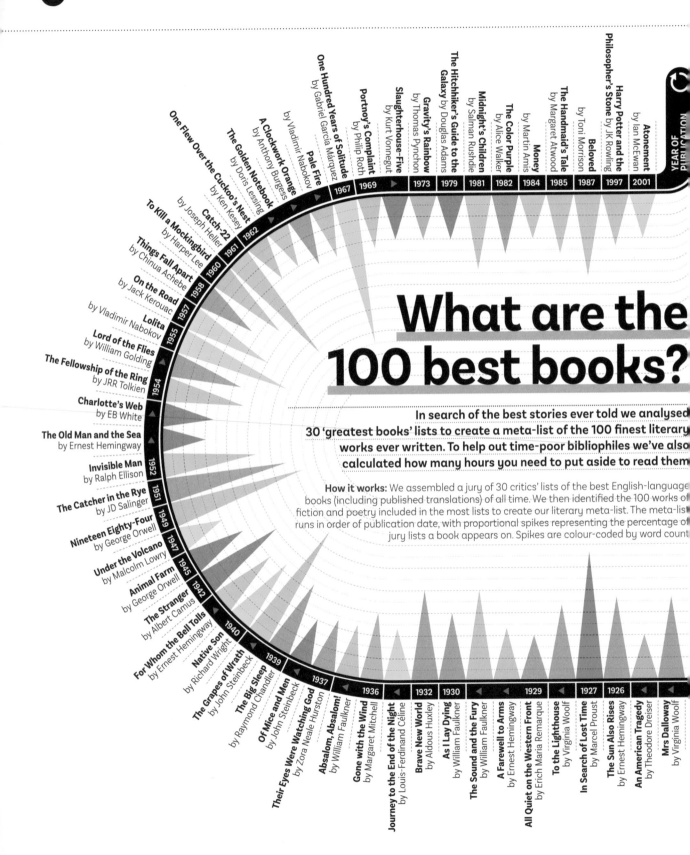

What are the 100 best books?

In search of the best stories ever told we analysed 30 'greatest books' lists to create a meta-list of the 100 finest literary works ever written. To help out time-poor bibliophiles we've also calculated how many hours you need to put aside to read them

How it works: We assembled a jury of 30 critics' lists of the best English-language books (including published translations) of all time. We then identified the 100 works of fiction and poetry included in the most lists to create our literary meta-list. The meta-list runs in order of publication date, with proportional spikes representing the percentage of jury lists a book appears on. Spikes are colour-coded by word count

YEAR OF PUBLICATION

Atonement
by Ian McEwan
2001

Harry Potter and the Philosopher's Stone by JK Rowling
1997

Beloved
by Toni Morrison
1987

The Handmaid's Tale
by Margaret Atwood
1985

Money
by Martin Amis
1984

The Color Purple
by Alice Walker
1982

Midnight's Children
by Salman Rushdie
1981

Gravity's Rainbow by Thomas Pynchon
1979

The Hitchhiker's Guide to the Galaxy by Douglas Adams
1973

Slaughterhouse-Five
by Kurt Vonnegut
1969

Portnoy's Complaint
by Philip Roth
1967

One Hundred Years of Solitude
by Gabriel García Márquez

Pale Fire
by Vladimir Nabokov

A Clockwork Orange
by Anthony Burgess

The Golden Notebook
by Doris Lessing
1962

One Flew Over the Cuckoo's Nest
by Ken Kesey
1961

Catch-22
by Joseph Heller
1960

To Kill a Mockingbird
by Harper Lee
1958

Things Fall Apart
by Chinua Achebe
1957

On the Road
by Jack Kerouac
1955

Lolita
by Vladimir Nabokov

Lord of the Flies
by William Golding
1954

The Fellowship of the Ring
by JRR Tolkien

Charlotte's Web
by EB White

The Old Man and the Sea
by Ernest Hemingway
1952

Invisible Man
by Ralph Ellison
1951

The Catcher in the Rye
by JD Salinger
1949

Nineteen Eighty-Four
by George Orwell
1947

Under the Volcano
by Malcolm Lowry
1945

Animal Farm
by George Orwell
1942

The Stranger
by Albert Camus
1940

For Whom the Bell Tolls
by Ernest Hemingway

Native Son
by Richard Wright
1939

The Grapes of Wrath
by John Steinbeck

The Big Sleep
by Raymond Chandler
1937

Of Mice and Men
by John Steinbeck

Their Eyes Were Watching God
by Zora Neale Hurston

Absalom, Absalom!
by William Faulkner
1936

Gone with the Wind
by Margaret Mitchell

Journey to the End of the Night
by Louis-Ferdinand Céline
1932

Brave New World
by Aldous Huxley
1930

As I Lay Dying
by William Faulkner

The Sound and the Fury
by William Faulkner
1929

A Farewell to Arms
by Ernest Hemingway

All Quiet on the Western Front
by Erich Maria Remarque

To the Lighthouse
by Virginia Woolf
1927

In Search of Lost Time
by Marcel Proust
1926

The Sun Also Rises
by Ernest Hemingway

An American Tragedy
by Theodore Dreiser

Mrs Dalloway
by Virginia Woolf

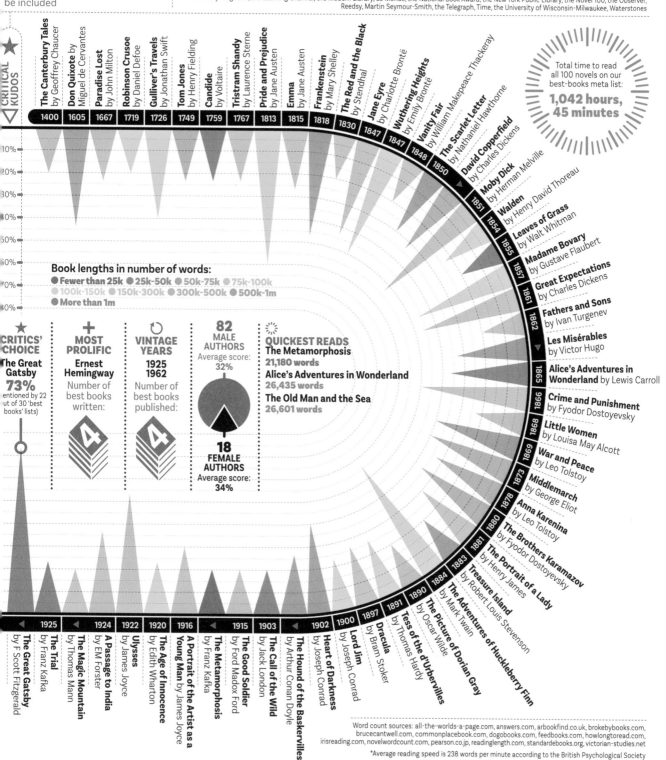

Books must appear on 20% or more of our 30 'best books' lists to be included

Jury sources: Amazon, BBC, Book Depository, Bookman, The Book of Great Books, Boston Public Library, Bravo! magazine, Counterpunch, Easton Press, Entertainment Weekly, For the Love of Books, Gardiner public library, Great Books Foundation, Great Books Guide, the Guardian, Harvard Book Store staff, January magazine, the Learning Channel, the Modern Library, Le Monde, the National Book Award, the New York Public Library, the Novel 100, the Observer, Reedsy, Martin Seymour-Smith, the Telegraph, Time, the University of Wisconsin-Milwaukee, Waterstones

CRITICAL KUDOS

The Canterbury Tales by Geoffrey Chaucer · 1400
Don Quixote by Miguel de Cervantes · 1605
Paradise Lost by John Milton · 1667
Robinson Crusoe by Daniel Defoe · 1719
Gulliver's Travels by Jonathan Swift · 1726
Tom Jones by Henry Fielding · 1749
Candide by Voltaire · 1759
Tristram Shandy by Laurence Sterne · 1767
Pride and Prejudice by Jane Austen · 1813
Emma by Jane Austen · 1815
Frankenstein by Mary Shelley · 1818
The Red and the Black by Stendhal · 1830
Jane Eyre by Charlotte Brontë · 1847
Wuthering Heights by Emily Brontë · 1847
Vanity Fair by William Makepeace Thackeray · 1848
The Scarlet Letter by Nathaniel Hawthorne · 1850
David Copperfield by Charles Dickens
Moby Dick by Herman Melville · 1851
Walden by Henry David Thoreau · 1854
Leaves of Grass by Walt Whitman · 1855
Madame Bovary by Gustave Flaubert · 1857
Great Expectations by Charles Dickens · 1861
Fathers and Sons by Ivan Turgenev · 1862
Les Misérables by Victor Hugo
Alice's Adventures in Wonderland by Lewis Carroll · 1865
Crime and Punishment by Fyodor Dostoyevsky · 1866
Little Women by Louisa May Alcott · 1868
War and Peace by Leo Tolstoy · 1869
Middlemarch by George Eliot · 1873
Anna Karenina by Leo Tolstoy · 1878
The Brothers Karamazov by Fyodor Dostoyevsky · 1880
The Portrait of a Lady by Henry James · 1881
Treasure Island by Robert Louis Stevenson · 1883
The Adventures of Huckleberry Finn by Mark Twain · 1884
The Picture of Dorian Gray by Oscar Wilde · 1890
Tess of the d'Urbervilles by Thomas Hardy · 1891
Dracula by Bram Stoker · 1897
Lord Jim by Joseph Conrad · 1900
Heart of Darkness by Joseph Conrad · 1902
The Hound of the Baskervilles by Arthur Conan Doyle
The Call of the Wild by Jack London · 1903
The Good Soldier by Ford Madox Ford · 1915
The Metamorphosis by Franz Kafka
A Portrait of the Artist as a Young Man by James Joyce · 1916
The Age of Innocence by Edith Wharton · 1920
Ulysses by James Joyce · 1922
A Passage to India by EM Forster · 1924
The Magic Mountain by Thomas Mann
The Trial by Franz Kafka · 1925
The Great Gatsby by F Scott Fitzgerald

Total time to read all 100 novels on our best-books meta list:
1,042 hours, 45 minutes

Book lengths in number of words:
- Fewer than 25k
- 25k-50k
- 50k-75k
- 75k-100k
- 100k-150k
- 150k-300k
- 300k-500k
- 500k-1m
- More than 1m

★ **CRITICS' CHOICE**
The Great Gatsby
73% (mentioned by 22 out of 30 'best books' lists)

+ **MOST PROLIFIC**
Ernest Hemingway
Number of best books written:
4

VINTAGE YEARS
1925 1962
Number of best books published:
4

82 MALE AUTHORS
Average score: **32%**

18 FEMALE AUTHORS
Average score: **34%**

QUICKEST READS
The Metamorphosis
21,180 words
Alice's Adventures in Wonderland
26,435 words
The Old Man and the Sea
26,601 words

Word count sources: all-the-worlds-a-page.com, answers.com, arbookfind.co.uk, brokebybooks.com, brucecantwell.com, commonplacebook.com, dogobooks.com, feedbooks.com, howlongtoread.com, irisreading.com, novelwordcount.com, pearson.co.jp, readinglength.com, standardbooks.org, victorian-studies.net

*Average reading speed is 238 words per minute according to the British Psychological Society

What's the deadliest soap opera?

The longest-running soap operas on UK television can be perilous places for their characters – but which has the highest mortality rates? And what's the most likely cause of death?

How it works: We took the longest-running soap operas (those with 5,000+ episodes) currently shown on UK terrestrial TV and analysed data of character deaths both on and off screen. Characters who never appeared alive in the shows are not included. Deaths are categorised by cause:

☠ **Murders** ⚠ **Accidents** ◓ **Natural causes** ○ **Other**

'Other' includes suicide, being shot by police marksmen and having your life support switched off

Source: Fandom UK

Coronation Street
Total deaths since launch, 9th December 1960:

👤✗ 201

Emmerdale
Total deaths since launch, 16th October 1972:

👤✗ 169

○ 29

◓ 51

⚠ 74

◓ 26

◓ 86

⚠ 75

☠ 14

☠ 15

Where do soap characters die?

Coronation Street has racked up the most deaths overall, with 201 of the combined death toll of 849. In terms of frequency of death, however, the clear winner is Hollyoaks

Average soap deaths per year:

🚶🚶🚶🚶🚶🚶🚶	7.04	**Hollyoaks**
🚶🚶🚶🚶	3.76	**EastEnders**
🚶🚶🚶	3.49	**Emmerdale**
🚶🚶🚶	3.34	**Coronation Street**
🚶🚶🚶	3.01	Home and Away
🚶🚶	1.78	Neighbours

Soap characters are much safer Down Under:

Neighbours and Home and Away have a combined total of 2.37 deaths per year: the average toll in English soaps is 70 percent higher, at 4.03 deaths per year

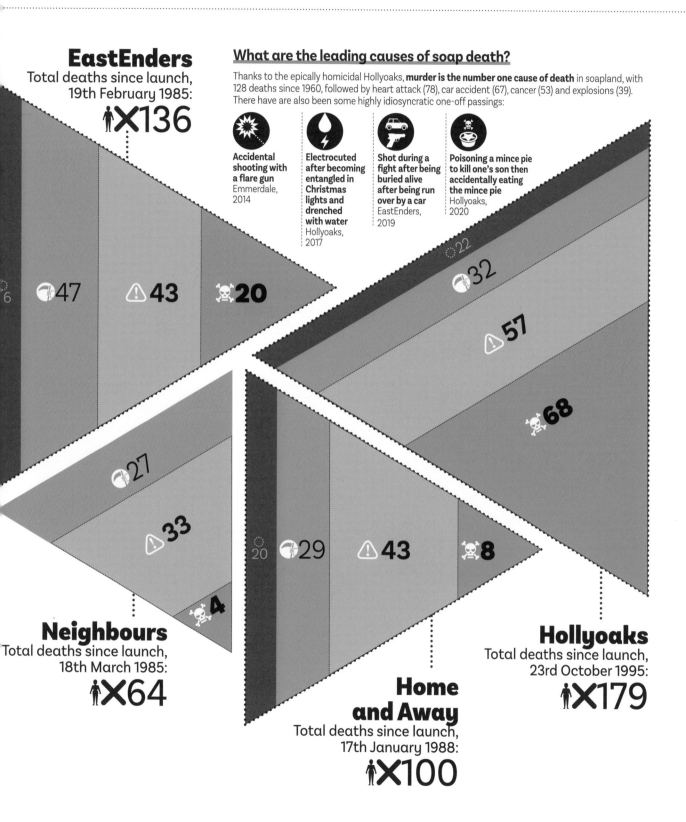

EastEnders
Total deaths since launch,
19th February 1985:
👤✕136

47 43 20

What are the leading causes of soap death?

Thanks to the epically homicidal Hollyoaks, **murder is the number one cause of death** in soapland, with 128 deaths since 1960, followed by heart attack (78), car accident (67), cancer (53) and explosions (39). There have are also been some highly idiosyncratic one-off passings:

Accidental shooting with a flare gun
Emmerdale, 2014

Electrocuted after becoming entangled in Christmas lights and drenched with water
Hollyoaks, 2017

Shot during a fight after being buried alive after being run over by a car
EastEnders, 2019

Poisoning a mince pie to kill one's son then accidentally eating the mince pie
Hollyoaks, 2020

22 32 57 68

27 33 4

20 29 43 8

Neighbours
Total deaths since launch,
18th March 1985:
👤✕64

Home and Away
Total deaths since launch,
17th January 1988:
👤✕100

Hollyoaks
Total deaths since launch,
23rd October 1995:
👤✕179

IS THERE ANYBODY OUT THERE

Questions about UFOs, space and conspiracy theories

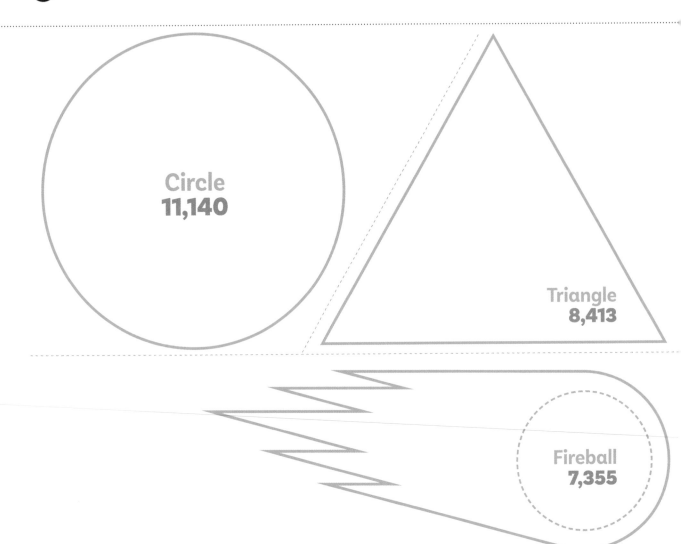

Circle
11,140

Triangle
8,413

Fireball
7,355

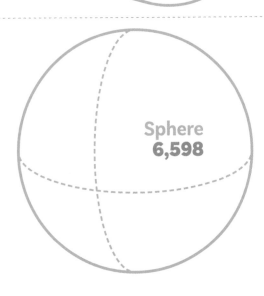

Sphere
6,598

What do UFOs look like?

Since 1974, the US National UFO Reporting Center
has logged thousands of sightings of unidentified flying objects.
We've ranked the most commonly cited shapes of these potential
alien-bearing craft according to the number
of times they have been reported

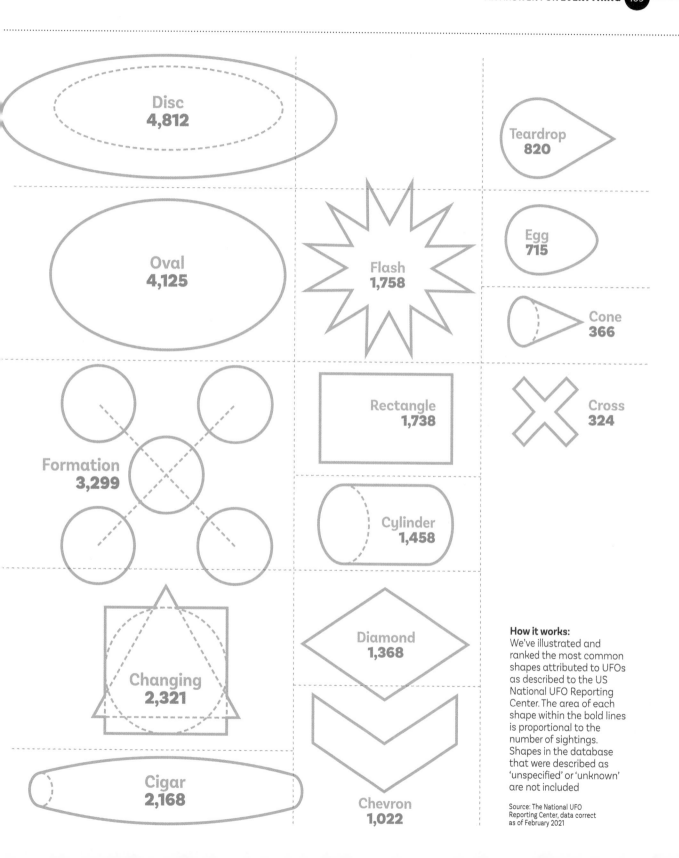

Disc
4,812

Teardrop
820

Oval
4,125

Flash
1,758

Egg
715

Cone
366

Formation
3,299

Rectangle
1,738

Cross
324

Cylinder
1,458

Changing
2,321

Diamond
1,368

How it works:
We've illustrated and ranked the most common shapes attributed to UFOs as described to the US National UFO Reporting Center. The area of each shape within the bold lines is proportional to the number of sightings. Shapes in the database that were described as 'unspecified' or 'unknown' are not included

Cigar
2,168

Chevron
1,022

Source: The National UFO Reporting Center, data correct as of February 2021

How many people have been to space?

Who's been to the moon?

Nine Apollo missions made the 384,400 kilometre trip to the moon. Six of them landed astronauts on the surface

Since Yuri Gagarin left Earth's atmosphere in 1961, hundreds of humans have been strapped into rockets and blasted out into the final frontier. We've tracked the first 60 years of human space flight, the missions flown and the most notable moments along the way

How it works: We've listed every mission that has crossed the Kármán line, which separates Earth from outer space. Each mission is listed in chronological order and colour-coded according to the organisation launching it:

Soviet Space Programme/Russian Space Agency   NASA   China National Space Administration   Space X

Crew members are shown below the mission name:
●Men ◆Women First time space travellers Subsequent trips ✖Fatalities Passengers who died before reaching space

Sources: China National Space Administration, NASA, Russian Space Agency, Soviet space programme, SpaceX

Who was the first man in space?

Soviet cosmonaut Yuri Gagarin completed one orbit of the Earth aboard *Vostok 1*, 12th April 1961. It was Gagarin's only space flight

Who was the first woman in space?

Cosmonaut Valentina Tereshkova spent almost three days in space, 16th June 1963

Cosmonauts, astronauts, taikonauts and tourists flying to space for the first time each year

1961
- Vostok 1
- Yuri Gagarin ●
- Mercury-Redstone 3
- Alan Shepherd ●
- Mercury-Redstone 4
- Virgil Grissom ●
- Vostok 2
- Gherman Titov ●

1962
- Mercury-Atlas 6
- John Glenn ●
- Mercury-Atlas 7
- Scott Carpenter ●
- Vostok 3
- Andriyan Nikolayev ●
- Vostok 4
- Pavel Popovich ●
- Mercury-Atlas 8
- Walter Schirra ●

1963
- Mercury-Atlas 9
- Gordon Cooper ●
- Vostok 5
- Valery Bykovsky ●
- Vostok 6
- Valentina Tereshkova ◆
- X-15 Flight 90
- Joseph Walker ●
- X-15 Flight 91
- Joseph Walker ●

1964
- Voskhod 1
- Vladimir Komarov ●
- Konstantin Feoktistov ●
- Boris Yegorov ●

1965
- Voskhod 2
- Pavel Belyayev ●
- Alexei Leonov ●
- Gemini 4
- James McDivitt ●
- Ed White ●
- Gemini 5
- Gordon Cooper ●
- Charles Conrad ●
- Gemini 7
- Frank Borman ●
- James Lovell ●
- Gemini 6A
- Walter Schirra ●
- Thomas Stafford ●

1966
- Gemini 8
- Neil Armstrong ●
- David Scott ●
- Gemini 9A
- Thomas Stafford ●
- Eugene Cernan ●
- Gemini 10
- John Young ●
- Michael Collins ●
- Gemini 11
- Charles Conrad ●
- Richard Gordon ●
- Gemini 12
- James Lovell ●
- Buzz Aldrin ●

1967
- Soyuz 1
- Vladimir Komarov ✖

1968
- Apollo 7
- Walter Schirra ●
- Donn Eisele ●
- Walter Cunningham ●
- Soyuz 3
- Georgy Beregovoy ●
- Apollo 8
- Frank Borman ●
- James Lovell ●
- William Anders ●

1969
- Soyuz 4
- Vladimir Shatalov ●
- Soyuz 5
- Boris Volynov ●
- Aleksei Yeliseyev ●
- Yevgeny Khrunov ●
- Apollo 9
- James McDivitt ●
- David Scott ●
- Russell Schweickart ●
- Apollo 10
- Thomas Stafford ●
- John Young ●
- Eugene Cernan ●
- Apollo 11
- Neil Armstrong ●
- Michael Collins ●
- Buzz Aldrin ●
- Soyuz 6
- Georgy Shonin ●
- Valery Kubasov ●
- Soyuz 7
- Anatoly Filipchenko ●
- Vladislav Volkov ●
- Viktor Gorbatko ●
- Soyuz 8
- Vladislav Shatalov ●
- Aleksei Yeliseyev ●
- Apollo 12
- Charles Conrad ●
- Richard Gordon ●
- Alan Bean ●

YEAR	1961	1962	1963	1964	1965	1966	1967	1968	1969
▶	4	5	4	3	9	7	0	4	11
	4	5	5	1	5	5	1	3	9
MISSIONS	4	5							

APOLLO MISSION NUMBER

- 8
- 10
- 11
- 12
- 13
- 14
- 15
- 16
- 17

24 individual astronauts flew to the moon – three, James Lovell, John Young and Eugene Cernan made the journey twice

12 astronauts landed on the moon

- 11 Neil Armstrong / Buzz Aldrin
- 12 Charles Conrad / Alan Bean
- 14 Alan Shepard / Edgar Mitchell
- 15 David Scott / James Irwin
- 16 John Young / Charles Duke
- 17 Eugene Cernan / Harrison Schmitt

What was the first space station?

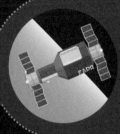

The first space station was the **Salyut 1**, launched by the USSR in 1971.
It spent a total of 175 days in orbit before being purposely crashed into the Pacific.
The first set of astronauts to arrive at the station, on the Soyuz 10 mission in
April 1971, had to return to Earth after being unable to get the hatch open.
Another attempt on Soyuz 11 in June 1971 was successful and three astronauts
spent more than three weeks aboard the station, but all died on their return
home after a ventilation valve broke open during re-entry

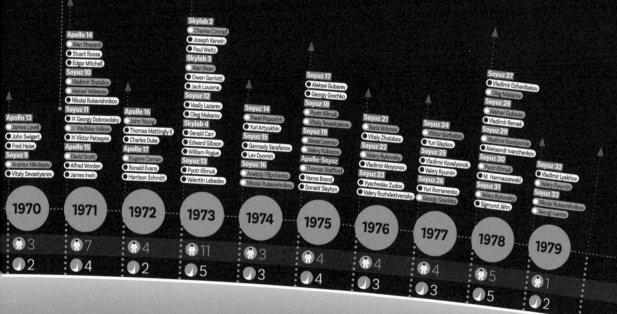

Apollo 13
- James Lovell
- John Swigert
- Fred Haise

Soyuz 9
- Andrian Nikolayev
- Vitaly Sevastyanov

Apollo 14
- Alan Shepard
- Stuart Roosa
- Edgar Mitchell

Soyuz 10
- Vladimir Shatalov
- Aleksei Yeliseyev
- Nikolai Rukavishnikov

Soyuz 11
- ✖ Georgy Dobrovolsky
- ✖ Vladislav Volkov
- ✖ Viktor Patsayev

Apollo 15
- David Scott
- Alfred Worden
- James Irwin

Apollo 16
- John Young
- Thomas Mattingly II
- Charles Duke

Apollo 17
- Eugene Cernan
- Ronald Evans
- Harrison Schmitt

Skylab 2
- Charles Conrad
- Joseph Kerwin
- Paul Weitz

Skylab 3
- Alan Bean
- Owen Garriott
- Jack Lousma

Soyuz 12
- Vasily Lazarev
- Oleg Makarov

Skylab 4
- Gerald Carr
- Edward Gibson
- William Pogue

Soyuz 13
- Pyotr Klimuk
- Valentin Lebedev

Soyuz 14
- Pavel Popovich
- Yuri Artyukhin

Soyuz 15
- Gennady Sarafanov
- Lev Dyomin

Soyuz 16
- Anatoly Filipchenko
- Nikolai Rukavishnikov

Soyuz 17
- Aleksei Gubarev
- Georgy Grechko

Soyuz 18
- Pyotr Klimuk
- Vitaly Sevastyanov

Soyuz 19
- Alexei Leonov
- Valery Kubasov

Apollo-Soyuz
- Thomas Stafford
- Vance Brand
- Donald Slayton

Soyuz 21
- Boris Volynov
- Vitaly Zholobov

Soyuz 22
- Valery Bykovsky
- Vladimir Aksyonov

Soyuz 23
- Vyacheslav Zudov
- Valery Rozhdestvensky

Soyuz 24
- Viktor Gorbatko
- Yuri Glazkov

Soyuz 25
- Vladimir Kovalyonok
- Valery Ryumin

Soyuz 26
- Yuri Romanenko
- Georgy Grechko

Soyuz 27
- Vladimir Dzhanibekov
- Oleg Makarov

Soyuz 28
- Aleksei Gubarev
- Vladimir Remek

Soyuz 29
- Vladimir Kovalyonok
- Aleksandr Ivanchenkov

Soyuz 30
- Pyotr Klimuk
- M. Hermaszewski

Soyuz 31
- Valery Bykovsky
- Sigmund Jähn

Soyuz 32
- Vladimir Lyakhov
- Valery Ryumin

Soyuz 33
- Nikolai Rukavishnikov
- Georgi Ivanov

1970	1971	1972	1973	1974	1975	1976	1977	1978	1979
3	7	4	11	3	4	4	4	5	1
2	4	2	5	3	4	3	3	5	2

When was the Space Shuttle launched?

NASA's first reusable spacecraft, designed to 'launch like a rocket and land like a plane', lifted off for the first time on **12th April 1981** from Florida's Kennedy Space Center. Space Shuttle *Columbia* was commanded by John Young, an astronaut who walked on the moon in 1972. It was powered by rocket boosters which could be recovered and used again after falling away: the only part which could not be reused was the fuel tank, which burned up as it returned to Earth

1985 was the **busiest year** for space travel so far, with 11 missions carrying 63 people – 40 of those for the first time

The **second and third women in space** travelled there almost 20 years after the first

What happened in 1986?

On 28th January 1986, Space Shuttle *Challenger* was launched for its tenth mission from Cape Canaveral in Florida. A failure of seals in one of the spacecraft's solid rocket boosters led to it breaking up 73 seconds after launch, killing the crew of seven. One of those on board was Christa McAuliffe, selected from more than 11,000 applicants to be the first teacher in space, who had planned to give lessons from orbit. It has been estimated that 17 percent of Americans watched the explosion live on television. The disaster led to a suspension of the shuttle programme for almost three years

1980

Soyuz 35
Leonid Popov
Valery Ryumin
Soyuz 36
Valery Kubasov
Bertalan Farkas
Soyuz T-2
Yury Malyshev
Vladimir Aksyonov
Soyuz 37
Viktor Gorbatko
Pham Tuân
Soyuz 38
Yuri Romanenko
Arnaldo Méndez
Soyuz T-3
Leonid Kizim
Oleg Makarov
Gennady Strekalov

1981

Soyuz T-4
Vladimir Kovalyonok
Viktor Savinykh
Soyuz 39
Vladimir Dzhanibekov
J. Gürragchaa
Columbia STS-1
John Young
Robert Crippen
Soyuz 40
Leonid Popov
Dumitru Prunariu
Columbia STS-2
Joe Engle
Richard Truly

1982

Columbia STS-3
Jack Lousma
Gordon Fullerton
Soyuz T-5
Anatoly Berezovoy
Valentin Lebedev
Soyuz T-6
Vladimir Dzhanibekov
Aleksandr Ivanchenkov
Jean-Loup Chrétien
Columbia STS-4
Thomas Mattingly
Henry Hartsfield
Soyuz T-7
Leonid Popov
Aleksandr Serebrov
Svetlana Savitskaya
Columbia STS-5
Vance Brand
Robert Overmyer
Joseph Allen
William Lenoir

1983

Challenger STS-6
Paul Weitz
Karol Bobko
Story Musgrave
Donald Peterson
Soyuz T-8
Vladimir Titov
Gennady Strekalov
Aleksandr Serebrov
Challenger STS-7
Robert Crippen
Frederick Hauck
John Fabian
Sally Ride
Norman Thagard
Soyuz T-9
Vladimir Lyakhov
Aleksandr Aleksandrov
Challenger STS-8
Richard Truly
Daniel Brandenstein
Guion Bluford
Dale Gardner
William Thornton
Columbia STS-9
John Young
Brewster Shaw
Owen Garriott
Robert Parker
Ulf Merbold
Byron Lichtenberg

1984

Challenger STS-41B
Vance Brand
Robert Gibson
Bruce McCandless
Robert Stewart
Ronald McNair
Soyuz T-10
Leonid Kizim
Vladimir Solovyov
Oleg Atkov
Soyuz T-11
Yuri Malyshev
Gennady Strekalov
Rakesh Sharma
Challenger STS-41C
Robert Crippen
Francis Scobee
Terry Hart
James van Hoften
George Nelson
Soyuz T-12
Vladimir Dzhanibekov
Svetlana Savitskaya
Igor Volk
Discovery STS-41D
Henry Hartsfield
Michael Coats
Richard Mullane
Steven Hawley
Judith Resnik
Charles Walker
Challenger STS-41G
Robert Crippen
Jon McBride
Kathryn Sullivan
Sally Ride
David Leestma
Paul Scully-Power
Marc Garneau
Discovery STS-51A
Frederick Hauck
David Walker
Joseph Allen
Anna Lee Fisher
Dale Gardner

1985

Discovery STS-51C
Thomas Mattingly
Loren Shriver
Ellison Onizuka
James Buchli
Gary Payton
Discovery STS-51D
Karol Bobko
Donald Williams
Rhea Seddon
David Griggs
Jeffrey Hoffman
Charles Walker
Edwin Garn
Challenger STS-51B
Robert Overmyer
Frederick Gregory
Don Lind
Norman Thagard
William Thornton
Lodewijk van den Berg
Taylor Wang
Soyuz T-13
Vladimir Dzhanibekov
Viktor Savinykh
Discovery STS-51G
Daniel Brandenstein
John Creighton
John Fabian
Steven Nagel
Shannon Lucid
Patrick Baudry
Sultan bin Salman Al Saud
Challenger STS-51F
Gordon Fullerton
Roy Bridges
Karl Henize
Story Musgrave
Anthony England
Loren Acton
John-David Bartoe
Discovery STS-51I
Joe Engle
Richard Covey
James van Hoften
John Lounge
William Fisher
Soyuz T-14
Vladimir Vasyutin
Georgy Grechko
Alexander Volkov
Atlantis STS-51J
Karol Bobko
Ronald Grabe
David Hilmers
Robert Stewart
William Pailes
Challenger STS-61A
Henry Hartsfield
Steven Nagel
Bonnie Dunbar
James Buchli
Guion Bluford
Reinhard Furrer
Wubbo Ockels
Ernst Messerschmid
Atlantis STS-61B
Brewster Shaw
Bryan O'Connor
Jerry Ross
Mary Cleave
Sherwood Spring
Charles Walker
Rodolfo Neri Vela

1986

Columbia STS-61C
Robert Gibson
Charles Bolden
George Nelson
Steven Hawley
Franklin Chang-Diaz
William Nelson
Robert Cenker
Challenger STS-51-L
Francis Scobee ✕
Michael Smith ✕
Ellison Onizuka ✕
Judith Resnik ✕
Ronald McNair ✕
Gregory Jarvis ✕
Christa McAuliffe ✕
Soyuz T-15
Leonid Kizim
Vladimir Solovyov

1987

Soyuz TM-2
Yuri Romanenko
Aleksandr Laveykin
Soyuz TM-3
Aleksandr Viktorenko
Aleksandr Aleksandrov
Muhammed Faris
Soyuz TM-4
Vladimir Titov
Musa Manarov
Anatoly Levchenko

1988

Soyuz TM-5
Anatoly Solovyev
Viktor Savinykh
Aleksandr Aleksandrov
Soyuz TM-6
Vladimir Lyakhov
Valeri Polyakov
Abdul Mohmand
Discovery STS-26
Frederick Hauck
Richard Covey
John Lounge
David Hilmers
George Nelson
Soyuz TM-7
Alexander Volkov
Sergei Krikalev
Jean-Loup Chrétien
Atlantis STS-27
Robert Gibson
Guy Gardner
Richard Mullane
Jerry Ross
William Shepherd

1989

Discovery STS-29
Michael Coats
John Blaha
Robert Springer
James Buchli
James Bagian
Columbia STS-30
David Walker
Ronald Grabe
Mark Lee
Norman Thagard
Mary Cleave
Atlantis STS-28
Brewster Shaw
Richard Richards
James Adamson
David Leestma
Mark Brown
Soyuz TM-8
Aleksandr Viktorenko
Aleksandr Serebrov
Atlantis STS-34
Donald Williams
Michael McCulley
Shannon Lucid
Franklin Chang-Diaz
Ellen Baker
Discovery STS-33
Frederick Gregory
John Blaha
Manley Carter
Story Musgrave
Kathryn Thornton

YEAR

NEW SPACE TRAVELLERS	1980	1981	1982	1983	1984	1985	1986	1987	1988	1989
					26	40	4	5	7	12
	7	6	9	17	8	11	3	3	5	6
MISSIONS	7	6	6	6						
	6	5								

Discovery STS-42
- Ronald Grabe
- Stephen Oswald
- Norman Thagard
- William Readdy
- David Hilmers
- Roberta Bondar
- Ulf Merbold

Soyuz TM-14
- Aleksandr Viktorenko
- Aleksandr Kaleri
- Klaus-Dietrich Flade

Atlantis STS-45
- Charles Bolden
- Brian Duffy
- Kathryn Sullivan
- David Leestma
- Michael Foale
- Dirk Frimout
- Byron Lichtenberg

Endeavour STS-49
- Daniel Brandenstein
- Kevin Chilton
- Richard Hieb
- Bruce Melnick
- Pierre Thuot
- Kathryn Thornton
- Thomas Akers

Columbia STS-50
- Richard Richards
- Kenneth Bowersox
- Bonnie Dunbar
- Ellen Baker
- Carl Meade
- Lawrence DeLucas
- Eugene Trinh

Soyuz TM-15
- Anatoly Solovyev
- Sergei Avdeyev
- Michel Tognini

Atlantis STS-46
- Loren Shriver
- Andrew Allen
- Claude Nicollier
- Marsha Ivins
- Jeffrey Hoffman
- Franklin Chang-Diaz
- Franco Malerba

Endeavour STS-47
- Robert Gibson
- Curtis Brown
- Mark Lee
- Jay Apt
- Jan Davis
- Mae Jemison
- Mamoru Mohri

Columbia STS-52
- James Wetherbee
- Michael Baker
- Charles Veach
- William Shepherd
- Tamara Jernigan
- Steven MacLean

Discovery STS-53
- David Walker
- Robert Cabana
- Guion Bluford
- Michael Clifford
- James Voss

Endeavour STS-54
- John Casper
- Donald McMonagle
- Mario Runco
- Gregory Harbaugh
- Susan Helms
- Gennadi Manakov
- Aleksandr Poleshchuk

Discovery STS-56
- Kenneth Cameron
- Stephen Oswald
- Michael Foale
- Kenneth Cockrell
- Ellen Ochoa

Columbia STS-55
- Steven Nagel
- Terence Henricks
- Jerry Ross
- Charles Precourt
- Bernard Harris
- Ulrich Walter
- Hans Schlegel

Endeavour STS-57
- Ronald Grabe
- Brian Duffy
- David Low
- Nancy Sherlock
- Peter Wisoff
- Janice Voss

Soyuz TM-17
- Vasili Tsibliyev
- Aleksandr Serebrov
- Jean-Pierre Haigneré

Discovery STS-51
- Frank Culbertson
- William Readdy
- James Newman
- Daniel Bursch
- Carl Walz

Columbia STS-58
- John Blaha
- Richard Searfoss
- Rhea Seddon
- William McArthur
- David Wolf
- Shannon Lucid
- Martin Fettman

Endeavour STS-61
- Richard Covey
- Kenneth Bowersox
- Kathryn Thornton
- Claude Nicollier
- Jeffrey Hoffman
- Story Musgrave
- Thomas Akers

Soyuz TM-18
- Viktor Afanasyev
- Yury Usachov
- Valeri Polyakov

Discovery STS-60
- Charles Bolden
- Kenneth Reightler
- Jan Davis
- Ronald Sega
- Franklin Chang-Diaz
- Sergei Krikalev

Columbia STS-62
- John Casper
- Andrew Allen
- Pierre Thuot
- Charles Gemar
- Marsha Ivins

Endeavour STS-59
- Sidney Gutierrez
- Kevin Chilton
- Jay Apt
- Michael Clifford
- Linda Godwin
- Thomas Jones

Soyuz TM-19
- Yuri Malenchenko
- Talgat Musabayev

Columbia STS-65
- Robert Cabana
- James Halsell
- Richard Hieb
- Carl Walz
- Leroy Chiao
- Donald Thomas
- Chiaki Mukai

Discovery STS-64
- Richard Richards
- Blaine Hammond
- Jerry Linenger
- Susan Helms
- Carl Meade
- Mark Lee

Endeavour STS-68
- Michael Baker
- Terrence Wilcutt
- Steven Smith
- Daniel Bursch
- Peter Wisoff
- Thomas Jones

Soyuz TM-20
- Aleksandr Viktorenko
- Yelena Kondakova
- Ulf Merbold

Atlantis STS-66
- Donald McMonagle
- Curtis Brown
- Ellen Ochoa
- Joseph Tanner
- Jean-François Clervoy
- Scott Parazynski

Discovery STS-63
- James Wetherbee
- Eileen Collins
- Bernard Harris
- Michael Foale
- Janice Voss
- Vladimir Titov

Endeavour STS-67
- Stephen Oswald
- William Gregory
- John Grunsfeld
- Wendy Lawrence
- Tamara Jernigan
- Samuel Durrance
- Ronald Parise

Soyuz TM-21
- Vladimir Dezhurov
- Gennady Strekalov
- Norman Thagard

Atlantis STS-71
- Robert Gibson
- Charles Precourt
- Ellen Baker
- Bonnie Dunbar
- Gregory Harbaugh
- Anatoly Solovyev
- Nikolai Budarin

Discovery STS-70
- Terence Henricks
- Kevin Kregel
- Donald Thomas
- Nancy Currie
- Mary Weber

Soyuz TM-22
- Yuri Gidzenko
- Sergei Avdeyev
- Thomas Reiter

Endeavour STS-69
- David Walker
- Kenneth Cockrell
- James Voss
- James Newman
- Michael Gernhardt

Columbia STS-73
- Kenneth Bowersox
- Kent Rominger
- Catherine Coleman
- Michael López-Alegría
- Kathryn Thornton
- Fred Leslie
- Albert Sacco

Atlantis STS-74
- Kenneth Cameron
- James Halsell
- Chris Hadfield
- Jerry Ross
- William McArthur

Endeavour STS-72
- Brian Duffy
- Brent Jett
- Leroy Chiao
- Winston Scott
- Koichi Wakata
- Daniel Barry

Soyuz TM-23
- Yuri Onufrienko
- Yury Usachov

Columbia STS-75
- Andrew Allen
- Scott Horowitz
- Jeffrey Hoffman
- Maurizio Cheli
- Claude Nicollier
- Franklin Chang-Diaz
- Umberto Guidoni

Atlantis STS-76
- Kevin Chilton
- Richard Searfoss
- Ronald Sega
- Michael Clifford
- Linda Godwin
- Shannon Lucid

Endeavour STS-77
- John Casper
- Curtis Brown
- Andrew Thomas
- Daniel Bursch
- Mario Runco
- Marc Garneau

Columbia STS-78
- Terence Henricks
- Kevin Kregel
- Richard Linnehan
- Susan Helms
- Charles Brady
- Jean-Jacques Favier
- Robert Thirsk

Soyuz TM-24
- Valery Korzun
- Aleksandr Kaleri
- Claudie André-Deshays

Atlantis STS-79
- William Readdy
- Terrence Wilcutt
- Scott Parazynski
- Jay Apt
- Thomas Akers
- Carl Walz
- John Blaha

Columbia STS-80
- Kenneth Cockrell
- Kent Rominger
- Story Musgrave
- Thomas Jones
- Tamara Jernigan

Atlantis STS-81
- Michael Baker
- Brent Jett
- Peter Wisoff
- John Grunsfeld
- Marsha S. Ivins
- Jerry Linenger

Discovery STS-82
- Kenneth Bowersox
- Scott Horowitz
- Joseph Tanner
- Steven Hawley
- Gregory Harbaugh
- Mark Lee
- Steven Smith

Columbia STS-83
- James Halsell
- Susan Still
- Janice Voss
- Michael Gernhardt
- Donald Thomas
- Roger Crouch
- Gregory Linteris

Atlantis STS-84
- Charles Precourt
- Eileen Collins
- Jean-François Clervoy
- Carlos Noriega
- Edward Lu
- Yelena Kondakova
- Michael Foale

Columbia STS-94
- James Halsell
- Susan Still
- Janice Voss
- Michael Gernhardt
- Donald Thomas
- Roger Crouch
- Greg Linteris

Soyuz TM-26
- Anatoly Solovyev
- Pavel Vinogradov

Discovery STS-85
- Curtis Brown
- Kent Rominger
- Jan Davis
- Robert Curbeam
- Stephen Robinson
- Bjarni Tryggvason

Atlantis STS-86
- James Wetherbee
- Michael Bloomfield
- Vladimir Titov
- Scott Parazynski
- Jean-Loup Chrétien
- Wendy Lawrence
- David Wolf

Columbia STS-87
- Kevin Kregel
- Steven Lindsey
- Kalpana Chawla
- Winston Scott
- Takao Doi
- Leonid Kadeniuk

Endeavour STS-89
- Terrence Wilcutt
- Joe Edwards
- James Reilly
- Michael Anderson
- Bonnie Dunbar
- Salizhan Sharipov
- Andrew Thomas

Soyuz TM-27
- Talgat Musabayev
- Nikolai Budarin
- Léopold Eyharts

Columbia STS-90
- Richard Searfoss
- Scott Altman
- Dafydd Williams
- Kathryn Hire
- Richard Linnehan
- Jay Buckey
- James Pawelczyk

Discovery STS-91
- Charles Precourt
- Dominic Pudwill Gorie
- Franklin Chang-Diaz
- Wendy Lawrence
- Janet Kavandi
- Valery Ryumin

Soyuz TM-28
- Gennady Padalka
- Sergei Avdeyev
- Yuri Baturin

Discovery STS-95
- Curtis Brown
- Steven Lindsey
- Pedro Duque
- Scott Parazynski
- Stephen Robinson
- Chiaki Mukai
- John Glenn

Endeavour STS-88
- Robert Cabana
- Frederick Sturckow
- Jerry Ross
- Nancy Currie
- James Newman
- Sergei Krikalev

Soyuz TM-29
- Viktor Afanasyev
- Jean-Pierre Haigneré
- Ivan Bella

Discovery STS-96
- Kent Rominger
- Rick Husband
- Daniel Barry
- Ellen Ochoa
- Tamara Jernigan
- Julie Payette
- Valeri Tokarev

Columbia STS-93
- Eileen Collins
- Jeffrey Ashby
- Michel Tognini
- Steven Hawley
- Catherine Coleman

Discovery STS-103
- Curtis Brown
- Scott Kelly
- John Grunsfeld
- Jean-François Clervoy
- Michael Foale
- Steven Smith
- Claude Nicollier

Columbia STS-32
- Daniel Brandenstein
- James Wetherbee
- Bonnie Dunbar
- Marsha Ivins
- David Low

Soyuz TM-9
- Anatoly Solovyev
- Aleksandr Balandin

Atlantis STS-36
- John Creighton
- John Casper
- Pierre Thuot
- David Hilmers
- Richard Mullane

Discovery STS-31
- Loren Shriver
- Charles Bolden
- Bruce McCandless
- Steven Hawley
- Kathryn Sullivan

Soyuz TM-10
- Gennady Manakov
- Gennady Strekalov

Discovery STS-41
- Richard Richards
- Robert Cabana
- Bruce Melnick
- William Shepherd
- Thomas Akers

Atlantis STS-38
- Richard Covey
- Frank Culbertson
- Carl Meade
- Robert Springer
- Charles Gemar

Columbia STS-35
- Vance Brand
- Guy Gardner
- Jeffrey Hoffman
- John Lounge
- Robert Parker
- Samuel Durrance
- Ronald Parise

Soyuz TM-11
- Viktor Afanasyev
- Musa Manarov
- Toyohiro Akiyama

Atlantis STS-37
- Steven Nagel
- Kenneth Cameron
- Linda Godwin
- Jerry Ross
- Jay Apt

Discovery STS-39
- Michael Coats
- Blaine Hammond
- Gregory Harbaugh
- Donald McMonagle
- Guion Bluford
- Charles Veach
- Richard Hieb

Soyuz TM-12
- Anatoly Artsebarsky
- Sergei Krikalev
- Helen Sharman

Columbia STS-40
- Bryan O'Connor
- Sidney Gutierrez
- James Bagian
- Tamara Jernigan
- Rhea Seddon
- Drew Gaffney
- Millie Hughes-Fulford

Atlantis STS-43
- John Blaha
- Michael Baker
- Shannon Lucid
- David Low
- James Adamson

Discovery STS-48
- John Creighton
- Kenneth Reightler
- Charles Gemar
- James Buchli
- Mark Brown

Soyuz TM-13
- Alexander Volkov
- Toktar Aubakirov
- Franz Viehböck

Atlantis STS-44
- Frederick Gregory
- Terence Henricks
- James Voss
- Story Musgrave
- Mario Runco
- Thomas Hennen

1990	1991	1992	1993	1994	1995	1996	1997	1998	1999
👤 17	👤 22	👤 23	👤 20	👤 16	👤 17	👤 15	👤 15	👤 16	👤 6
🌓 9	🌓 9	🌓 10	🌓 9	🌓 10	🌓 9	🌓 9	🌓 9	🌓 7	🌓 4

Mark Lee and Jan Davis are the only married couple to fly together in space so far

Valeri Polyakov has spent the longest continuous time in space – 437 days, 17 hours, 58 minutes and 16 seconds

Who's the oldest person to orbit the Earth?

American John Glenn was 77 years old when he took his second trip to space in October 1998 – his first was in 1962

Who was the first space tourist?

On 28th April 2001 multi-millionaire US businessman and space enthusiast **Dennis Tito** was launched into space on a Soyuz rocket having paid $20 million to the Russian space agency for the privilege. He spent eight days on the International Space Station, much to the irritation of NASA, which had advised the Russians against taking him, believing it was no place for a 60-year-old who had received only limited training and preparation

What happened in 2003?

On **1st February 2003**, the Space Shuttle **Columbia** disintegrated during re-entry to Earth's atmosphere during its 28th mission, killing the crew of seven. During the shuttle's launch a piece of insulation had broken off from its external tank, smashing into its wing: the damage allowed atmospheric gas to make its way through the heat shield and destroy the wing on re-entry, leading to the disaster

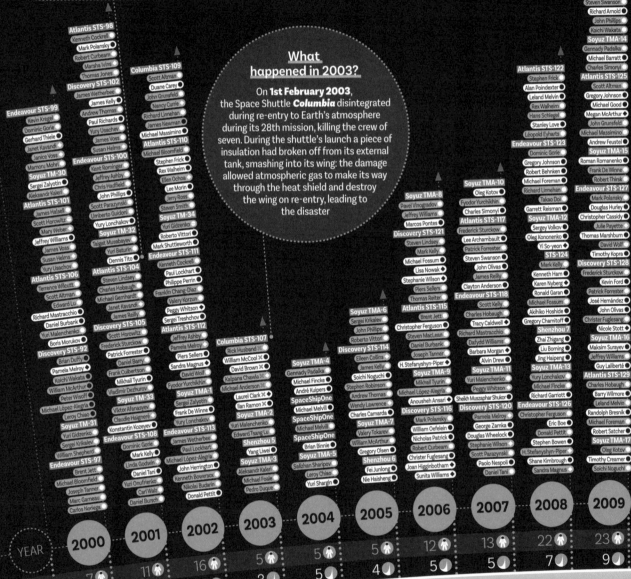

Discovery STS-119
Lee Archambault
Dominic Antonelli
Joseph Acaba
Steven Swanson
Richard Arnold
John Phillips
Koichi Wakata

Soyuz TMA-14
Gennady Padalka
Michael Barratt
Charles Simonyi

Atlantis STS-125
Scott Altman
Gregory Johnson
Michael Good
Megan McArthur
John Grunsfeld
Michael Massimino
Andrew Feustel

Soyuz TMA-15
Roman Romanenko
Frank De Winne
Robert Thirsk

Endeavour STS-127
Mark Polansky
Douglas Hurley
Christopher Cassidy
Julie Payette
Thomas Marshburn
David Wolf
Timothy Kopra

Discovery STS-128
Frederick Sturckow
Kevin Ford
Patrick Forrester
José Hernández
John Olivas
Christer Fuglesang
Nicole Stott

Soyuz TMA-16
Maksim Surayev
Jeffrey Williams
Guy Laliberté

Atlantis STS-129
Charles Hobaugh
Barry Wilmore
Leland Melvin
Randolph Bresnik
Michael Foreman
Robert Satcher

Soyuz TMA-17
Oleg Kotov
Timothy Creamer
Soichi Noguchi

Atlantis STS-122
Stephen Frick
Alan Poindexter
Leland Melvin
Rex Walheim
Hans Schlegel
Stanley Love
Léopold Eyharts

Endeavour STS-123
Dominic Gorie
Gregory Johnson
Robert Behnken
Michael Foreman
Richard Linnehan
Takao Doi
Garrett Reisman

Soyuz TMA-12
Sergey Volkov
Oleg Kononenko
Yi So-yeon

STS-124
Mark Kelly
Kenneth Ham
Karen Nyberg
Ronald Garan
Michael Fossum
Akihiko Hoshide
Gregory Chamitoff

Shenzhou 7
Zhai Zhigang
Liu Boming
Jing Haipeng

Soyuz TMA-13
Yury Lonchakov
Michael Fincke
Richard Garriott

Endeavour STS-126
Christopher Ferguson
Eric Boe
Donald Pettit
Stephen Bowen
H. Stefanyshyn-Piper
Shane Kimbrough
Sandra Magnus

Soyuz TMA-10
Oleg Kotov
Fyodor Yurchikhin
Charles Simonyi

Atlantis STS-117
Frederick Sturckow
Lee Archambault
Patrick Forrester
Steven Swanson
John Olivas
James Reilly
Clayton Anderson

Endeavour STS-118
Scott Kelly
Charles Hobaugh
Tracy Caldwell
Richard Mastracchio
Dafydd Williams
Barbara Morgan
Alvin Drew

Soyuz TMA-11
Yuri Malenchenko
Peggy Whitson
Sheikh Muszaphar Shukor

Discovery STS-120
Pamela Melroy
George Zamka
Douglas Wheelock
Stephanie Wilson
Scott Parazynski
Paolo Nespoli
Daniel Tani

Soyuz TMA-8
Pavel Vinogradov
Jeffrey Williams
Marcos Pontes

Discovery STS-121
Steven Lindsey
Mark Kelly
Michael Fossum
Lisa Nowak
Stephanie Wilson
Piers Sellers
Thomas Reiter

Atlantis STS-115
Brent Jett
Christopher Ferguson
Steven MacLean
Daniel Burbank
Joseph Tanner
H. Stefanyshyn-Piper

Soyuz TMA-9
Mikhail Tyurin
Michael López-Alegría
Anousheh Ansari

Discovery STS-116
Mark Polansky
William Oefelein
Nicholas Patrick
Robert Curbeam
Christer Fuglesang
Joan Higginbotham
Sunita Williams

Soyuz TMA-6
Sergei Krikalev
John Phillips
Roberto Vittori

Discovery STS-114
Eileen Collins
James Kelly
Soichi Noguchi
Stephen Robinson
Andrew Thomas
Wendy Lawrence
Charles Camarda

Soyuz TMA-7
Valery Tokarev
William McArthur
Gregory Olsen

Shenzhou 6
Fei Junlong
Nie Haisheng

Soyuz TMA-4
Gennady Padalka
Michael Fincke
André Kuipers

SpaceShipOne
Michael Melvill

SpaceShipOne
Michael Melvill

SpaceShipOne
Brian Binnie

Soyuz TMA-5
Salizhan Sharipov
Leroy Chiao
Yuri Shargin

Columbia STS-107
Rick Husband
William McCool
David Brown
Kalpana Chawla
Michael Anderson
Laurel Clark
Ilan Ramon

Soyuz TMA-2
Yuri Malenchenko
Edward Tsang Lu

Shenzhou 5
Yang Liwei

Soyuz TMA-3
Aleksandr Kaleri
Michael Foale
Pedro Duque

Columbia STS-109
Scott Altman
Duane Carey
John Grunsfeld
Nancy Currie
Richard Linnehan
James Newman
Michael Massimino

Atlantis STS-110
Michael Bloomfield
Stephen Frick
Rex Walheim
Ellen Ochoa
Lee Morin
Jerry Ross
Steven Smith

Soyuz TM-34
Yuri Gidzenko
Roberto Vittori
Mark Shuttleworth

Endeavour STS-111
Kenneth Cockrell
Paul Lockhart
Philippe Perrin
Franklin Chang-Diaz
Valery Korzun
Peggy Whitson
Sergei Treshchov

Atlantis STS-112
Jeffrey Ashby
Pamela Melroy
Piers Sellers
Sandra Magnus
David Wolf
Fyodor Yurchikhin

Soyuz TMA-1
Sergei Zalyotin
Frank De Winne
Yury Lonchakov

Endeavour STS-113
James Wetherbee
Paul Lockhart
Michael López-Alegría
John Herrington
Kenneth Bowersox
Nikolai Budarin
Donald Pettit

Atlantis STS-98
Kenneth Cockrell
Mark Polansky
Robert Curbeam
Marsha Ivins
Thomas Jones

Discovery STS-102
James Wetherbee
James Kelly
Andrew Thomas
Paul Richards
Yury Usachev
James Voss
Susan Helms

Endeavour STS-100
Kent Rominger
Jeffrey Ashby
Chris Hadfield
John Phillips
Scott Parazynski
Umberto Guidoni
Yury Lonchakov

Soyuz TM-32
Talgat Musabayev
Yuri Baturin
Dennis Tito

Atlantis STS-104
Steven Lindsey
Charles Hobaugh
Michael Gernhardt
Janet Kavandi
James Reilly

Discovery STS-105
Scott Horowitz
Frederick Sturckow
Patrick Forrester
Daniel Barry
Frank Culbertson
Mikhail Tyurin
Vladimir Dezhurov

Soyuz TM-33
Viktor Afanasyev
Claudie Haigneré
Konstantin Kozeyev

Endeavour STS-108
Dominic Gorie
Mark Kelly
Linda Godwin
Daniel Tani
Yuri Onufrienko
Carl Walz
Daniel Bursch

Endeavour STS-99
Kevin Kregel
Dominic Gorie
Gerhard Thiele
Janet Kavandi
Janice Voss
Mamoru Mohri

Soyuz TM-30
Sergei Zalyotin
Aleksandr Kaleri

Atlantis STS-101
James Halsell
Scott Horowitz
Mary Weber
Jeffrey Williams
James Voss
Susan Helms
Yury Usachev

Atlantis STS-106
Terrence Wilcutt
Scott Altman
Edward Lu
Richard Mastracchio
Daniel Burbank
Yuri Malenchenko
Boris Morukov

Discovery STS-92
Brian Duffy
Pamela Melroy
Koichi Wakata
William McArthur
Peter Wisoff
Michael López-Alegría
Leroy Chiao

Soyuz TM-31
Yuri Gidzenko
Sergei Krikalev
William Shepherd

Endeavour STS-97
Brent Jett
Michael Bloomfield
Joseph Tanner
Marc Garneau
Carlos Noriega

YEAR	2000	2001	2002	2003	2004	2005	2006	2007	2008	2009
NEW SPACE TRAVELLERS	7	11	16	5	5	5	12	13	22	23
	7	8	5	3	5	4	5	5	7	9
MISSIONS	7	7	5		5					

How many people flew on the Space Shuttle?

The final Shuttle flight launched on **8th July 2011** after 31 years in service, with 135 missions carrying 852 people:

62% of all people who have been to space flew at least one way on the Shuttle

355 individual people, ● **306** men and ◆ **49** women from **16** different countries

283 of the flyers (80%) were United States citizens

UNITED STATES

Los Angeles
New York
Washington
Orlando

A
B
C
D

Where can I see a Space Shuttle?

Of the five Shuttles that flew into space three survive, plus the original atmospheric test-flight vehicle, *Enterprise*:

A	B	C	D
Enterprise	**Discovery**	**Atlantis**	**Endeavour**
Launched: **12th Aug 1977**	Launched: **30th Aug 1984**	Launched: **3rd Oct 1985**	Launched: **7th May 1992**
Flights: **5**	Flights: **39**	Flights: **33**	Flights: **25**
Intrepid Sea, Air & Space Museum, Manhattan, New York	**Steven F Udvar-Hazy Center,** Chantilly, Virginia	**Kennedy Space Center Visitor Complex,** Cape Canaveral, Florida	**California Science Center,** Los Angeles, California

STS-130
● George Zamka
● Terry Virts
● Kathryn Hire
● Stephen Robinson
● Nicholas Patrick
● Robert Behnken
Soyuz TMA-18
● Aleksandr Skvortsov
● Mikhail Korniyenko
● Tracy Caldwell Dyson
STS-131
● Alan Poindexter
● James Dutton
● Richard Mastracchio
◆ D. Metcalf-Lindenburger
◆ Stephanie Wilson
◆ Naoko Yamazaki
● Clayton Anderson
STS-132
● Kenneth Ham
● Dominic Antonelli
● Garrett Reisman
● Michael Good
● Stephen Bowen
● Piers Sellers
Soyuz TMA-19
● Fyodor Yurchikhin
◆ Shannon Walker
● Douglas Wheelock
Soyuz TMA-01M
● Aleksandr Kaleri
● Oleg Skripochka
● Scott Kelly
Soyuz TMA-20
● Dmitri Kondratyev
● Catherine Coleman
● Paolo Nespoli

STS-133
● Steven Lindsey
● Eric Boe
● Nicole Stott
● Alvin Drew
● Michael Barratt
● Stephen Bowen
Soyuz TMA-21
● Aleksandr Samokutyayev
● Andrei Borisenko
● Ronald Garan
STS-134
● Mark Kelly
● Gregory Johnson
● Michael Fincke
● Roberto Vittori
● Andrew Feustel
● Gregory Chamitoff
Soyuz TMA-02M
● Sergey Volkov
● Michael Fossum
● Satoshi Furukawa
STS-135
● Christopher Ferguson
● Douglas Hurley
● Sandra Magnus
● Rex Walheim
Soyuz TMA-22
● Anton Shkaplerov
● Anatoli Ivanishin
● Daniel Burbank
Soyuz TMA-03M
● Oleg Kononenko
● André Kuipers
● Donald Pettit

Soyuz TMA-04M
● Gennady Padalka
● Sergei Revin
● Joseph Acaba
Shenzhou 9
● Jing Haipeng
● Liu Wang
● Liu Yang
Soyuz TMA-05M
● Yuri Malenchenko
● Sunita Williams
● Akihiko Hoshide
Soyuz TMA-06M
● Oleg Novitskiy
● Evgeny Tarelkin
● Kevin Ford
Soyuz TMA-07M
● Roman Romanenko
● Chris Hadfield
● Thomas Marshburn

Soyuz TMA-08M
● Pavel Vinogradov
● Alexander Misurkin
● Christopher Cassidy
Soyuz TMA-09M
● Fyodor Yurchikhin
● Karen Nyberg
● Luca Parmitano
Shenzhou 10
● Nie Haisheng
● Zhang Xiaoguang
◆ Wang Yaping
Soyuz TMA-10M
● Oleg Kotov
● Sergey Ryazansky
● Michael Hopkins
Soyuz TMA-11M
● Mikhail Tyurin
● Richard Mastracchio
● Koichi Wakata

Soyuz TMA-12M
● Oleg Artemyev
● Aleksandr Skvortsov
● Steven Swanson
Soyuz TMA-13M
● Maksim Surayev
● Gregory Reid Wiseman
● Alexander Gerst
Soyuz TMA-14M
● Aleksandr Samokutyayev
◆ Yelena Serova
● Barry Wilmore
Soyuz TMA-15M
● Anton Shkaplerov
◆ Samantha Cristoforetti
● Terry Virts

Soyuz TMA-16M
● Gennady Padalka
● Mikhail Kornienko
● Scott Kelly
Soyuz TMA-17M
● Oleg Kononenko
● Kimiya Yui
● Kjell Lindgren
Soyuz TMA-18M
● Sergey Volkov
● Andreas Mogensen
● Aidyn Aimbetov
Soyuz TMA-19M
● Yuri Malenchenko
● Timothy Kopra
● Tim Peake

Soyuz TMA-20M
● Aleksey Ovchinin
● Oleg Skripochka
● Jeffrey Williams
Soyuz MS-01
● Anatoli Ivanishin
● Takuya Onishi
◆ Kathleen Rubins
Shenzhou 11
● Jing Haipeng
● Chen Dong
Soyuz MS-02
● Sergey Ryzhikov
● Andrei Borisenko
● Shane Kimbrough
Soyuz MS-03
● Oleg Novitskiy
● Thomas Pesquet
◆ Peggy Whitson

Soyuz MS-04
● Fyodor Yurchikhin
● Jack Fischer
Soyuz MS-05
● Sergey Ryazansky
● Randolph Bresnik
● Paolo Nespoli
Soyuz MS-06
● Alexander Misurkin
● Mark Vande Hei
● Joseph Acaba
Soyuz MS-07
● Anton Shkaplerov
● Scott Tingle
● Norishige Kanai

Soyuz MS-08
● Oleg Artemyev
● Andrew Feustel
● Richard Arnold
Soyuz MS-09
● Sergey Prokopyev
● Alexander Gerst
◆ Serena Auñón-Chancellor
Soyuz MS-11
● Oleg Kononenko
● David Saint-Jacques
◆ Anne McClain

Soyuz MS-12
● Aleksey Ovchinin
● Nick Hague
◆ Christina Koch
Soyuz MS-13
● Aleksandr Skvortsov
● Luca Parmitano
● Andrew R. Morgan
Soyuz MS-15
● Oleg Skripochka
◆ Jessica Meir
● Hazza Al Mansouri

2010	**2011**	**2012**	**2013**	**2014**	**2015**	**2016**	**2017**	**2018**	**2019**
9	5	5	6	5	5	6	4	4	5
7	7	5	5	4	5	5	4	3	3

353 UNITED STATES CITIZENS
(including 11 with dual nationality)

96 RUSSIAN
(including one with dual nationality)

In the first 60 years of
human spaceflight

569 PEOPLE
travelled to space

508 MEN **61 WOMEN**

14 UKRAINIAN
12 JAPANESE
11 CHINESE
10 GERMAN
10 FRENCH
10 CANADIAN
7 ITALIAN
6 KAZAKH

Six countries have sent
two people into space:
**Belarus, Belgium,
Latvia, the Netherlands,
the UK and Uzbekistan**

A further 28 countries
have sent one person

Soyuz MS-16
Anatoli Ivanishin
Ivan Vagner
Christopher Cassidy
**Crew Dragon
Endeavour**
Doug Hurley
Bob Behnken
Soyuz MS-17
Sergey Ryzhikov
Sergey Kud-Sverchkov
Kathleen Rubins
**Crew Dragon
Resilience**
Michael Hopkins
Victor Glover
Soichi Noguchi
Shannon Walker

**Crew Dragon
Endeavour**
Shane Kimbrough
Megan McArthur
Akihiko Hoshide
Thomas Pesquet

Missions up to 12th April
2021, the 60th anniversary
of the first successful
human spaceflight

YEAR

2020 **2021**

NEW SPACE
TRAVELLERS ▶ 3 0

MISSIONS ▶ 3 1

Who's going to space next?
On 11th July 2021 British billionaire
Richard Branson flew 50 miles above the
Earth aboard his spaceship VSS Unity, beating
fellow billionaires **Jeff Bezos** and **Elon Musk**
to the edge of space. Branson claims to have
signed up over **600 space tourists**, with
Virgin Galactic flights starting in 2022

Who's actually been in space?

Not everyone who got to space actually ventured out of their rocket or space station, and even fewer got to bounce around on the moon: these are the spacewalkers, moonwalkers and record-setters of the wild black yonder

227 SPACEWALKERS 🚶🚶

12 MOONWALKERS 🧑🧑🧑🧑🧑🧑🧑🧑🧑🧑🧑🧑

18th March 1965
First ever spacewalk
☀ 12 minutes
🌑 Alexei Leonov

3rd June 1965
First American to spacewalk
☀ 23 minutes
🌑 Ed White

20th July 1969
First ever moonwalk
☀ 21 hours
🌑 Neil Armstrong

6th February 1971
Only person to play golf on the moon
☀ 4 hours 43 minutes
🌑 Alan Shepard

7th February 1984
First untethered spacewalk
☀ 5 hours 55 minutes
🌑 Bruce McCandless

25th July 1984
First woman to walk in space
☀ 3 hours 35 minutes
🌑 Svetlana Savitskaya

16th January 1998
Most spacewalks and longest total time spacewalking
☀ 82 hours 22 minutes
🌑 Anatoly Solovyev

11th March 2001
Longest single spacewalk
☀ 8 hours 56 minutes
🌑 Susan Helms
🌑 James S Voss

27th September 2008
First Chinese spacewalk
☀ 22 minutes
🌑 Zhai Zhigang

15th January 2016
First spacewalk by a British astronaut
☀ 4 hours 43 minutes
🌑 Tim Peake

Who's got the biggest rocket?

Earth's largest spacecraft of the past, present and near future

Statue of Liberty, New York, **46m**

Nelson's Column, London, **52m**

Height in metres

What's the biggest rocket ever launched?

E Saturn V 1967–1973

Maximum payload: **118,000 kg**

Launch cost: **$1.23 billion** (adjusted)

Saturn V remains the tallest and most powerful rocket ever. It was used by NASA to send astronauts to the moon and to launch America's first space station, Skylab, in 1973. Fifteen such vehicles were built with 13 successfully launched into space.

How it works: We've compared some of the biggest rockets ever built (or about to be built) and illustrated them to scale

Sources: NASA, SpaceX. Data correct as of April 2021

What's the biggest rocket never launched?

D N1 1969–1972

Maximum payload: **95,000 kg**

The N1 was the Soviet Union's answer to America's Saturn V, a super-heavy-lift rocket intended to launch cosmonauts to the moon. Ten were built, but after four failed attempts to launch between 1969 and 1972 the project was cancelled in 1974.

What's the biggest rocket launching now?

A Falcon 9 2018–

Maximum payload: **22,800 kg**

Launch cost: **$50 million** (on re-use)

B Falcon Heavy 2018–

Maximum payload: **63,800 kg**

Launch cost: **$90 million** (on re-use)

SpaceX's reusable Falcon 9 is the biggest rocket certified to carry humans into space today. Its Falcon Heavy has the heaviest payload capacity currently operating and famously launched Elon Musk's Tesla electric car into space.

What's the biggest rocket launching next?

C SLS 2021–

Maximum payload: **70,000 kg**

Launch cost: **$2 billion** (estimated)

After the moon, NASA's Space Launch System is hoped to send crews to Mars

F SpaceX Starship 2023

Maximum payload: **100,000+ kg**

Launch cost: **$2 million** (aim per mission)

The moon- and Mars-ready Starship is also being considered by NASA for the Artemis programme, and includes a spacecraft and landing vehicle

Why is there so much junk in space?

The Earth is orbited by many broken-up pieces of satellite – several thousand tonnes' worth of debris, according to the European Space Agency. But what caused them to disintegrate in the first place?

Approximate number of satellites launched since Sputnik 1 at the start of the space age in 1957:
11,370

Estimated total number of satellites still orbiting the Earth today:
6,900

Estimated number of those orbiting satellites that are now defunct and at risk of breaking up:
2,900

Debris objects regularly tracked by space surveillance networks and maintained in their catalogue:
28,160

Estimated number of events that have resulted in fragmentation: **560+**

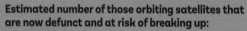

Deliberate destruction	Propulsion incident	Accidental collisions	Battery incident	Unknown causes
32.7%	**30.5%**	**14.3%**	**8.7%**	**13.8%**

9,300 tonnes

Estimated total mass of all space objects in Earth orbit, about the same as 66 blue whales

How it works: The chart around the globe is a representation of the total number of satellites estimated to be currently orbiting the Earth, with functioning satellites in yellow and those which are defunct and at risk of breaking up in black

Source: European Space Agency, data correct as of April 2021, NASA

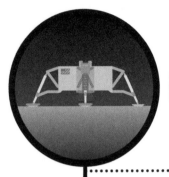

44 American spacecraft

Including six intact Apollo lunar lander descent stages and the debris of craft intentionally crashed into the moon

At least 33 other spacecraft

21 from the Soviet Union, four Chinese, four Japanese, two Indian, one Israeli and one European

27 cameras

Including seven TV cameras and an additional 18 lenses

20 sick bags

Plus an additional 25 'defecation collection devices', 18 'urine collection assemblies' and receptacles and other waste deposited in bags at the foot of the lunar landers

7 flags

Six Stars and Stripes and one US Marine Corps flag

7 hammers

Plus nine tongs

6 tributes to dead colleagues

Including silver astronaut wing pins, and medals commemorating Russian cosmonauts

5+ personal items

Including a photograph of astronaut Charles Duke and his family, a bible and a document proclaiming 'University of Michigan Alumni of the Moon'

1 stack of two-dollar bills

The Apollo 15 crew took 100 two-dollar bills to photograph on the moon and take back as souvenirs, but forgot to take them back to Earth

1 falcon feather

Used in a hammer vs feather physics experiment

1 gold olive branch

Symbolising peace and left alongside a silicone disc inscribed with comments from the leaders of 74 countries

1 human

Ashes of NASA geologist Eugene Shoemaker were shot onto the moon's surface in 1999 – Shoemaker's ambition to go to the moon had been thwarted due to a medical condition

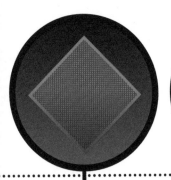

20 towels

10 blue, 10 red plus one bar of soap and 11 wet wipes

14 pairs of moonboots

Plus an additional three helmets, six jackets and nine spacesuit life support backpacks

9 seismic experiments

Including two grenade launchers, plus more than 30 pieces of scientific equipment and five retroreflectors still used to precisely measure the Earth-moon distance

9 hammocks

Plus an additional 11 'sleeping restraints'

5 robotic rovers

Comprising two intact Soviet remote controlled rovers (the first from 1970), two Chinese and one Indian

3 moon buggies

NASA's Lunar Roving Vehicles, deployed by Apollo 15, 16 and 17 in 1971 and 1972, could carry two astronauts and covered an average distance of 30km across the moon

3 pieces of sporting equipment

Two golf balls, and a makeshift javelin used in the 'First Lunar Olympics', won by Edgar Mitchell in 1971 during the Apollo 14 mission

3 rakes

For use in the collection of samples from the lunar surface

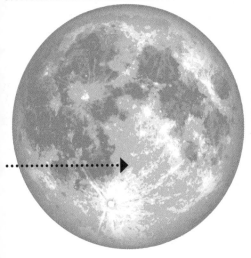

What have we left on the moon?

The Apollo 11 crew deposited at least 106 items on the moon's surface which have been added to by subsequent missions. Here's a selection of manmade items that are orbiting us on our nearest celestial body

How it works: We've illustrated some of the categories of object that have been left on the moon and placed them in order of the number of objects in each category

Sources: China National Space Administration, European Space Agency, Indian Space Research Organisation, NASA, SpaceIL. Data correct as of June 2021

Americans who believe 9/11 was an 'inside job'
23%

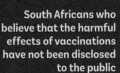

South Africans who believe that the harmful effects of vaccinations have not been disclosed to the public
32%

Paul McCartney 1942-1966

Americans who believe that Paul McCartney died in 1966
5%

Britons who believe the Earth is 'probably' or 'definitely' flat
3%

Americans who believe the government is mandating the switch to compact fluorescent light bulbs because they make people easier to control*
11%

Americans who believe the government is using aircraft 'chemtrails' to control the population
19%

Britons who believe in guardian angels
31%

Scots who think the Loch Ness monster could be real
24%

26%
Mexicans who believe that aliens have made contact and this has been hidden from the public

13%
Americans who believe that vampires 'probably' or 'definitely' exist

6%
Americans who believe the 1969 moon landing was staged

4%
Americans who believe that lizard people control politics

15%
Indians who think manmade global warming is a hoax

21%
Americans who believe Bigfoot is real

32%
French people who believe that the virus that causes AIDS was created in a lab

 Proportion
of adult...

Who believes the moon landing was faked?

According to polls, significant numbers of people give credence to conspiracy theories, cryptozoological beasts and supernatural hypotheses...

How it works: The graphic shows answers to questions asked in opinion polls between 2010 and 2020, with each icon of a person representing one percentage point

Sources: American Journal of Political Science, The Atlantic, Essential Research, FiveThirtyEight, France 24, The Independent, Ipsos, Pew Research Center, Tass, University of Oxford, YouGov
*Theory made up by researchers to test subjects' susceptibility to a previously unspread theory

Turks who believe the US government helped make 9/11 happen
36%

Thais who believe 'slightly' or 'seriously' in ghosts
43%

Russians who believe the 1969 moon landing was staged
49%

41%
Americans who believe in extrasensory perception

46%
Nigerians who believe that there is a single group of people who secretly control events and rule the world together

58%
Americans who believe a house can be haunted

61%
Americans who believe that Lee Harvey Oswald didn't act alone in the assassination of JFK

65%
Americans who believe in supernatural phenomena including reincarnation, the 'evil eye', astrology and making contact with the dead

Who's seen the Loch Ness monster?

Is Nessie out there? We've charted every sighting of the legendary beast of Loch Ness going back to the sixth century AD

How it works: We've illustrated the number of sightings every year since 1900 as logged by the Official Loch Ness Sightings Register and highlighted some key moments in the hunt to prove Nessie's existence

Sources: BBC, CNN, Gary Campbell, Maritime and Coastguard Agency, Natural Environment Research Council, the Official Loch Ness Sightings Register

Total number of recorded sightings
(Up to 31st December 2020)

1,078

Most sightings in a single year
142

Number of recorded sightings each year since 1900

Recorded sightings before 1900 **18**

First recorded sighting:
The seventh-century book *Life of Saint Columba* reports that the Irish monk encountered a 'water beast' on the River Ness in the year 565

First use of the word 'monster' to refer to the supposed creature occurs on 2nd May 1933 in an *Inverness Courier* report by Alex Campbell, water bailiff for Loch Ness. The article, 'Strange Spectacle on Loch Ness. What Was It?', tells of a sighting by Aldie Mackay on 14th April - kicking off a spate of 77 sightings that year

1900 01 02 03 04 05 06 07 08 09

19 18 17 16 15 14 13 12 11 1910

1920 21 22 23 24 25 26 27 28 29 1930 31 32 33 34 35 36

50
40
30
20
10

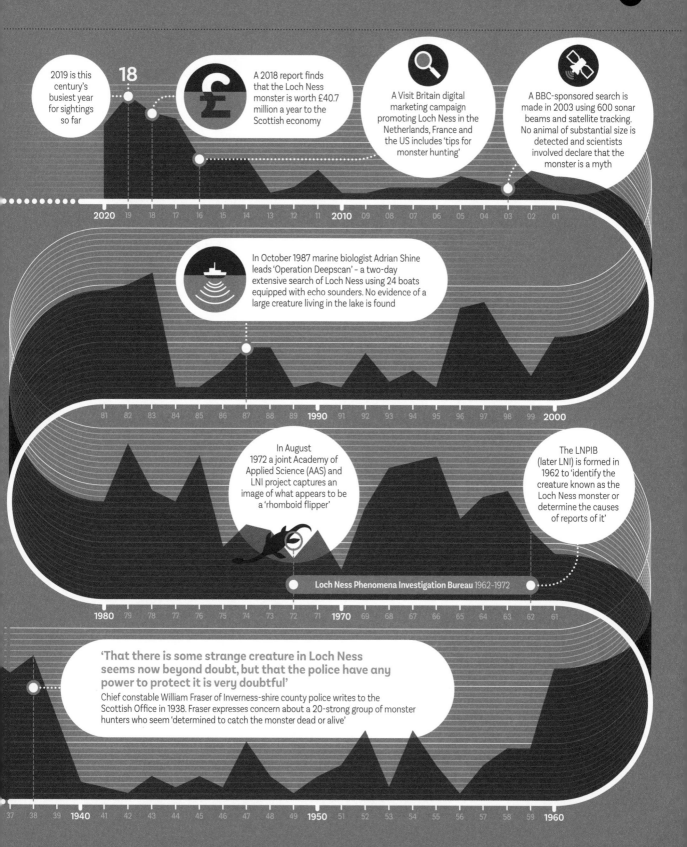

2019 is this century's busiest year for sightings so far

18

A 2018 report finds that the Loch Ness monster is worth £40.7 million a year to the Scottish economy

A Visit Britain digital marketing campaign promoting Loch Ness in the Netherlands, France and the US includes 'tips for monster hunting'

A BBC-sponsored search is made in 2003 using 600 sonar beams and satellite tracking. No animal of substantial size is detected and scientists involved declare that the monster is a myth

2020 19 18 17 16 15 14 13 12 11 2010 09 08 07 06 05 04 03 02 01

In October 1987 marine biologist Adrian Shine leads 'Operation Deepscan' – a two-day extensive search of Loch Ness using 24 boats equipped with echo sounders. No evidence of a large creature living in the lake is found

81 82 83 84 85 86 87 88 89 1990 91 92 93 94 95 96 97 98 99 2000

In August 1972 a joint Academy of Applied Science (AAS) and LNI project captures an image of what appears to be a 'rhomboid flipper'

The LNPIB (later LNI) is formed in 1962 to 'identify the creature known as the Loch Ness monster or determine the causes of reports of it'

Loch Ness Phenomena Investigation Bureau 1962-1972

1980 79 78 77 76 75 74 73 72 71 1970 69 68 67 66 65 64 63 62 61

'That there is some strange creature in Loch Ness seems now beyond doubt, but that the police have any power to protect it is very doubtful'

Chief constable William Fraser of Inverness-shire county police writes to the Scottish Office in 1938. Fraser expresses concern about a 20-strong group of monster hunters who seem 'determined to catch the monster dead or alive'

37 38 39 1940 41 42 43 44 45 46 47 48 49 1950 51 52 53 54 55 56 57 58 59 1960

Who believes in God?

(Or other deities, idols or higher spiritual powers)

Levels of religiosity fluctuate significantly across the globe, but there are clear patterns for where you'll find the largest concentrations of self-declared believers

How it works: The map shows countries and territories colour-coded according to the estimated percentage of their populations identifying as a follower of any religion

Source: Pew Research Center

NORTH AMERICA

SOUTH AMERICA

Almost everyone here is a believer
Countries and territories in which over 90% of the population identify as being a follower of a religion

Most people here believe
Countries and territories in which between 50% and 90% of the population identify as being a follower of a religion

Most people here don't believe
Countries and territories in which less than 50% of the population are affiliated with a religion

What do most countries believe in?

Number of countries and territories where the majority of the population identifies as being a follower of:

● **Christianity** (161)
● **Islam** (51)
● **Something else** (15)

ASIA

EUROPE

AFRICA

OCEANIA

WHERE ARE THE MOST RELIGIOUS PLACES? ✷

The 14 countries and territories where 99.5% or more of the population identify as followers of the nation's major religion

● Christian countries ● Muslim countries

Ⓐ **Afghanistan** Ⓑ **Iran** Ⓒ **Iraq** Ⓓ **Mauritania**
Ⓔ **Morocco** Ⓕ Papua New Guinea Ⓖ Romania
Ⓗ **Somalia** Ⓘ Timor-Leste Ⓙ Tokelau Ⓚ **Tunisia**
Ⓛ Vatican City Ⓜ **Western Sahara** Ⓝ **Yemen**

✕ WHERE ARE THE LEAST RELIGIOUS PLACES?

Ⓤ 51.8% no religious affiliation: China
Ⓥ 54.7% Hong Kong
Ⓦ 60% Japan
Ⓧ 60.2% **Estonia**
Ⓨ 71.3% **North Korea**
Ⓩ 78.4% **Czech Republic**

HOW DO I MAKE FRIENDS AND INFLUENCE PEOPLE

Questions about power, politics and Putin's poses

Who gets to be president of the United States?

The vital statistics of all the commanders-in-chief compared to see which Americans get the top political job

PRESIDENTS		INAUGURATED
George Washington	1	1789
John Adams	2	1797
Thomas Jefferson	3	1801
James Madison	4	1809
James Monroe	5	1817
John Quincy Adams	6	1825
Andrew Jackson	7	1829
William Henry Harrison	9	1841
John Tyler	10	1841
James K Polk	11	1845
Zachary Taylor	12	1849
Millard Fillmore	13	1850
Franklin Pierce	14	1853
James Buchanan	15	1857
Abraham Lincoln	16	1861
Andrew Johnson	17	1865
Ulysses S Grant	18	1869
Rutherford B Hayes	19	1877
James A Garfield	20	1881
Chester A Arthur	21	1881
Grover Cleveland	22	1885
Benjamin Harrison	23	1889
Grover Cleveland (re-elected)	24	1893
William McKinley	25	1897
Theodore Roosevelt	26	1901
William Howard Taft	27	1909
Woodrow Wilson	28	1913
Warren G Harding	29	1921
Calvin Coolidge	30	1923
Herbert Hoover	31	1929
Franklin D Roosevelt	32	1933
Harry S Truman	33	1945
Dwight D Eisenhower	34	1953
John F Kennedy	35	1961
Lyndon B Johnson	36	1963
Richard Nixon	37	1969
Gerald Ford	38	1974
Jimmy Carter	39	1977
Ronald Reagan	40	1981
George H W Bush	41	1989
Bill Clinton	42	1993
George W Bush	43	2001
Barack Obama	44	2009
Donald Trump	45	2017
Joe Biden	46	2021

SHORTEST PRESIDENCY
Harrison became ill and died after just 31 days in office

MOST TYPICAL
Hayes matches six out of eight of the top categories

LEAST TYPICAL
In his first presidency Cleveland matched only one of the top categories

LONGEST PRESIDENCY
Franklin D Roosevelt was elected four times and served 4,422 days. In 1951 the 22nd amendment was ratified restricting presidents to two terms – a maximum of eight years

How it works: Presidents are listed chronologically on the left. On the right is a list of some of their characteristics at the time of their first inaugurations, bracketed into proportional segments. In the case of Grover Cleveland, who served as both the 22nd and 24th president, the entries are correct as of his two inauguration dates

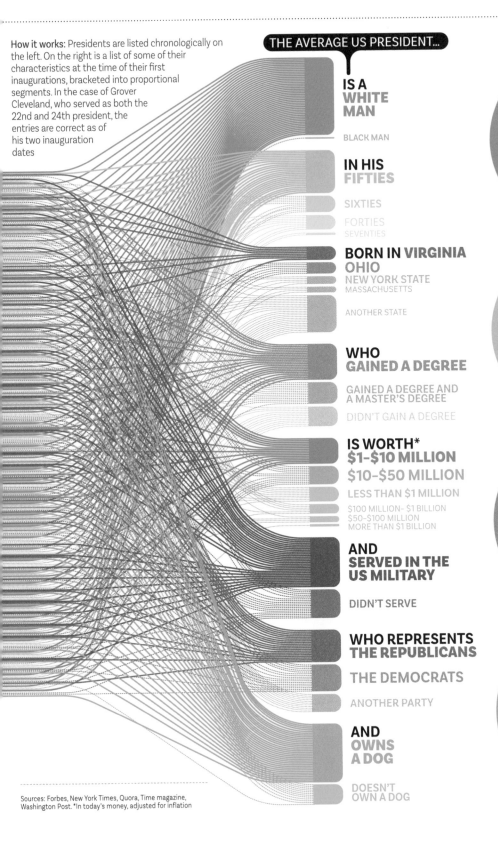

THE AVERAGE US PRESIDENT...

IS A WHITE MAN

BLACK MAN

IN HIS FIFTIES

SIXTIES

FORTIES

SEVENTIES

BORN IN VIRGINIA
OHIO
NEW YORK STATE
MASSACHUSETTS

ANOTHER STATE

WHO GAINED A DEGREE

GAINED A DEGREE AND A MASTER'S DEGREE

DIDN'T GAIN A DEGREE

IS WORTH*
$1–$10 MILLION

$10–$50 MILLION

LESS THAN $1 MILLION

$100 MILLION– $1 BILLION
$50–$100 MILLION
MORE THAN $1 BILLION

AND SERVED IN THE US MILITARY

DIDN'T SERVE

WHO REPRESENTS THE REPUBLICANS

THE DEMOCRATS

ANOTHER PARTY

AND OWNS A DOG

DOESN'T OWN A DOG

Certain names have proved propitious for presidents: almost a third have been called James, John, George or William

JAMES 𝕚𝕚𝕚𝕚𝕚
JOHN 𝕚𝕚𝕚𝕚
GEORGE 𝕚𝕚𝕚
WILLIAM 𝕚𝕚𝕚

27 percent of presidents had facial hair during their time in office, with five – **Abraham Lincoln, Ulysses S Grant**, **Rutherford B Hayes, James Garfield** and **Benjamin Harrison** – sporting full beards

33 percent of presidents graduated from an **Ivy League** university, compared with an estimated 0.2 percent of the general population

Pet-loving president **Calvin Coolidge** owned 12 dogs, three canaries, a thrush, a goose, a mockingbird, two cats, two racoons, a donkey, a bobcat, two lion cubs, a wallaby, a pygmy hippo and a black bear

Sources: Forbes, New York Times, Quora, Time magazine, Washington Post. *In today's money, adjusted for inflation

Who gets to be British prime minister?

Former British PM Benjamin Disraeli described the position as the 'top of the greasy pole': we've identified the common attributes of those who have climbed it

PRIME MINISTERS	First year in power
○ **Robert Walpole**	1721
Earl of Wilmington, **Spencer Compton**	1742
Henry Pelham	1743
Duke of Newcastle, **Thomas Pelham-Holles**	1754
Duke of Devonshire, **William Cavendish**	1756
Earl of Bute, **John Stuart**	1762
George Grenville	1763
Marquess of Rockingham, **Charles Watson-Wentworth**	1765
Earl of Chatham, **William Pitt the Elder**	1766
Duke of Grafton, **Augustus FitzRoy**	1768
Lord North, **Frederick North**	1770
Earl of Shelburne, **William Petty**	1782
Duke of Portland, **William Cavendish-Bentinck**	1783
William Pitt the Younger	1783
Henry Addington	1801
Baron Grenville, **William Grenville**	1806
Spencer Perceval	1809
Earl of Liverpool, **Robert Jenkinson**	1812
○ **George Canning**	1827
Viscount Goderich, **Frederick John Robinson**	1827
Duke of Wellington, **Arthur Wellesley**	1828
Earl Grey, **Charles Grey**	1830
Viscount Melbourne, **William Lamb**	1834
Robert Peel	1834
Lord Russell, **John Russell**	1846
Earl of Derby, **Edward Smith-Stanley**	1852
Earl of Aberdeen, **George Hamilton-Gordon**	1852
Viscount Palmerston, **Henry John Temple**	1855
Benjamin Disraeli	1868
William Ewart Gladstone	1868
Marquess of Salisbury, **Robert Gascoyne-Cecil**	1885
Earl of Rosebery, **Archibald Primrose**	1894
Arthur Balfour	1902
Henry Campbell-Bannerman	1905
Herbert Asquith	1908
David Lloyd George	1916
Andrew Bonar Law	1922
Stanley Baldwin	1923
Ramsay MacDonald	1924
Neville Chamberlain	1937
Winston Churchill	1940
Clement Attlee	1945
Anthony Eden	1955
Maurice Harold Macmillan	1957
Alec Douglas-Home	1963
Harold Wilson	1964
Edward Heath	1970
James Callaghan	1976
Margaret Thatcher	1979
John Major	1990
Tony Blair	1997
Gordon Brown	2007
David Cameron	2010
Theresa May	2016
○ **Boris Johnson**	2019

MOST TYPICAL

Four prime ministers match all of the top categories: Robert Peel, Edward Smith-Stanley, Robert Gascoyne-Cecil and Anthony Eden

LEAST TYPICAL

William Pitt the Younger, Henry Campbell-Bannerman, James Callaghan and Gordon Brown all match only three top categories

THE AVERAGE BRITISH PRIME MINISTER...

IS A WHITE MAN

WHITE WOMAN

IN THEIR FORTIES OR FIFTIES

SIXTIES OR SEVENTIES
TWENTIES OR THIRTIES

BORN IN ENGLAND

SCOTLAND
IRELAND
NORTH AMERICA

INTO AN ARISTOCRATIC FAMILY

A NON-ARISTOCRATIC FAMILY

WHO WAS EDUCATED AT PRIVATE SCHOOL

GRAMMAR SCHOOL
CHURCH SCHOOL/COMPREHENSIVE
HOME

AND ATTENDED* OXFORD UNIVERSITY

CAMBRIDGE UNIVERSITY

ANOTHER UNIVERSITY
NO UNIVERSITY
SANDHURST

WHO REPRESENTS THE CONSERVATIVES

THE WHIGS

THE TORIES
LABOUR
THE LIBERALS

AND FIRST BECAME PM WITHOUT WINNING A GENERAL ELECTION OUTRIGHT

BY WINNING A GENERAL ELECTION OUTRIGHT

How it works:
Prime ministers are listed chronologically on the left by the date they first took office. On the right we show key characteristics at the time they came to power, bracketed into proportional segments

Sources: BBC, Britannica. Gov.uk.
*First university attended only

There have been eight British prime ministers named William – four times the number of women that have held the post
WILLIAM
HENRY
ROBERT
GEORGE
JOHN

33% of prime ministers sported facial hair during their time in office, but only one, **Robert Gascoyne-Cecil**, had a full beard

While there has been one Welsh prime minister, **David Lloyd George**, Britain has never had a prime minister born in Wales – Lloyd George was born in Manchester

Over a third of British prime ministers went to Eton – 20 in total – with Harrow and Westminster schools educating seven each

Who gets to be supreme leader?

A brief profile of the three men who have led the secretive and repressive country of North Korea since it was established in 1948

How it works: Leaders of the Democratic People's Republic of Korea are listed chronologically on the left. On the right we show their characteristics, with the most common listed first

THE AVERAGE SUPREME LEADER...

KIM IL-SUNG
Time in power:
1948-1994

Current status:
Eternal president

KIM JONG-IL
Time in power:
1994-2011

Current status:
Eternal general secretary of the Workers' Party of Korea (WPK)

KIM JONG-UN
Time in power:
2011-

Current status:
Supreme leader, first secretary of the WPK, chairman of the central military commission

IS A
NORTH KOREAN MAN
KOREAN MAN

FROM
THE KIM FAMILY

EDUCATED TO
UNIVERSITY LEVEL
SCHOOL LEVEL

WHO DOES NOT
FIGHT IN THE MILITARY
FIGHTS IN THE MILITARY

AND COMES TO POWER
AFTER THE DEATH OF HIS FATHER
BY BEING INSTALLED BY THE SOVIET UNION

WHO TAKES UP OFFICE
BEFORE THE AGE OF FORTY
IN HIS FIFTIES

AND REMAINS IN POWER
UNTIL HIS DEATH
UNTIL TODAY

WHO CONDUCTS
NUCLEAR TESTS
NO NUCLEAR TESTS

AND WHOSE PEOPLE LIVE TEN YEARS
LESS THAN SOUTH KOREANS*
FIVE YEARS LESS THAN SOUTH KOREANS*

*Average life expectancies at birth at the time of Kim Il-sung and Kim Jong-il's death and as of 2020 in the case of Kim Jong-un

Who died and made you King?

(And, on six occasions, Queen)

Some are born great, some have greatness thrust upon them, others amass an army and take greatness for themselves. Here's how the great monarchs of English history came to the throne

How it works: Kings and queens are listed chronologically according to the first time they took the throne and colour coded by who died so that they could come to power. The central pie chart shows each category proportionally.

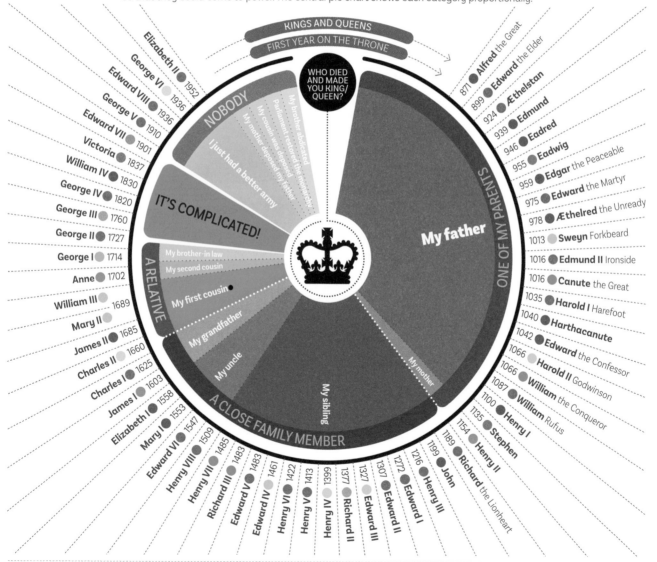

KINGS AND QUEENS
FIRST YEAR ON THE THRONE

WHO DIED AND MADE YOU KING/ QUEEN?

NOBODY
My brother abdicated
Parliament restored the monarchy
My cousin was deposed
My mother deposed my father
I just had a better army

IT'S COMPLICATED!

A RELATIVE
My brother-in-law
My second cousin
My first cousin
My grandfather
My uncle

A CLOSE FAMILY MEMBER
My sibling

ONE OF MY PARENTS
My father
My mother

Elizabeth II ● 1952
George VI ● 1936
Edward VIII ● 1936
George V ● 1910
Edward VII ● 1901
Victoria ● 1837
William IV ● 1830
George IV ● 1820
George III ● 1760
George II ● 1727
George I ● 1714
Anne ● 1702
William III ● 1689
Mary II ● 1685
James II ● 1685
Charles II ● 1660
Charles I ● 1625
James I ● 1603
Elizabeth I ● 1558
Mary I ● 1553
Edward VI ● 1547
Henry VIII ● 1509
Henry VII ● 1485
Richard III ● 1483
Edward V ● 1483
Edward IV ● 1461
Henry VI ● 1422
Henry V ● 1413
Henry IV ● 1399
Richard II ● 1377
Edward III ● 1327
Edward II ● 1307
Edward I ● 1272
Henry III ● 1216
John ● 1199
Richard the Lionheart ● 1189
Henry II ● 1154
Stephen ● 1135
Henry I ● 1100
William Rufus ● 1087
William the Conqueror ● 1066
Harold II Godwinson ● 1066
Edward the Confessor ● 1042
Harthacanute ● 1040
Harold I Harefoot ● 1035
Canute the Great ● 1016
Edmund II Ironside ● 1016
Sweyn Forkbeard ● 1013
Æthelred the Unready ● 978
Edward the Martyr ● 975
Edgar the Peaceable ● 959
Eadwig ● 955
Eadred ● 946
Eadred ● 939
Edmund ● 924
Æthelstan ● 899
Edward the Elder ● 871
Alfred the Great

Sources: Britannica, royal.uk. 'It's complicated' includes: 'My future wife's uncle' and 'My brother died and I probably killed my nephew'. Disputed rulers Lady Jane Grey and Empress Matilda are discounted. While not all of England was ruled by Alfred the Great and Edward the Elder, they are included as the House of Wessex was the dominant power and became the ruling dynasty ● Includes first cousins once and twice removed

What makes a memorable speech?

An oration evaluation:
how sophistication, self-abnegation
and abbreviation can create
sensation in communication

Greta Thunberg
'Our house is
on fire'
To the Davos
World Economic
Forum,
25th Jan 2019

Charlie Chaplin
'You are not machines!
You are not cattle!
You are men!'
As Adenoid Hynkel in
The Great Dictator,
7th Mar 1941

Malcolm X
'The ballot or
the bullet'
Civil rights speech,
3rd Apr 1964

Robin Williams
'Carpe diem, boys'
As John Keating in *Dead Poets Society*,
2nd Jun 1989

SIMPLE LANGUAGE ◄ ···················· 10 ········· 11 ········· 12 ········· 13 ········· 14 ········· 15

Mel Gibson
'They will never take
our freedom'
As William Wallace in
Braveheart, 8th Sep 1995

Malala Yousafzai
'They thought that the
bullets would silence us.
But they failed'
United Nations address,
12th Jul 2013

How it works: We put each speech through the
Gunning fog index, which determines the reading
age needed to comprehend a text. These scores are
charted on the x axis. We then determined the ratio
between mentions of the words 'me', 'myself' and 'I' and
'you', 'we' and 'us' in each speech. These results
are plotted on the y axis

Muhammad Ali
'I am the greatest'
Before his world title fight
against Sonny Liston,
25th Feb 1964

Speeches by:
● Politicians ● Campaigners and activists
● Characters in fiction ● Monarchs ● Sportspeople
● Philosophers ● Entrepreneurs

Speech length in number of words:

Steve Jobs
'Death is very likely
the single best invention of life'
Stanford commencement address,
12th Jun 2005

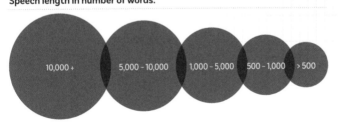

10,000 +   5,000 – 10,000   1,000 – 5,000   500 – 1,000   > 500

Donald Trump
'From this day forward, it's going to be only America first'
Inaugural speech, 20th Jan 2017

Abraham Lincoln
'This nation, under God, shall have a new birth of freedom'
The Gettysburg Address, 19th Nov 1863

John F Kennedy
'Ask not what your country can do for you...'
Inaugural speech, 20th Jan 1961

Amanda Gorman
'We ask ourselves where can we find light in this never-ending shade?'
Reading her poem *The Hill We Climb* at the presidential inauguration of Joe Biden, 20th Jan 2021

Emmeline Pankhurst
'They will have to choose between giving us freedom or giving us death'
Suffragette speech to supporters, 13th Nov 1913

Martin Luther King
'I have a dream'
At the March on Washington for Jobs and Freedom, 28th Aug 1963

Henry V
'Gentlemen in England now a-bed shall think themselves accursed they were not here'
By William Shakespeare, circa 1599

Winston Churchill
'We shall fight on the beaches'
Prime ministerial speech to parliament, 4th Jun 1940

15 — 16 — 17 — 18 — 19 — 20 — 21 ▶ SOPHISTICATED LANGUAGE

Kamala Harris
'I may be the first woman in this office; I won't be the last'
Vice-presidential acceptance speech, 7th Nov 2020

Queen Elizabeth II
'We will meet again'
Coronavirus broadcast to the nation, 5th Apr 2020

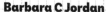

Margaret Thatcher
'The lady's not for turning'
Conservative Party conference speech, 10th Oct 1980

Barbara C Jordan
'Through the process of amendment, interpretation, and court decision, I have finally been included in 'We, the people''
The constitutional basis for impeachment, 25th Jul 1974

Queen Elizabeth I
'I have the body of a weak and feeble woman; but I have the heart and stomach of a king'
To English troops at Tilbury, 9th Aug 1588

Ronald Reagan
'Mr Gorbachev, tear down this wall'
At the Berlin Wall, 12th Jun 1987

Socrates
'The unexamined life is not worth living'
'Apology', by Plato, 4th century BCE

Nelson Mandela
'It is an ideal for which I am prepared to die'
From the dock at the Rivonia trial, 20th Apr 1964

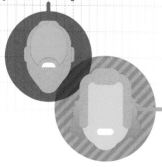

William Wilberforce
'Let us make a reparation to Africa'
On the abolition of the slave trade, 12th May 1789

How does Vladimir Putin want to be seen?

Every year a raft of calendars are released featuring Kremlin-approved photos of Putin at work, rest and play. So what sort of image of the Russian president is being projected?

How it works: The charts below show the most frequent categories of photo with a proportional breakdown of common types of shot in each

Sensitive Putin

72 Photos of Putin posing with children or animals

- 50% dogs
- 15% horses
- 10% leopards

Shootin' Putin

66 Engaging in military activity

- 27% in uniform
- 23% meeting soldiers
- 20% holding a gun

Athletic Putin

51 Photos of Putin playing sport

- 33% ice hockey
- 20% fishing
- 18% judo

Alfresco Putin

47 Enjoying the Russian landscape

- 34% in forests
- 15% by or on lakes
- 4% sitting in a tree

Movin' Putin

32 Photos of Putin in forms of transport

- 47% aircraft
- 44% boats
- 6% motorbikes

Diplomatic Putin

26 Meeting heads of state

- 38% Donald Trump
- 15% Emmanuel Macron
- 4% The Queen

Smilin' Putin

22 Photos of Putin with a smile on his face

Topless Putin

21 Photos of Putin where he is bare-chested

Source: putin-calendar.ru. Analysis based on 401 pictures published across 30 calendars. Some pictures appeared in more than one calendar. We have excluded pictures that do not belong to the listed categories

How is **Nelson Mandela** remembered?

The South African leader's name lives on in many tributes around the world, from nuclear particles to car parks and spiders. Here are some of the highlights

How it works: We've illustrated some of the most interesting monuments and tributes to Nelson Mandela as of December 2020

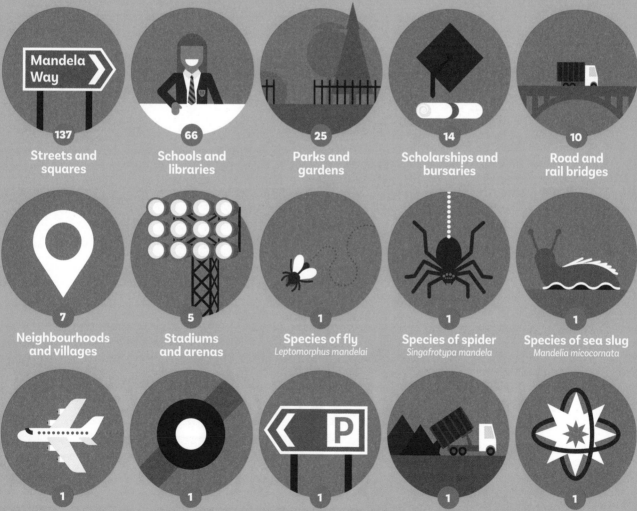

137
Streets and squares

66
Schools and libraries

25
Parks and gardens

14
Scholarships and bursaries

10
Road and rail bridges

7
Neighbourhoods and villages

5
Stadiums and arenas

1
Species of fly
Leptomorphus mandelai

1
Species of spider
Singafrotypa mandela

1
Species of sea slug
Mandelia micocornata

1
Airport
Nelson Mandela International Airport, Santiago Island, Cape Verde

1
Metro station
Nelson Mandela Station, Line 2, Tunis, Tunisia

1
Car park
Nelson-Mandela-Platz, Nuremberg, Germany

1
Landfill site
Mandela Landfill, Georgetown, Guyana

1
Nuclear particle
Mandela particle

Source: The Nelson Mandela Foundation Archive

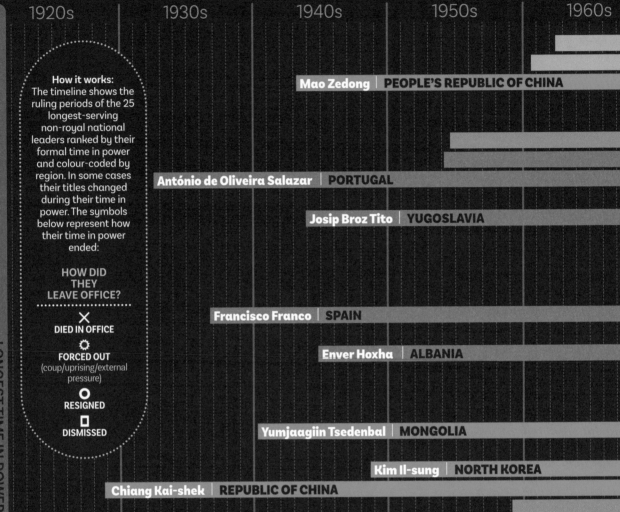

1920s   1930s   1940s   1950s   1960s

LONGEST TIME IN POWER ▼

How it works:
The timeline shows the ruling periods of the 25 longest-serving non-royal national leaders ranked by their formal time in power and colour-coded by region. In some cases their titles changed during their time in power. The symbols below represent how their time in power ended:

HOW DID THEY LEAVE OFFICE?

✕ **DIED IN OFFICE**

✿ **FORCED OUT**
(coup/uprising/external pressure)

◉ **RESIGNED**

◻ **DISMISSED**

Mao Zedong | PEOPLE'S REPUBLIC OF CHINA

António de Oliveira Salazar | PORTUGAL

Josip Broz Tito | YUGOSLAVIA

Francisco Franco | SPAIN

Enver Hoxha | ALBANIA

Yumjaagiin Tsedenbal | MONGOLIA

Kim Il-sung | NORTH KOREA

Chiang Kai-shek | REPUBLIC OF CHINA

Which leader lasted the longest?

A line-up of the 25 non-royal rulers who have shown the most staying power since 1900 – all of them men, most of them dictators, many of them brutal

Sources: Axios, BBC, Encyclopedia Britannica, Freedom House. *Ratings started in 1973 so exclude Salazar's Portugal

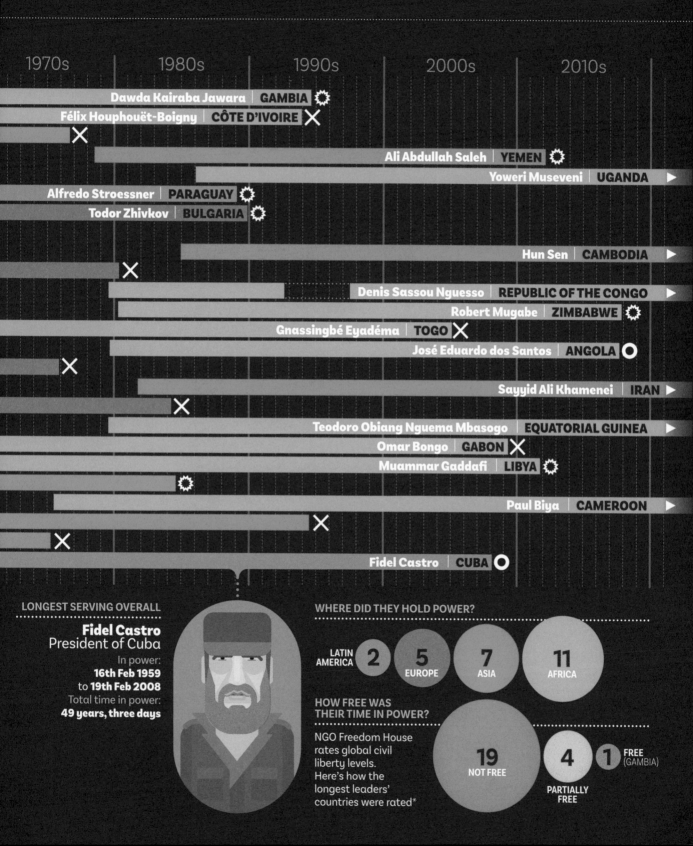

1970s | 1980s | 1990s | 2000s | 2010s

Dawda Kairaba Jawara | GAMBIA
Félix Houphouët-Boigny | CÔTE D'IVOIRE
Ali Abdullah Saleh | YEMEN
Yoweri Museveni | UGANDA
Alfredo Stroessner | PARAGUAY
Todor Zhivkov | BULGARIA
Hun Sen | CAMBODIA
Denis Sassou Nguesso | REPUBLIC OF THE CONGO
Robert Mugabe | ZIMBABWE
Gnassingbé Eyadéma | TOGO
José Eduardo dos Santos | ANGOLA
Sayyid Ali Khamenei | IRAN
Teodoro Obiang Nguema Mbasogo | EQUATORIAL GUINEA
Omar Bongo | GABON
Muammar Gaddafi | LIBYA
Paul Biya | CAMEROON
Fidel Castro | CUBA

LONGEST SERVING OVERALL

Fidel Castro
President of Cuba
In power:
16th Feb 1959
to **19th Feb 2008**
Total time in power:
49 years, three days

WHERE DID THEY HOLD POWER?

2 LATIN AMERICA
5 EUROPE
7 ASIA
11 AFRICA

HOW FREE WAS THEIR TIME IN POWER?

NGO Freedom House rates global civil liberty levels. Here's how the longest leaders' countries were rated*

19 NOT FREE
4 PARTIALLY FREE
1 FREE (GAMBIA)

Who's had a female leader?

NORTH
AMERICA

SOUTH
AMERICA

Out of 195 countries and territories featured in the Women's Power Index, only 36 percent have had a female leader since World War II and only 13 percent have had more than one

How it works: The map highlights countries and territories that have had an elected or appointed female head of state or government between January 1946 and April 2021*. ■ Grey areas = no data from source

Source: Council on Foreign Relations Women's Power Index

**Have had
a female
leader**

**Have not
had a female
leader**

*Defined by source as excluding monarchs or governors appointed by monarchs, acting or interim heads of state or government who were not subsequently elected or confirmed, honorary heads of state or government, co-presidents, joint heads of state, heads of government of a constituent country, and women who were or are not constitutionally the head of government but rather serve or served in a position akin to a deputy to the president. In countries with collective heads of state, the list includes only presiding members (often called the chairperson)

Who was the longest serving female leader?

Vigdís Finnbogadóttir is the longest continuously serving elected female leader in history, serving 16 years and 1 day as president of Iceland from 1980 to 1996

EUROPE

ASIA

AFRICA

OCEANIA

COUNTRIES
THAT HAVEN'T
HAD A
FEMALE LEADER

125

ONE FEMALE
LEADER

45

19

TWO FEMALE
LEADERS

COUNTRIES THAT HAVE HAD MORE
THAN TWO FEMALE LEADERS

6
Ⓐ **Switzerland**
Ⓑ **Finland**
Ⓒ **Iceland**
Ⓓ **Lithuania**
Ⓔ **New Zealand**
Ⓕ **Poland**

Which is better, Oxford or Cambridge?

England's ancient, elite academic institutions go head-to-head to see which has turned out the greatest number of high-flyers

Oxford University Ⓥ **Cambridge University**

SPORT

	Oxford		Cambridge	
✕	80	Winning men's boat race teams	85	★
✕	30	Winning women's boat race teams	45	★
★	70	Olympic gold medallists	66	✕

ARTS & SCIENCES

	Oxford		Cambridge	
✕	3	Oscar-winning actors and directors	4	★
✕	56	Nobel laureates*	110	★

RECOGNITION

	Oxford		Cambridge	
★	13	Canonised saints of the Roman Catholic church	10	✕
=	12	People on BBC's 100 Greatest Britons list	12	=

POWER

	Oxford		Cambridge	
★	20	Archbishops of Canterbury	18	✕
★	28	British prime ministers	14	✕

MONEY

	Oxford		Cambridge	
✕	218	Multimillionaires (Known to have a net worth above $30 million)	259	★

4 Ⓥ **5**

How it works: We've compared the latest available figures across ten categories, awarding a point to the winner of each. The difference between the two is shown proportionally, with the larger number occupying the full bar

Sources: 100 Greatest Britons (2002), Blavatnik School of Government, University of Cambridge, University of Oxford, WealthX estimate.
*Includes alumni, academics carrying out research at the university in postdoctoral or faculty positions, and official appointments

Is the honours system even?

In its twice-yearly honours lists the UK salutes some of its most outstanding citizens.
The top tier of gongs, however, has not been equally shared between the sexes

The Most Excellent Order of the British Empire is a series of honours awarded by the monarch

The order has five levels with the highest being Knight Grand Cross or Dame Grand Cross of the British Empire

MBE
Member of the British Empire

OBE
Officer of the British Empire

CBE
Commander of the British Empire

KBE/DBE
Knight or Dame Commander of the British Empire

GBE
Knight or Dame Grand Cross of the British Empire

766 recipients of the highest honour in the reign of Queen Elizabeth II ◄

Recipients called John: 70

Recipients who are women: 53

How it works: We've illustrated all recipients of the GBE during the reign of Queen Elizabeth II and added subdivisions into female recipients and men called John

Source: The Gazette, Official Public Record, thegazette.co.uk

Who's got all the money?

The 20 richest people on the planet have a combined total of almost $2 trillion in assets. Here's a breakdown of who gets their hands on such extraordinarily large amounts of wealth

How it works: The illustration shows the combined wealth of the 20 richest Forbes Real Time Billionaires as of 6th January 2021. The billionaires are further subdivided according to categories of sex, age, race, nationality and whether or not they are Warren Buffett

Wealth owned by the world's top 20 billionaires

$**1,821** billion

Who are **men** – 18 out of 20

$**1,679** billion

Who are **white** – 16 out of 20

$**1,587** billion

Who are **American** (US citizens) – 12 out of 20

$**1,169** billion

Who are **old** (over 70) – 8 out of 20

$**661** billion

Who are **old, white, American men** – 4 out of 20

$**308** billion

Who is an old, white, American man named **Warren Buffett** – 1 out of 20

$**86** billion

Source: Forbes Real Time Billionaires

Who's got all the gold?

An estimated 197,576 tonnes of gold has been mined since it first became a valued resource. But who has it all? And what's left to extract?

How it works: The illustrations are proportional. Estimates of the amount of gold in the ocean vary wildly, with some as high as 20 million tonnes

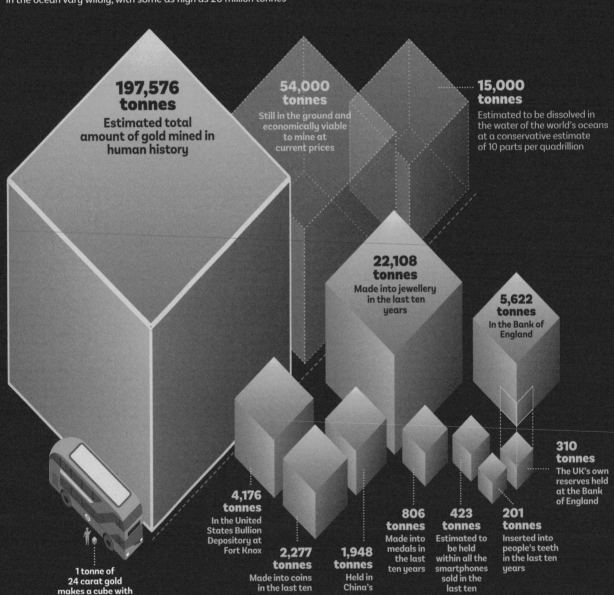

197,576 tonnes
Estimated total amount of gold mined in human history

54,000 tonnes
Still in the ground and economically viable to mine at current prices

15,000 tonnes
Estimated to be dissolved in the water of the world's oceans at a conservative estimate of 10 parts per quadrillion

22,108 tonnes
Made into jewellery in the last ten years

5,622 tonnes
In the Bank of England

310 tonnes
The UK's own reserves held at the Bank of England

4,176 tonnes
In the United States Bullion Depository at Fort Knox

2,277 tonnes
Made into coins in the last ten years

1,948 tonnes
Held in China's reserves

806 tonnes
Made into medals in the last ten years

423 tonnes
Estimated to be held within all the smartphones sold in the last ten years

201 tonnes
Inserted into people's teeth in the last ten years

1 tonne of 24 carat gold makes a cube with 37 cm-long sides

Sources: Bank of England, BBC, US Money Reserve, World Gold Council

How rich is China?

Charting the country's breakneck economic growth since 2000

How it works: We've illustrated the annual GDP of the largest economies in the world since 2000 and marked key moments in China's development

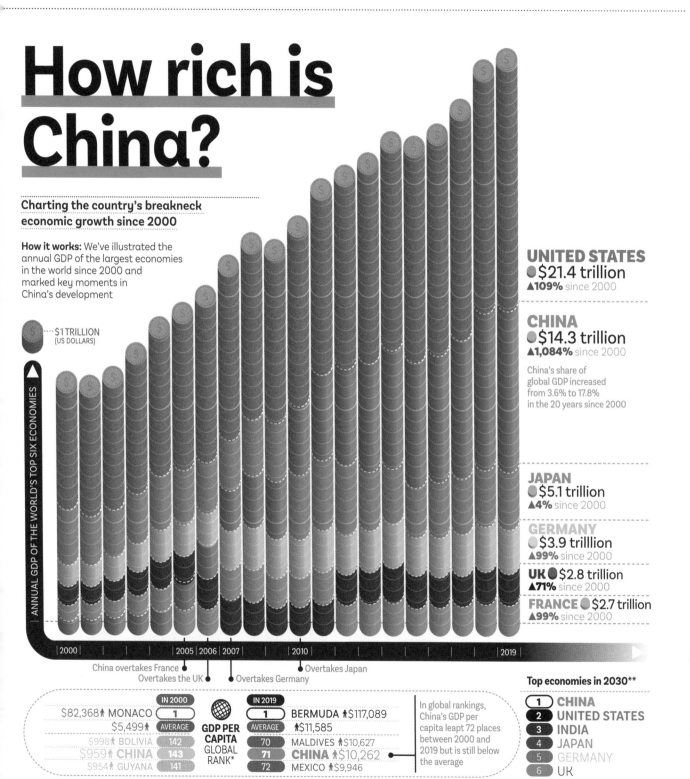

···· $1 TRILLION (US DOLLARS)

ANNUAL GDP OF THE WORLD'S TOP SIX ECONOMIES

UNITED STATES
● $21.4 trillion
▲**109%** since 2000

CHINA
● $14.3 trillion
▲**1,084%** since 2000

China's share of global GDP increased from 3.6% to 17.8% in the 20 years since 2000

JAPAN
● $5.1 trillion
▲**4%** since 2000

GERMANY
● $3.9 trilllion
▲**99%** since 2000

UK ● $2.8 trillion
▲**71%** since 2000

FRANCE ● $2.7 trillion
▲**99%** since 2000

2000 | 2005 | 2006 | 2007 | 2010 | 2019

China overtakes France
Overtakes the UK
Overtakes Germany
Overtakes Japan

	IN 2000		GDP PER CAPITA GLOBAL RANK*	IN 2019	
$82,368↑ MONACO	1			1	BERMUDA ↑$117,089
$5,499↑ AVERAGE	AVERAGE			AVERAGE	↑$11,585
$998↑ BOLIVIA	142			70	MALDIVES ↑$10,627
$959↑ CHINA	143			71	CHINA ↑$10,262
$954↑ GUYANA	141			72	MEXICO ↑$9,946

In global rankings, China's GDP per capita leapt 72 places between 2000 and 2019 but is still below the average

Top economies in 2030**

1 CHINA
2 UNITED STATES
3 INDIA
4 JAPAN
5 GERMANY
6 UK

Source: World Bank. *In current US dollars. **Estimated by Centre for Economics and Business Research

How is China changing?

The people of China have grown healthier and more prosperous in recent years, but this has not been accompanied by a move to a freer society

PEOPLE IN CHINA TODAY: (according to the most recent data available)

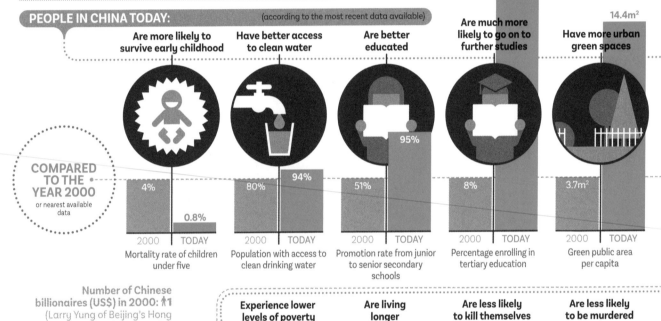

Are more likely to survive early childhood

Have better access to clean water

Are better educated

Are much more likely to go on to further studies

54%

Have more urban green spaces

14.4m²

COMPARED TO THE YEAR 2000
or nearest available data

	2000	TODAY
	4%	0.8%

Mortality rate of children under five

	2000	TODAY
	80%	94%

Population with access to clean drinking water

	2000	TODAY
	51%	95%

Promotion rate from junior to senior secondary schools

	2000	TODAY
	8%	

Percentage enrolling in tertiary education

	2000	TODAY
	3.7m²	

Green public area per capita

Number of Chinese billionaires (US$) in 2000: ↑1
(Larry Yung of Beijing's Hong Kong-listed Citic Pacific)

In 2020:

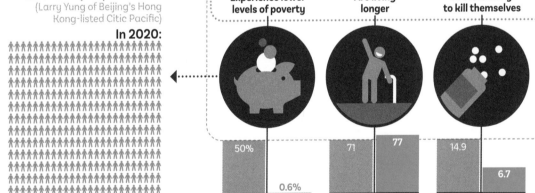

Experience lower levels of poverty

Are living longer

Are less likely to kill themselves

Are less likely to be murdered

↟↟↟↟↟↟↟↟↟↟↟↟↟↟↟↟↟↟↟↟
↟↟↟↟↟↟↟↟↟↟↟↟↟↟↟↟↟↟↟↟
↟↟↟↟↟↟↟↟↟↟↟↟↟↟↟↟↟↟↟↟
↟↟↟↟↟↟↟↟↟↟↟↟↟↟↟↟↟↟↟↟
↟↟↟↟↟↟↟↟↟↟↟↟↟↟↟↟↟↟↟↟
↟↟↟↟↟↟↟↟↟↟↟↟↟↟↟↟↟↟↟↟
↟↟↟↟↟↟↟↟↟↟↟↟↟↟↟↟↟↟↟↟
↟↟↟↟↟↟↟↟↟↟↟↟↟↟↟↟↟↟↟↟
↟↟↟↟↟↟↟↟↟↟↟↟↟↟↟↟↟↟↟↟
↟↟↟↟↟↟↟↟↟↟↟↟↟↟↟↟↟↟↟↟
↟↟↟↟↟↟↟↟↟↟↟↟↟↟↟↟↟↟↟↟
↟↟↟↟↟↟↟↟↟↟↟↟↟↟↟↟↟↟↟↟
↟↟↟↟↟↟↟↟↟↟↟↟↟**388**

	2000	TODAY
	50%	0.6%

Percentage of rural population classed as living in poverty

	2000	TODAY
	71	77

Average life expectancy

	2000	TODAY
	14.9	6.7

Suicide rate (per 100,000 people)

	2005	TODAY
	1.6	0.5

Murder rate (per 100,000 people)

Sources: National Bureau of Statistics of China, New York Times, NPR, Pew Research Center, Transparency International, WENR, WHO

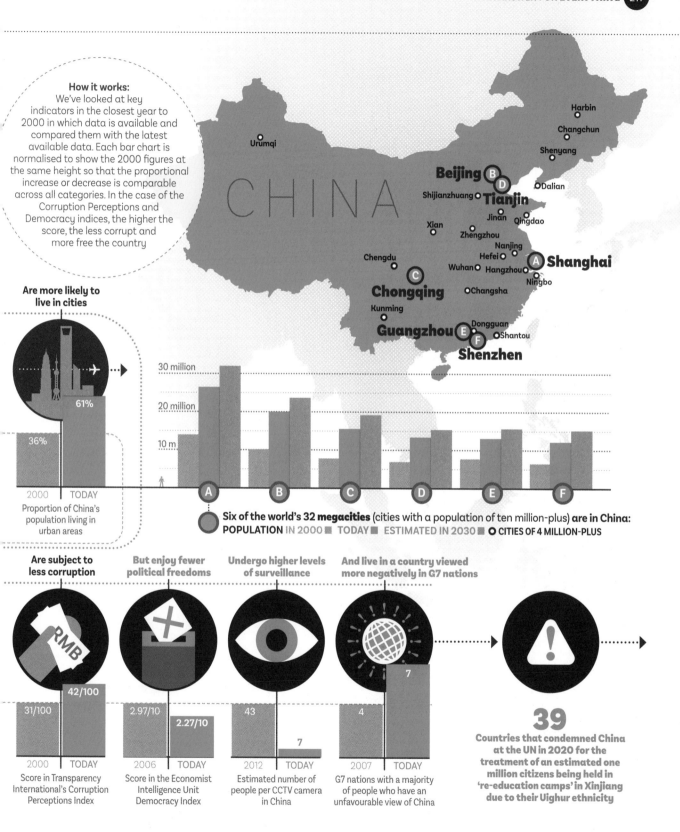

How it works:
We've looked at key indicators in the closest year to 2000 in which data is available and compared them with the latest available data. Each bar chart is normalised to show the 2000 figures at the same height so that the proportional increase or decrease is comparable across all categories. In the case of the Corruption Perceptions and Democracy indices, the higher the score, the less corrupt and more free the country

CHINA

Harbin
Changchun
Shenyang
Urumqi
Beijing **B** **D**
Shijianzhuang Dalian
Tianjin
Jinan Qingdao
Xian
Zhengzhou
Nanjing
Chengdu Hefei
Wuhan Hangzhou **A** Shanghai
Chongqing **C** Changsha Ningbo
Kunming
Dongguan
Guangzhou **E** **F** Shantou
Shenzhen

Are more likely to live in cities

61%

36%

2000 | TODAY

Proportion of China's population living in urban areas

30 million
20 million
10 m

A B C D E F

Six of the world's 32 megacities (cities with a population of ten million-plus) **are in China:**
POPULATION IN 2000 ■ TODAY ■ ESTIMATED IN 2030 ■ ○ CITIES OF 4 MILLION-PLUS

Are subject to less corruption

42/100

31/100

2000 | TODAY

Score in Transparency International's Corruption Perceptions Index

But enjoy fewer political freedoms

2.97/10

2.27/10

2006 | TODAY

Score in the Economist Intelligence Unit Democracy Index

Undergo higher levels of surveillance

43

7

2012 | TODAY

Estimated number of people per CCTV camera in China

And live in a country viewed more negatively in G7 nations

7

4

2007 | TODAY

G7 nations with a majority of people who have an unfavourable view of China

39
Countries that condemned China at the UN in 2020 for the treatment of an estimated one million citizens being held in 're-education camps' in Xinjiang due to their Uighur ethnicity

How is China changing the world?

China's commercial, military, diplomatic and soft power reach is immense. The country's influence has spread across the world – and is soon to spread outside it

How it works: We've illustrated some of the key numbers that represent the extent of China's global influence

Number of foreign airlines that agreed to list Taiwan as part of China in 20

72 Countries involved in China's Belt and Road initiative, creating trade routes and infrastructure covering 60 percent of the world's population

276 Chinese diplomatic missions around the world, making China the world's largest diplomatic power

59 Countries where China has dona*

$153 billion
Total loans made by China to 51 out of 54 African countries between 2000 and 2019

155 million Trips abroad made by Chinese tourists each year

662,100 Chinese people studying abroad each year

13km

Sources: Asia Maritime Transparency Initiative, Bain, BBC, China Africa Research Initiative, CNBC, Economist Intelligence Unit, The Guardian, Institute for Energy Research, Lowy Institute Global Diplomacy Index, OECD, Space News, Variety, World Bank

er pressure from Beijing **44** ✈

't or helped fund a football stadium

Up to $190bn

Predicted annual amount the Chinese people will spend on luxury fashion, jewellery and beauty by 2025 – half the global total

China is planning a moon base to be ready by 2036

China has launched the first module of a 66 tonne orbital space station that will be operational in 2022

China plans to send humans to the surface of Mars in 2033

74%
Of the world's new lithium-ion battery plants planned to open by 2029 will be in China – 101 out of 136

$9.2 billion
China's cinema box office sales in 2019, second only to the US with $11.4 billion

Nations that have changed their diplomatic recognition from Taipei to Beijing since 1970 – Taiwan is currently recognised by only 15 countries

w land created by China in the Spratly Islands
ce 2013 in a programme of artificial island-building

66
Articles in the Hong Kong security law passed in June 2020, which give Beijing sweeping new powers in the territory

🌐 **75**

Mn
93% of the world's manganese refining is by China

Co
80% of the world's cobalt refinining is controlled by China

C
64% of the world's graphite is produced by China

AM I LIVING MY BEST LIFE

?

Questions about hopes, dreams
and filthy lucre

Are you happy?

Every year the UN's *World Happiness Report* attempts to quantify joy. We've mapped the results of the 2021 edition to find the happiest places on Earth

How it works: The United Nations Sustainable Development Solutions Network's *World Happiness Report* ranks 149 countries and territories based on residents' responses to the Gallup World Poll and assorted quality of life factors. We have banded the countries according to whether they are above or below the average score in the World Happiness Report, with those above marked on the map in green and those below in black. Scores are based on a three-year average, 2018–2020. ■ Grey areas represent countries and territories with no data available from source

Source: World Happiness Report 2021

NORTH AMERICA

SOUTH AMERICA

Happy
Countries and territories that scored above average in the *World Happiness Report 2021*

Unhappy
Countries and territories that scored below average in the *World Happiness Report 2021*

Who's up and who's down?

Biggest change in happiness levels between 2020 and 2021:

 Armenia +12.96%

 Pakistan -13.33%

ASIA

EUROPE

AFRICA

OCEANIA

Where are the happiest places on Earth? 😊

Finland Ⓐ

Denmark Ⓑ

Switzerland Ⓒ

Iceland Ⓓ

Netherlands Ⓔ

HAPPIEST ▲

Where are the unhappiest places on Earth? 😟

UNHAPPIEST ▼

Ⓕ Lesotho

Ⓖ Botswana

Ⓗ Rwanda

Ⓘ Zimbabwe

Ⓙ **Afghanistan**

WHO'S THE OLDEST PERSON TO...

Score a goal at the World Cup finals?
▶28th June 1994

Roger Milla
Cameroon
◀Born: 20th May 1952

Win a Wimbledon championship
▶6th July 2003

Martina Navratilova US
◀Born: 18th October 1956

Play for their country at cricket?
▶29th August 2019

Osman Göker
Turkey
◀Born: 1st March 1960

Be a *Playboy* model?
▶10th December 2009

Patricia Paay
Netherlands
◀Born: 7th April 1949

AGED: ▶

42

46

59

60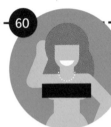

Have I left it too late?

Be elected pope?
▶29th April 1670

Pope Clement X
Papal States (now Italy)
◀Born: 13th Jul 1590

79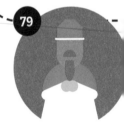

Worried you don't have time to leave a lasting legacy? Fear not – we've tracked down some late-blooming high achievers to inspire you

How it works: We've illustrated a selection of world record holders as of May 2021. They are listed in order of their age at the time of their achievement and colour-coded by its type

● Sport and physical achievements ● Entertainment and fashion ● Life events
● Professional and educational achievement ● Politics and religion ● Crime

Source: Guinness World Records

Be a flying trapeze artist?
▶1st July 2017

Betty Goedhart
US
◀Born: 25th October 1932

Be on the cover of *Vogue*?
▶7th May 2020

Dame Judi Dench
UK
◀Born: 9th December 1934

Be convicted as a bank robber?
▶23rd January 2004

JL Hunter Rountree
US
◀Born: 16th December 1911

Top the UK album charts?
▶19th September 2009

Dame Vera Lynn
UK
◀Born: 20th March 1917

Become a father?
▶1st July 1992

Les Colley
Australia
◀Born: 1st September 1899

84

85

92

92

92

Become a mother?
▶ 29th December 2006

Maria del Carmen Bousada Spain

◀ Born: 5th January 1940

66

Swim the English Channel?
▶ 21st August 2018

Linda Ashmore UK

◀ Born: 21st October 1946

71

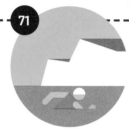

Win an Olympic medal
▶ 27th July 1920

Oscar Swahn Sweden

◀ Born: 20th October 1847

72

Row across the Atlantic solo?
▶ 29th April 2020

Graham Walters UK

◀ Born: 17th July 1947

72

Become US president?
▶ 20th January 2021

Joe Biden US

◀ Born: 20th Nov 1942

78

Climb Mount Everest?
▶ 23rd May 2013

Yuichiro Miura Japan

◀ Born: 12th Oct 1932

80

Cycle the length of the UK?
▶ 24th May 2019

Mavis Margaret Paterson UK

◀ Born: 24th May 1938

81

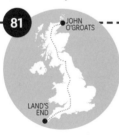

JOHN O'GROATS

LAND'S END

Be elected PM for the first time?
▶ 24th March 1977

Morarji Ranchhodji Desai India

◀ Born: 29th Feb 1896

81

Win an Oscar for acting?
▶ 26th February 2012

Christopher Plummer US

◀ Born: 13th Dec 1929

82

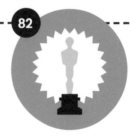

Go into space?
▶ 20th July 2021

Wally Funk US

◀ Born: 1st Feb 1939

82

Star in a film?
▶ 16th October 1987

Lillian Gish US

◀ Born: 14th October 1893

94

Get a doctorate?
▶ 29th September 2008

Heinz Wenderoth Germany

◀ Born: 11th January 1911

97

Top the UK singles chart?
▶ 24th April 2020

Captain Tom Moore UK

◀ Born: 30th April 1920

99

Become a published author?
▶ 15th February 2016

Jim Downing US

◀ Born: 22nd August 1913

102

THE OTHER SIDE OF INFAMY JIM DOWNING

Get married?
▶ 3rd December 1984

Harry Stevens US

◀ Born: 13th September 1881

103

How do you pull off a high wire act?

High wire walks capture the world's imagination and ensure the reputation of those brave enough to walk the line. Here are some of the record-breaking funambulists we've looked up to in the past

How it works: The illustration shows the height △ and length ▷ of a selection of record-breaking high-wire walks in proportion

Sources: Associated Press, Guinness World Records, Reuters, Vanguard

Nik Wallenda, USA

📍 2013, Nevada, US

First person to high wire walk across a Grand Canyon area gorge

△ 457m

▷ 427m

(A)

Philippe Petit, FRA

📍 1974, New York City, US

Only person to high wire walk between the twin towers of the World Trade Center

△ 417m

▷ 61m

(B)

Jay Cochrane, CAN

📍 1995, Three Gorges, China

First person to high wire walk across Qutang Gorge above the Yangtze River

△ 410m

▷ 640m

(C)

Karl Wallenda, GER/USA

📍 1970, Georgia, US

First person to high wire walk across Tallulah Gorge. Did a handstand while doing so

△ 213m

▷ 366m

(D)

Mustafa Danger, MAR

📍 2010, Benidorm, Spain

World record for highest tightrope crossed on a motorcycle

△ 130m

▷ 666m

(E)

Charles Blondin, FRA

📍 1859, Niagara Gorge, New York, US and Ontario, Canada

First high wire walk over Niagara Falls. Later repeated blindfolded, pushing a wheelbarrow and making an omelette halfway

△ 48m

▷ 335m

(F)

Didier Pasquette, FRA, and **Jade Kindar-Martin**, USA

📍 1997, London, UK

Longest dual high wire walk over the Thames, crossing paths en route

△ 30m

▷ 366m

(G)

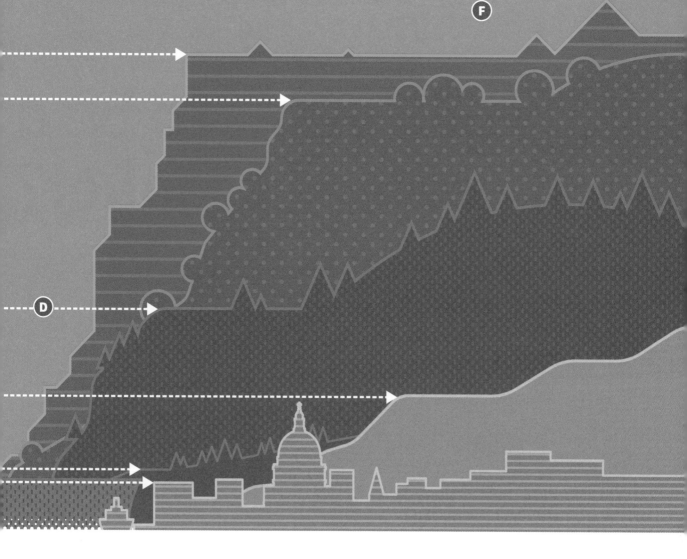

4
Most people
crammed in a
regular-sized
swimming cap

8
Most dogs in
a conga line

8
Most magic tricks
performed in a
wind tunnel in
three minutes

9
Most hotdogs
consumed in
three minutes

13
Most paper
aircraft thrown
into watermelons
in one minute

14
Most apples
crushed with
one's bicep in one
minute

36
Most traffic cones
balanced on
the chin

49
Most coconuts
smashed around a
person in a minute
while blindfolded

52
Most drinks cans
crushed by hand in
30 seconds while
holding an egg

55
Most shuttlecocks
caught with
chopsticks in one
minute

67.8
Loudest purr of
a domestic cat
(decibels)

84.6
Loudest crunch of
an apple (decibels)

Do you want to be a record breaker?

195
Most juggling catches
in one minute while
hanging by the teeth

254
Greatest variety
of cheeses on
a pizza

284
Most walnuts
crushed by hand
in one minute

435
Most eyebrow
waxes performed
in eight hours

437
Most finger snaps
in one minute

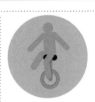

439
Most consecutive
bunny hops on a
unicycle

1,370
Most people
simultaneously
throwing napkins

1,452
Participants in the
biggest hole-digging
competition

1,624
Most people making
sand angels at the
same time

2,019
Participants in largest
game of human
mattress dominoes

2,036
Most snowmen
built in one hour

2,101
Most living figures
in a nativity scene

17
Most pairs of underpants pulled on in 30 seconds

18
Most soft toys caught blindfolded in 30 seconds

19
Most playing cards removed from between two bottles with nunchaku

20
Most drinks cans attached to a human body using only suction

21
Most swimming trunks pulled on over clothes in 30 seconds

33
People in the longest human tunnel traversed by a dog on a skateboard

100
Most lit candles in the mouth

103
Most whoopee cushions sat on in one minute

156
Most times to put on and remove a T-shirt while controlling a football with the head

163
Most cups kicked off someone's head in one minute

168
Most bridesmaids for one bride

174
Most skips of a rope in one minute while wearing clogs

Breaking a world record is a fine achievement for anyone's CV – but, regrettably, it often demands long-term dedication, athletic prowess and bottomless reserves of mental strength. Canoeing up the Amazon, parachute jumping from the edge of space and running a sub-two-hour marathon are all very well, but for those who don't have the time, energy or knee strength to take on such mainstream challenges, we've dived into the Guinness database to find some of the dafter, more attainable-sounding records waiting to be broken

How it works: Records are listed in ascending order numerically and colour-coded by participants needed and our judgement of risk involved:
● **You can break it on your own** ● **You'll need some help** ● **You'll need an animal** ○ **A bit dangerous**
Source: Guinness World Records

450
Most pencils in a beard

470
Most people hammering in a nail simultaneously

541
Largest gathering of people dressed as Albert Einstein

574
Most people eating breakfast in bed

697
Most whip cracks with two whips in one minute

710
Most dogs in the largest canine photoshoot

2,495
Largest gathering of people dressed as scarecrows

2,499
Most people wearing high-vis vests

2,505
Most people taking part in a skinny dip

2,586
Most participants in a rugby scrum

8,065
People in the largest ukulele ensemble

79,467
Most Instagram followers for a duck (Ben Afquack)

How does the other half live?

Denise Coates is the best-rewarded CEO in the UK. The founder of gambling company Bet365, she earned a reported £469 million in 2020. If you're earning the UK's average salary as your sole source of income, she'll be earning 15,820 times more than you. Here's how that translates into relative purchasing power

How it works: We've illustrated a series of purchases for someone on the average weekly salary of £567 and what Coates could buy with an equivalent proportion of her earnings. Calculations are based on earnings before tax and deductions. In 2020 Coates was the UK's biggest taxpayer

WHEN YOU BUY...

A pint of milk

For **50p**

A Filet-O-Fish sandwich at McDonald's

For **£3.19**

An advance off-peak single train ticket from London to Milton Keynes and a cup of tea

For **£11.05**

A large Ikea Björksta picture with frame and a nail to hang it on

For **£65.80**

A second-hand Vauxhall Astra

For **£1,440**

IT'S THE EQUIVALENT OF DENISE COATES BUYING...

11 magnums of 1998 vintage Moët & Chandon's Dom Pérignon Champagne and one tonne of ice

For **£7,910**

10.5 kilograms of imperial beluga caviar

For **£50,466**

A trip to space on Virgin Galactic

For **£175,000**

Banksy's 'Girl with Balloon'

For **£1,042,000**

A 1956 Ferrari 290 MM race car once owned by legendary Formula 1 driver Juan Manuel Fangio

For **£22,843,633**

Sources: AutoTrader, BBC, British Airways, Ikea, londonfinefoods.co.uk, McDonald's, National Rail Enquiries, Ocado, Office for National Statistics, the Sun, Visit London

Do you need some overtime?

In July 2020 Jeff Bezos made $13 billion in a single day thanks to Amazon's soaring share value. It's a figure the average Amazon warehouse worker can only dream of...

How it works: We've divided the $13 billion US dollars Jeff Bezos was reported to have gained on 20th July 2020 by 1,440 (the number of minutes in a day) and then divided that number by the estimated average annual salary of an Amazon warehouse worker in the US in 2021

Estimated annual salary of an Amazon warehouse worker: **$32,055**

282 YEARS

How long the average Amazon warehouse worker would have to work to earn the same as Jeff Bezos did in one minute on 20th July 2020

Sources: Bloomberg, Zip Recruiter

Can I get Ariana Grande to play at my party?

Nothing says you've made it like paying for a private concert by your favourite musician. We've dug through the numbers quoted by an American booking agency to find out how much a selection of A-listers, and Vanilla Ice, would set you back

How it works: We've compared quoted costs for a selection of musical artists to play at your event, with the circles behind each artist sized proportionally to the cost. The agency quotes a range of prices for each artist and we've used the highest price quoted for each

Source: Celebrity Talent International

For the same price as one Ariana Grande performance you could get:

Ariana Grande
$6,000,000

Billie Eilish
$1,499,000

Harry Styles
$1,499,000

Coldplay
$1,499,000

Pharrell Williams
$1,499,000

Or you could get:

Dolly Parton
$1,499,000

+

Ricky Martin
$999,998

Kiss
$749,000

+

Lenny Kravitz
$749,000

Pet Shop Boys
$499,000

+

Meatloaf
$499,000

Susan Boyle
$299,000

+

Blondie
$299,000

Snoop
$299,000

+

Chaka Khan
$149,999

Or even:

150 performances by Vanilla Ice
$39,999 each

How can I have a hit song?

Many people dream of being a pop star but have no idea where to start. To set you on the path to stardom, we've tracked every winner of the 'Record of the Year' category at the Grammy awards since 1959 to tell you what to write about, what style to choose and whether you should go solo or start a group

How it works: Winning songs are listed in chronological order on the left-hand page. On the right we show key characteristics of the singers and songs, bracketed into proportional segments

Sources: Apple Music, The Recording Academy (grammy.com), tunebat.com

★

WHO'S HAD A GRAMMY DOUBLE WHAMMY?

Artists who have won more than once

(Excluding artists who performed We Are the World as a member of USA for Africa in 1986)

Records of the year	Year awarded
Nel Blu Dipinto Di Blu (Volare) by **Domenico Modugno**	1959
Mack the Knife by **Bobby Darin**	1960
Theme from A Summer Place by **Percy Faith**	1961
Moon River by **Henry Mancini** ★	1962
I Left My Heart in San Francisco by **Tony Bennett**	1963
Days of Wine and Roses by **Henry Mancini** ★	1964
The Girl from Ipanema by **Astrud Gilberto, João Gilberto & Stan Getz**	1965
A Taste of Honey by **Herb Alpert & The Tijuana Brass**	1966
Strangers in the Night by **Frank Sinatra**	1967
Up, Up and Away by **The 5th Dimension** ★	1968
Mrs Robinson by **Simon & Garfunkel** ★	1969
Aquarius/Let the Sunshine In by **The 5th Dimension** ★	1970
Bridge over Troubled Water by **Simon & Garfunkel** ★	1971
It's Too Late by **Carole King**	1972
The First Time Ever I Saw Your Face by **Roberta Flack** ★	1973
Killing Me Softly with His Song by **Roberta Flack** ★	1974
I Honestly Love You by **Olivia Newton-John**	1975
Love Will Keep Us Together by **Captain & Tennille**	1976
This Masquerade by **George Benson**	1977
Hotel California by **The Eagles**	1978
Just the Way You Are by **Billy Joel**	1979
What a Fool Believes by **The Doobie Brothers**	1980
Sailing by **Christopher Cross**	1981
Bette Davis Eyes by **Kim Carnes**	1982
Rosanna by **Toto**	1983
Beat It by **Michael Jackson**	1984
What's Love Got to Do with It by **Tina Turner**	1985
We Are the World by **USA for Africa**	1986
Higher Love by **Steve Winwood**	1987
Graceland by **Paul Simon** ★	1988
Don't Worry, Be Happy by **Bobby McFerrin**	1989
Wind Beneath My Wings by **Bette Midler**	1990
Another Day in Paradise by **Phil Collins**	1991
Unforgettable by Natalie Cole with **Nat King Cole**	1992
Tears in Heaven by **Eric Clapton** ★	1993
I Will Always Love You by **Whitney Houston**	1994
All I Wanna Do by **Sheryl Crow**	1995
Kiss from a Rose by **Seal**	1996
Change the World by **Eric Clapton** ★	1997
Sunny Came Home by **Shawn Colvin**	1998
My Heart Will Go On by **Celine Dion**	1999
Smooth by **Santana feat Rob Thomas**	2000
Beautiful Day by **U2** ★	2001
Walk On by **U2** ★	2002
Don't Know Why by **Norah Jones** ★	2003
Clocks by **Coldplay**	2004
Here We Go Again by Ray Charles and **Norah Jones** ★	2005
Boulevard of Broken Dreams by **Green Day**	2006
Not Ready to Make Nice by **Dixie Chicks**	2007
Rehab by **Amy Winehouse**	2008
Please Read the Letter by **Robert Plant and Alison Krauss**	2009
Use Somebody by **Kings of Leon**	2010
Need You Now by **Lady Antebellum**	2011
Rolling in the Deep by **Adele** ★	2012
Somebody That I Used to Know by **Gotye feat Kimbra**	2013
Get Lucky by **Daft Punk feat Pharrell Williams & Nile Rodgers**	2014
Stay With Me by **Sam Smith**	2015
Uptown Funk by **Mark Ronson feat Bruno Mars** ★	2016
Hello by **Adele** ★	2017
24K Magic by **Bruno Mars** ★	2018
This Is America by **Childish Gambino**	2019
○ Bad Guy by **Billie Eilish** ★	2020
○ Everything I Wanted by **Billie Eilish** ★	2021

THE AVERAGE RECORD OF THE YEAR AWARD

IS WON BY
A MAN

A WOMAN

BOTH MEN AND WOMEN

FROM
THE UNITED STATES

THE UNITED KINGDOM

SOMEWHERE ELSE

PERFORMING
AS A SOLO ARTIST

IN A BAND

IN A DUO

SINGING
A POP SONG

A ROCK SONG

A JAZZ SONG
A SOUL SONG

SOMETHING ELSE

IN A
MAJOR KEY

MINOR KEY

WHICH IS ABOUT
A ROMANTIC SPLIT
LOVE
HEDONISM
LONELINESS/UNREQUITED LOVE
SOCIAL ISSUES
SOMETHING ELSE

AND IS WRITTEN BY
THEMSELVES

SOMEONE ELSE

The first female solo artist to win Record of the Year was **Carole King** in 1972, 13 years after the first ceremony

Between 1966 and 1990 only two non-American acts won Record of the Year, **Olivia Newton-John** and **Steve Winwood**

Between 1987 and 1999 no songs by groups won Record of the Year

Only two cover versions have won the Record of the Year, both of which were performed by Norah Jones

How do I write a Christmas hit?

If writing a Grammy-winner is beyond you (see previous page), a Christmas number one might have a lower barrier to entry and the promise of a bumper royalty payment every time December rolls around. We've analysed the most-streamed festive hits of all time in the UK to reveal the recipe for the perfect seasonal song. Don't forget the sleigh bells...

How it works: The Official Charts Company's most-streamed seasonal songs as of December 2020 are listed below in reverse order of popularity, followed by symbols showing which Christmassy criteria each fulfils

THE UK'S TOP 12 CHRISTMAS HITS

MUSICAL AND LYRICAL INGREDIENTS

Song	#	Bells	Choir	Cold weather	Gifts/toys	Mistletoe/kissing	Wine/drinking	Children	Santa	Tree	Jesus
Merry Xmas Everybody by Slade	12	✗	✓	✓	✓	✓	✓	✗	✓	✗	✗
Driving Home for Christmas by Chris Rea	11	✓	✗	✗	✗	✗	✗	✗	✗	✗	✗
Rockin' Around the Christmas Tree by Brenda Lee	10	✓	✓	✗	✗	✓	✗	✗	✗	✓	✗
I Wish It Could Be Christmas Everyday by Wizzard	9	✓	✓	✓	✗	✗	✗	✓	✓	✗	✗
Santa Tell Me by Ariana Grande	8	✓	✓	✓	✓	✓	✗	✗	✓	✗	✗
Step into Christmas by Elton John	7	✓	✓	✓	✗	✗	✓	✗	✗	✗	✗
It's Beginning to Look a Lot Like... by Michael Bublé	6	✓	✗	✓	✓	✗	✓	✓	✗	✓	✗
Do They Know It's Christmas? by Band Aid	5	✓	✓	✓	✓	✗	✓	✗	✗	✗	✗
Merry Christmas Everyone by Shakin' Stevens	4	✓	✓	✓	✓	✓	✗	✓	✗	✗	✗
Fairytale of New York by The Pogues featuring Kirsty MacColl	3	✗	✗	✓	✗	✓	✓	✗	✗	✗	✗
Last Christmas by Wham!	2	✓	✗	✗	✓	✗	✗	✗	✗	✗	✗
All I Want for Christmas Is You by Mariah Carey	1	✓	✓	✓	✓	✓	✗	✓	✓	✓	✗

Sources: Official Charts Company, genius.com

Should I climb Everest?

Whether you call it Chomolungma, Sagarmatha or Everest, summiting Earth's highest peak is a life goal for many an adventurer – but if you do tackle it, you might find it a bit crowded up there

How it works: The pie chart represents everyone who has reached the summit of Mount Everest, split between those who did so from 29th May 1953–31st December 2015 and those who did so from 1st January 2016–31st December 2020

Total number of people summiting Everest for the first time between 1953 and 2020

5,788

Average 1953–2020:
85 per year

29%

First-time summiters of Everest 2016–2020 **1,691** Average 2016–2020:
338 per year

Source: The Himalayan Database

876
men have
been awarded
Nobel Prizes

28
organisations
have been
awarded
Nobel Prizes

-57 women have been
awarded Nobel Prizes

Who were the first women to win the Nobel Prizes?

Initial female winners of each Nobel Prize:

 Physics
Marie Curie, 1903

The first female Nobel laureate, Marie Curie
was also the first person to be awarded
two Nobel Prize

 Peace
Bertha von Suttner, 1905

The fifth Peace Prize was awarded to von Suttner,
author of the influential 1889 anti-war novel
Lay Down Your Arms, 'for her audacity to oppose the
horrors of war'

 Literature
Selma Lagerlöf, 1909

Selma Lagerlöf's first and most successful novel,
The Saga of Gösta Berling, was the basis for the 1924 film
that launched the career of Greta Garbo

 Chemistry
Marie Curie, 1911

Curie's daughter Irène also received the Chemistry Prize in 1935

 Physiology or Medicine
Gerty Cori, 1947

Cori was recognised for her role in identifying the process by which glucose is
metabolised in the human body and broken down into lactic acid in muscle tissue

 Economics
Elinor Ostrom, 2009

A pioneer in sustainability theory, Ostrom's field studies showed how small,
local communities manage shared natural resources in economical and ecological ways

ALFR·
NOBEL

Wh
the Nob

Bagging a Nobel Prize is usually th
pinnacle of a career. To find out what so
of person is most likely to take th
prestigious Swedish gong, we hav
crunched the numbers for eve
laureate to date. It appears it
still a man's worl

Source: Nobel Foundation. Strictly speaking there is
Nobel Prize in economics, it is the Bank of Swed
Prize in Economic Sciences in Memory of Alf
Nobel, but is widely treated as a Nobel P

1900s
1910s
1920s
1930s
1940s
1950s

Men and organisations

Women

2020s

2010s

2000s

1990s

1980s

1970s

1960s

NAT•
MDCCC
XXXIII

OB•
MDCCC
XCVI

gets
el Prize?

ow it works: The chart shows, in chronological
der, the number of ● **men**, ■ **women** and
organisations which have received
Nobel Prize each year since the inaugural
wards in 1901. For shared awards each
cipient is represented. Prizes are
lour-coded by category:

Physics
Chemistry
Literature
Physiology/Medicine
Peace
Economics

The **United States** has been the
country of birth of the greatest
number of Nobel laureates,
with **282** recipients.
The UK comes
second with 105

The youngest person to be made a
Nobel laureate is **Malala Yousafzai**,
who was 17 when she was awarded
the Peace Prize in 2014. The oldest is
John Goodenough, who was 97
when he won the Chemistry
Prize in 2019

Linus Pauling is the only recipient of
two 'undivided' prizes (Chemistry in
1954, Peace in 1962). The other
double recipients – **John Bardeen**,
Marie Curie and **Frederick
Sanger** – shared at least
one of their prizes

Two Nobel laureates have declined
the Prize: **Jean-Paul Sartre**
(Literature, 1964) and **Le Duc Tho**,
who was awarded the 1973 Peace
Prize with US secretary of state
Henry Kissinger, but said he
was not in a position
to accept

What's on your bucket list?

Everyone has an idea of the things they want to do before they die. Here are the most popular pre-mortality action points on the planet – and the percentage of people who have fulfilled their ambition

How it works: Bucketlist.org is an open platform where people submit their life goals. We've taken the 15 most popular entries and illustrated them; the bar below each shows the percentage of people who have ticked them off their lists on the site

#15 12% ✔
Ride a gondola In Venice, Italy

#14 14% ✔
Do a road trip with friends

#13 0% ✔
Throw a dart at a map and travel there

#12 20% ✔
See the Grand Canyon

#11 6% ✔
Float in the Dead Sea

#10 5% ✔
Ride in a hot air balloon

#9 14% ✔
Get married

#8 23% ✔
Visit Niagara Falls

#7 18% ✔
Visit a volcano

#6 8% ✔
Do a bungee jump

#5 11% ✔
Go skydiving

#4 4% ✔
See the Northern Lights

#3 25% ✔
Go on a cruise

#2 17% ✔
Learn a new language

Jeg lærer at tale dansk

#1 15% ✔
Swim with dolphins

Source: bucketlist.org

Which films should I watch before I die?

If swimming with dolphins seems like a lot of effort, there's lower-hanging fruit on the 'things to do before you die' tree. We've created a meta-list of the most-featured films on movie bucket lists to help plan your rest-of-life viewing schedule

How it works: We've analysed five 'films to watch before you die' lists to create our meta-list. The bigger the name, the more times it featured on the lists. Directors with multiple entries get a namecheck; film genres are colour-coded by category:

● **Action/adventure** ● **Comedy** ● **Crime** ● **Horror** ● **Mystery** ● **Noir** ● **Romance** ● **Sci-fi/fantasy** ● **War**

The Wizard of Oz

Alien

Martin Scorsese

GoodFellas   Taxi Driver   Pink Flamingos   It's a Wonderful Life

Citizen Kane   The Godfather

Francis Ford Coppola

Back to the Future   Apocalypse Now

Vertigo   Psycho   North by Northwest

Billy Wilder

Alfred Hitchcock

Double Indemnity   Sunset Boulevard

Casablanca   Pulp Fiction

Modern Times

Chinatown   2001: A Space Odyssey

Scarface   Dr Strangelove   **Stanley Kubrick**

A Clockwork Orange

Sources: Channel 4, Complex, IMDB, Roger Ebert, Stylist

WHAT'S THE WORST THAT COULD HAPPEN

?

Questions about pandemics, locusts and giant asteroids

3.3%

TODAY: (Most recent data available)

We're feeling worse than we used to

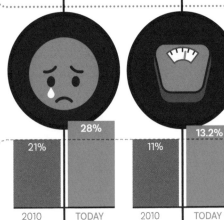

28%

21%

2010 | TODAY

Proportion of those in the Gallup World Poll who reported feelings of worry, sadness and anger

Obesity levels are rising

13.2%

11%

2010 | TODAY

Global prevalence of obesity (BMI of 30+) among adults

We're more likely to have diabetes

8.8%

6.5%

2010 | TODAY

Proportion of the population aged 20-79 diagnosed with diabetes

Jobs in the West are becoming more precarious

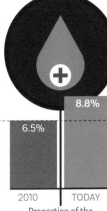

CV

3.3%

0.6%

2010 | TODAY

Proportion of people in the UK in employment on a zero-hours contract

Bosses in the West are earning ever more than their workers

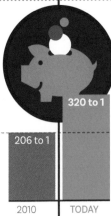

320 to 1

206 to 1

2010 | TODAY

CEO-to-worker compensation ratio in the US's top 350 companies

• COMPARED TO THE YEAR 2010

Is everything getting worse?

Yes! Things have deteriorated significantly for humanity over the past ten years (although see also overleaf)

How it works: We've looked at key indicators in 2010 and compared them with the latest available data to see how we're doing today. Each bar chart has been normalised to show the 2010 figures at the same height, which makes the proportional increase or decrease more clearly comparable across all categories

There are far more refugees and asylum-seekers

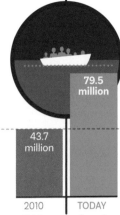

79.5 million

43.7 million

2010 | TODAY

Total number of people forcibly displaced worldwide

Sources: Amnesty, Economic Policy Institute, Emissions Database for Global Atmospheric Research (EDGAR), Freedom House, Gallup, Mongabay, National Oceanic and Atmospheric Administration, National Snow and Ice Data Center, Office for National Statistics, UNHCR, WHO, World Bank

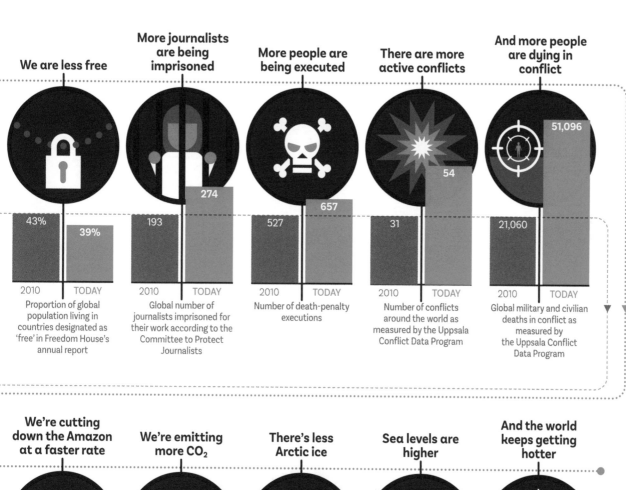

We are less free

43% (2010)
39% (TODAY)

Proportion of global population living in countries designated as 'free' in Freedom House's annual report

More journalists are being imprisoned

193 (2010)
274 (TODAY)

Global number of journalists imprisoned for their work according to the Committee to Protect Journalists

More people are being executed

527 (2010)
657 (TODAY)

Number of death-penalty executions

There are more active conflicts

31 (2010)
54 (TODAY)

Number of conflicts around the world as measured by the Uppsala Conflict Data Program

And more people are dying in conflict

21,060 (2010)
51,096 (TODAY)

Global military and civilian deaths in conflict as measured by the Uppsala Conflict Data Program

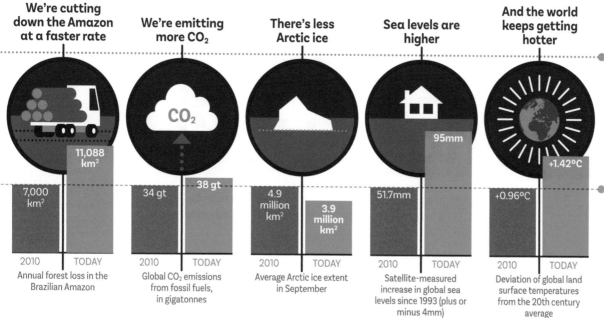

We're cutting down the Amazon at a faster rate

7,000 km² (2010)
11,088 km² (TODAY)

Annual forest loss in the Brazilian Amazon

We're emitting more CO₂

34 gt (2010)
38 gt (TODAY)

Global CO_2 emissions from fossil fuels, in gigatonnes

There's less Arctic ice

4.9 million km² (2010)
3.9 million km² (TODAY)

Average Arctic ice extent in September

Sea levels are higher

51.7mm (2010)
95mm (TODAY)

Satellite-measured increase in global sea levels since 1993 (plus or minus 4mm)

And the world keeps getting hotter

+0.96°C (2010)
+1.42°C (TODAY)

Deviation of global land surface temperatures from the 20th century average

TODAY: (Most recent data available)

Humans are having more successful births

We're less likely to catch TB

HIV infection rates are falling

We're less likely to be bankrupted by medical bills

There's less extreme poverty

37	158	2.1 million	35.2%	16%
28.2	130	1.5 million	21.3%	9.3%
2010 — TODAY	2010 — TODAY	2010 — TODAY	2010 — TODAY	2010 — TODAY

Global infant mortality rate per 1,000 births

Incidence of tuberculosis per 100,000 people

Estimated new HIV infections

Proportion of global population at risk of catastrophic expenditure for surgical care

Global population living on $1.90 or less a day as a measure of purchasing power in international dollars

● COMPARED TO THE YEAR 2010

Is anything getting better?

Yes! Things have improved significantly for humanity in the last ten years (although see also previous page)

How it works: We've looked at key indicators in 2010 and compared them with the latest available data to see how we're doing today. Each bar chart has been normalised to show the 2010 figures at the same height, which makes the proportional increase or decrease more clearly comparable across all categories

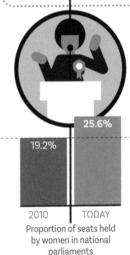

There are more women in politics

19.2% 25.6%

2010 — TODAY

Proportion of seats held by women in national parliaments

Sources: Amnesty, Bulletin of the Atomic Scientists, Cranfield School of Management Female FTSE Index, Earth Policy Institute, Federation of American Scientists, Heidrick & Struggles Board Monitor, Pew Research Center, pv magazine, UN, World Bank, WWEA

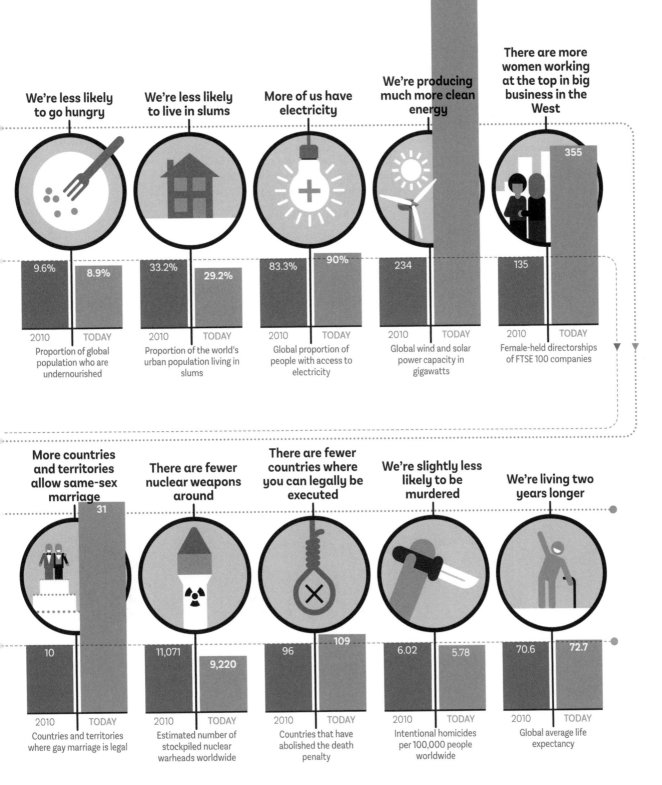

We're less likely to go hungry

9.6% — 2010
8.9% — TODAY

Proportion of global population who are undernourished

We're less likely to live in slums

33.2% — 2010
29.2% — TODAY

Proportion of the world's urban population living in slums

More of us have electricity

83.3% — 2010
90% — TODAY

Global proportion of people with access to electricity

We're producing much more clean energy

1,234

234 — 2010
TODAY

Global wind and solar power capacity in gigawatts

There are more women working at the top in big business in the West

355

135 — 2010
TODAY

Female-held directorships of FTSE 100 companies

More countries and territories allow same-sex marriage

31

10 — 2010
TODAY

Countries and territories where gay marriage is legal

There are fewer nuclear weapons around

11,071 — 2010
9,220 — TODAY

Estimated number of stockpiled nuclear warheads worldwide

There are fewer countries where you can legally be executed

109

96 — 2010
TODAY

Countries that have abolished the death penalty

We're slightly less likely to be murdered

6.02 — 2010
5.78 — TODAY

Intentional homicides per 100,000 people worldwide

We're living two years longer

70.6 — 2010
72.7 — TODAY

Global average life expectancy

What should I be worried about?

Every year since 2007 the World Economic Forum in Davos, Switzerland, has issued a *Global Risks Report*, which charts the top five planetary hazards in terms of likelihood. We've crunched the numbers to see what they say we should fear the most

How it works: We've counted every entry on *Global Risks Reports* since 2007, grouping the risks identified into parent categories where relevant. We've then illustrated the ten risk factors that had the most entries overall and placed them in order of number of mentions. If risks have equal numbers of mentions, the one most recently featured in a Global Risks Report ranks higher. Risks can appear multiple times in one report

10th

Interstate conflict with regional consequences

Includes: Middle East instability

▶ Entries: **3**

◀ Latest entry: **2016**

▲ Highest entry: **1st in 2015**

9th

Biodiversity loss

Includes: Ecosystem collapse

▶ Entries: **3**

◀ Latest entry: **2021**

▲ Highest entry: **4th in 2020**

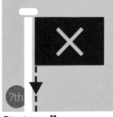

8th

Income disparity

Includes: Severe income disparity, unemployment or underemployment and chronic fiscal imbalances

▶ Entries: **5**

◀ Latest entry: **2015**

▲ Highest entry: **1st in 2014**

7th

State collapse or crisis

Includes: Large-scale involuntary migration, failure of national governance and failed and failing states

▶ Entries: **5**

◀ Latest entry: **2017**

▲ Highest entry: **1st in 2016**

6th

Natural disasters

Includes: Earthquakes, tsunamis and volcanic eruptions

▶ Entries: **5**

◀ Latest entry: **2020**

▲ Highest entry: **2nd in 2018**

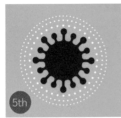

5th

Infectious diseases

Includes: Chronic disease

▶ Entries: **5**

◀ Latest entry: **2021**

▲ Highest entry: **2nd in 2007**

4th

Information infrastructure vulnerabilities

Includes: Cyber attack, data fraud or theft and breakdown of critical information infrastructure

▶ Entries: **8**

◀ Latest entry: **2019**

▲ Highest entry: **1st in 2007**

3rd

Financial and fiscal crises

Includes: Asset price collapse, fiscal crises, chronic fiscal imbalances and oil and gas price spike/shock

▶ Entries: **9**

◀ Latest entry: **2013**

▲ Highest entry: **1st in 2010**

2nd

Extreme weather events

Includes: Meteorological catastrophes and flooding

▶ Entries: **10**

◀ Latest entry: **2021**

▲ Highest entry: **1st in 2021**

1st

Climate change

Includes: Human environmental disaster, rising greenhouse gas emissions, failure of climate-change mitigation and adaptation

▶ Entries: **11**

◀ Latest entry: **2021**

▲ Highest entry: **2nd in 2021**

Source: World Economic Forum's Global Risks Report

How much damage can a hurricane do?

Hurricanes cost the US economy more than droughts, floods, freezes, wildfires and winter storms combined. They are also becoming more frequent. Here's the scale of damage each category of hurricane is capable of causing

What's the strongest category of hurricane?

How it works: The Saffir-Simpson hurricane wind scale rates hurricane intensity from 1 to 5. In general, damage rises by about a factor of four for every category increase

1	**2**	**3**	**4**	**5**
Some minor damage	**Moderate damage**	**Excessive damage**	**Extreme damage**	**Catastrophic damage**
Winds: **75–95 mph**	Winds: **96–110mph**	Winds: **111–129mph**	Winds: **130–156mph**	Winds: **157+ mph**
Roof tiles and tree branches blown off, damage to power lines with outages for days	Roof damage, some trees uprooted, roads blocked, power loss for days or weeks	Structural roof damage, areas isolated, electricity and water unavailable for days or weeks	Major property and infrastructure damage. Much of the area uninhabitable for weeks	Destruction of property, power and water supply. Areas uninhabitable for months

How much does it cost to clean up after a hurricane?

The five most expensive US hurricane seasons in billions of dollars (adjusted for inflation)

2017	Hurricanes Harvey, Irma, Jose, Maria	**$283.6 bn**
2005	Hurricanes Dennis, Katrina, Ophelia, Rita, Wilma	**$227.7 bn**
1926	The Great Miami hurricane	**$184.3 bn**
1900	The Great Galveston hurricane	$113.5 bn
1915	Galveston, New Orleans hurricanes	$80.8 bn

DEADLIEST ON RECORD
8,000 FATALITIES

Sources: National Hurricane Center, National Oceanic and Atmospheric Administration, Time magazine

Is it hot or is it just me?

Global warming is arguably the biggest challenge humankind has ever faced, with rising temperatures threatening food production, habitats, political and economic stability and access to clean water. While the effects of climate change will be felt long into the future, the world is already considerably hotter than it used to be

How it works: The map divides the world's countries and territories into three bands according to the difference between their average temperatures in 2020 and their average temperatures from 1951 to 1980. 2020 saw the warmest annual average temperatures since instrumental records began in 45 countries. ■ Grey areas represent countries for which no data are available

Source: Berkeley Earth

NORTH AMERICA

H

L

SOUTH AMERICA

A bit hotter
Countries and territories in which 2020 was 0-1.49°C warmer than the 1951-1980 average

Considerably hotter
Countries and territories in which 2020 was 1.5-2.99°C warmer than the 1951-1980 average

A lot hotter
Countries and territories in which 2020 was over 3°C warmer than the 1951-1980 average

Has it been hot lately?

Since 2010 the planet's seen eight of the ten hottest years since records began in 1850

2010   2011   2012   2013   2014   2015
2016   2017   2018   2019   2020

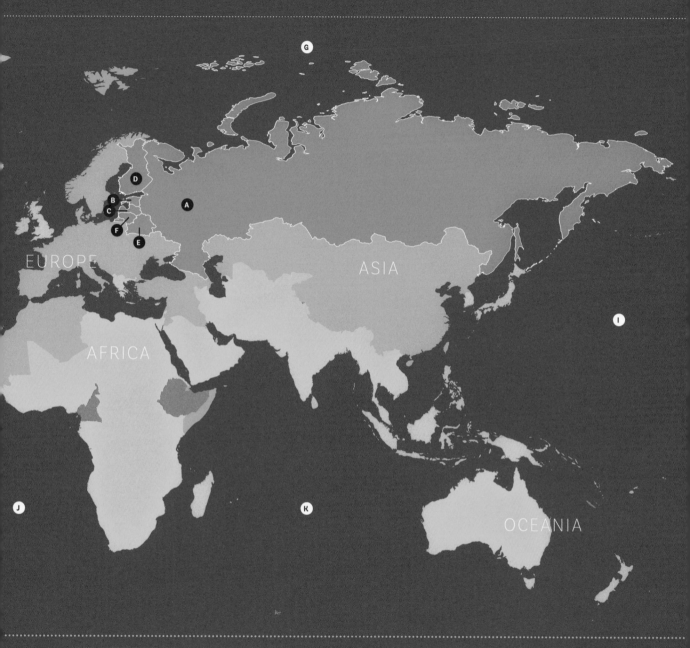

G

D

B
C
F
E
A

EUROPE

AFRICA

ASIA

I

J

K

OCEANIA

Who's getting hotter?
The places with the greatest increase in average
temperatures in 2020 compared to 1951-1980 (°C)

+3.6	**Russia**	A
+3.4	**Estonia**	B
+3.3	**Latvia**	C
+3.2	**Finland**	D
+3.1	Belarus	E
+3.1	Lithuania	F

What's it like in the water?
The oceans with the greatest increase in average
temperatures in 2020 compared to 1951-1980 (°C)

G	**Arctic Ocean**	+2.7
H	**North Atlantic**	+0.8
I	**North Pacific**	+0.8
J	South Atlantic	+0.5
K	Indian Ocean	+0.5
L	South Pacific	+0.4

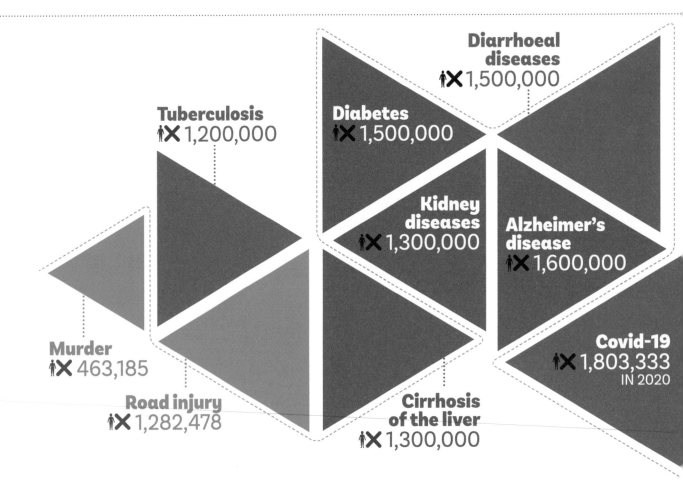

Diarrhoeal diseases
✝✗ 1,500,000

Tuberculosis
✝✗ 1,200,000

Diabetes
✝✗ 1,500,000

Kidney diseases
✝✗ 1,300,000

Alzheimer's disease
✝✗ 1,600,000

Murder
✝✗ 463,185

Road injury
✝✗ 1,282,478

Cirrhosis of the liver
✝✗ 1,300,000

Covid-19
✝✗ 1,803,333
IN 2020

What's going to kill me?

According to the World Health Organization, around 55.4 million people die each year. Here are the most likely causes of being shuffled off this mortal coil

How it works: We've visualised the **annual global fatality numbers (✝✗)** for the world's leading causes of death according to the World Health Organization in 2019, as well as the number of people whose deaths were recorded as Covid 19-related* in 2020. Murder is not a leading cause of death, but has been included as a point of comparison. Causes of death are colour-coded by category:

▶ **Communicable, maternal, perinatal and nutritional conditions** (including infectious and parasitic diseases)
▶ **Noncommunicable** (influenced by factors including age, sex, diet, environment, lifestyle and genetics)
▶ **Injuries** (accidental and intentional causes of death)

Sources: World Health Organization, World Bank
*Defined by WHO as 'a death resulting from a clinically compatible illness in a probable or confirmed Covid-19 case, unless there is a clear alternative cause of death that cannot be related to the disease (eg trauma)'

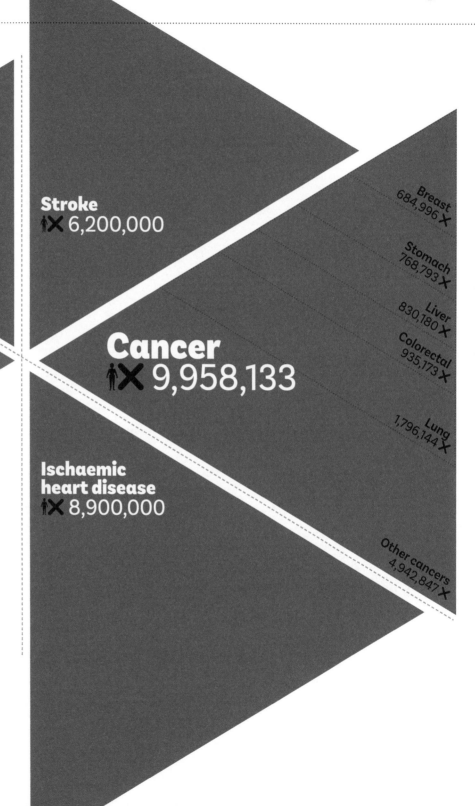

Chronic obstructive pulmonary disease
👤✖ 3,200,000

Stroke
👤✖ 6,200,000

Lower respiratory tract infections
👤✖ 2,600,000

Cancer
👤✖ 9,958,133

Neonatal conditions
👤✖ 2,000,000

Ischaemic heart disease
👤✖ 8,900,000

Breast
684,996 ✖

Stomach
768,793 ✖

Liver
830,180 ✖

Colorectal
935,173 ✖

Lung
1,796,144 ✖

Other cancers
4,942,847 ✖

☠

122,675
AVERAGE DAILY
FATALITIES FROM
LISTED CAUSES
OF DEATH

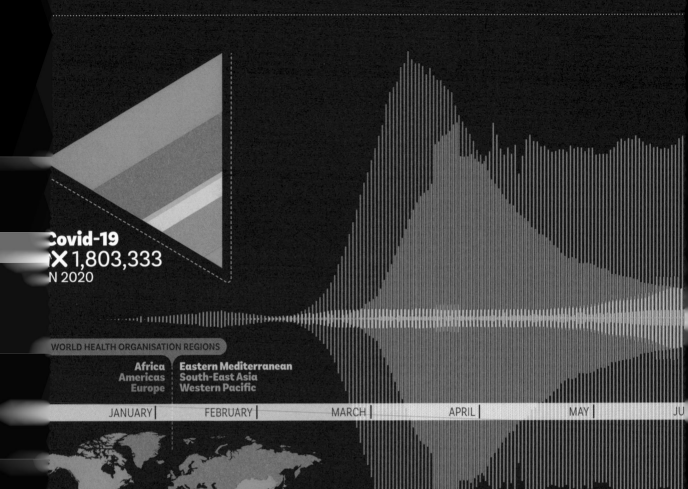

Covid-19
X 1,803,333
N 2020

WORLD HEALTH ORGANISATION REGIONS

Africa **Eastern Mediterranean**
Americas **South-East Asia**
Europe **Western Pacific**

JANUARY | FEBRUARY | MARCH | APRIL | MAY | JU

How did Covid-19 spread across the world?

On 12th January 2020 the first death from Covid-19 was reported. By the end of the year 1,803,333 people had died from it. We've visualised where and when those deaths took place as the disease made its way across the world

How it works: The graph shows a proportional representation of the number of deaths reported to the WHO between 16th January 2020 and 31st December 2020. A rolling seven-day average is applied after the death toll reaches 100 in each region. Lines are colour-coded by WHO region as illustrated on the map. The total deaths for each region in 2020 are represented within the triangle at the top of this page

Source: World Health Organization. Covid deaths are defined by WHO as 'a death resulting from a clinically compatible illness in a probable or confirmed Covid-19 case,

12th Jan	First reported death in the **Western Pacific**
13th Feb	First reported death in **Europe**
20th Feb	First reported death in the **Eastern Mediterranean**
1st Mar	First reported death in **South-East Asia**
3rd Mar	First reported death in **the Americas**
12th Mar	First reported death in **Africa**

24th Apr	Worst day in the **Western Pacific**, 229 deaths
22nd Sep	Worst day in **South-East Asia**, 1,336 deaths
25th Nov	Worst day in the **Eastern Mediterranean**, 903 deaths
19th Dec	Worst day in **Europe**, 5,427 deaths
24th Dec	Worst day globally, 11,663 deaths
25th Dec	Worst day in **the Americas**, 4,824 deaths
31st Dec	Worst day in **Africa**, 414 deaths

Global search peak:

🔍 **SEARCH TOPICS:**

▲ **% INCREASE:**

☀ 'Breakout' topics are defined by Google as search terms with a year on year increase of 5,000% or more

12 days before

Hoarding

▲ **1,307%**

Searches on the topic of hoarding, which included panic buying and stock levels, peaked early

On day 1

Pandemic

☀ **BREAKOUT**

Pandemic was the first topic to 'break out', with a 26,000% increase in searches peaking on the same day that the global pandemic was declared

3 days later

Toilet paper

▲ **355%**

Fears of a shortage saw a spike in toilet roll searches, including 'how do I make my own toilet paper?'

5 days later

Coronavirus

☀ **BREAKOUT**

Coronavirus was the first new topic in years to become the most searched on Google

GLOBAL PANDEMIC DECLARED 11TH MARCH 2020

What was life like in lockdown?

In an attempt to combat the first wave of Covid-19 infections, governments around the world ordered their citizens to stay at home. The billions cooped up indoors took to the internet to help them navigate a world that had changed at speed. We've mapped the shifting concerns of locked-down humanity to create a timeline of life in the early days of the pandemic

How it works: Using Google Trends, which brings together clusters of related search terms in different languages, we compared the year-on-year growth in Google searches of relevant topics and questions in the period from February to July 2020. We then identified the day on which each search term hit its peak interest level worldwide

Search topics: ● Shopping ● Health ● Regulations ● Entertainment and lifestyle ● Home and work

Source: Google Trends

24 days later

Surgical mask

▲ **1,904%**

As face coverings became commonplace, surgical-mask interest hit its peak

25 days later

Cut your own hair

☀ **BREAKOUT**

The closure of hairdressing establishments the world over saw people going DIY

26 days later

Unemployment benefits

▲ **98%**

The economic impact of lockdown hits. Denmark searched the most

28 days later

Permit to go outside

☀ **BREAKOUT**

The UAE topped searches on whether people could leave their homes

31 days later

Baker's yeast

▲ **224%**

Searches for 'where to buy' and 'how to use' drove the rise of baker's yeast

33 days later

Café sounds, YouTube

☀ **BREAKOUT**

Australia led the way in the hunt for some ambience

Hand sanitiser
▲ 1,703%

Panic buying saw hand sanitiser supplies dip and searches relating to the product peak

1 week later

Vaccine
▲ 118%

As the extent of the crisis became clear, people started searching for answers

9 days later

Curfew
▲ 1,266%

Nationwide and local curfews were new to a lot of people

Hydroxychloroquine
▲ 1,195%

Interest in the drug jumped when it was touted as a treatment by President Trump

Quarantine
▲ 4,791%

Searches included 'how to quarantine', 'quarantine offence report' and 'quarantine dating ideas'

10 days later

Ammunition
▲ 64%

The US led the way in searches relating to ammunition, looking for availability and shelf life

---

11 days later

Boredom
▲ 42%

As the 'new normal' set in, boredom-related searches, including simply 'I'm bored', spiked

Exercise bike
▲ 182%

A rush in people looking to get fit without leaving the house drove an uptick in stationary-bike searches

Paint roller
▲ 348%

Others sought the tools to spruce up their houses as they faced spending more time in them

Virtual tour
▲ 223%

Many looked to virtual culture, particularly in France, which saw the biggest spike

12 days later

Homeschooling
▲ 82%

The reality of school closures saw people educating themselves on how to educate others...

When will schools open?
☀ BREAKOUT

...before asking the question on nearly every parent's mind

17 days later

Board game
▲ 33%

Interest in classic board games saw a resurgence during the pandemic

18 days later

Banana bread
▲ 106%

The comfort cake spiked worldwide, but Ireland and Slovakia saw the biggest search increases

Webcam
▲ 63%

As Zoom became a buzzword, people looked for the best kit

19 days later

Social distancing
☀ BREAKOUT

Another 'new normal' term enters the global vocabulary

3 weeks later

Zoom dating
☀ BREAKOUT

Because love will find a way... Sweden saw the highest percentage increase in searches

24 days later

Paint by numbers
▲ 187%

Old-school entertainment made a return worldwide, but Ukraine saw the biggest rise in searches

---

36 days later

Unmute on Zoom
☀ BREAKOUT

Ireland struggled the most with this recurring videocall problem

38 days later

Drive-by birthday party
☀ BREAKOUT

A new tradition was born, the US leading the world in searches

52 days later

How to make McDonald's
☀ BREAKOUT

Meanwhile the UK apparently couldn't live without Big Macs...

60 days later

Take-out
▲ 108%

...although some were prepared to brave the outside world to get their favourite comfort food

67 days later

Bicycle
▲ 46%

As restrictions eased, cycling interest soared. Belgians were the biggest bike searchers

142 days later

How many people can attend a funeral?
☀ BREAKOUT

The UK led the way in the saddest search of all

Do worse things happen at sea?

The sinking of the *Titanic* might be the most famous maritime disaster, but it is far from the most deadly. We've compared the 1912 tragedy with five more of the world's worst shipwrecks

How it works: We've drawn the RMS Titanic and five other ill-fated ships to scale to enable comparison and put the length of the longest one in perspective below

Sources: Britannica, The Daily Telegraph, History.com, The Maritime Executive, Smithsonian magazine

Seawise Giant was also the longest ship ever built – tipped on its end, at 458 metres, it would overshadow the Eiffel Tower in Paris, New York City's Empire State Building and London's Shard

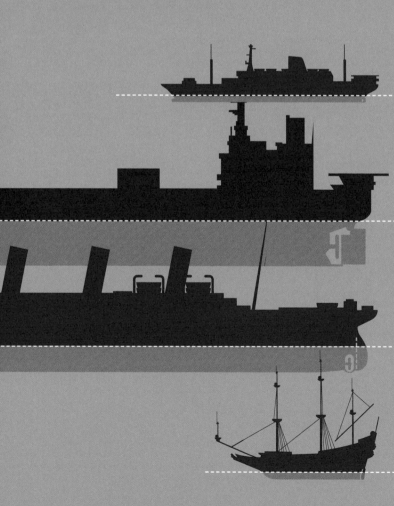

What's the most famous ship ever sunk?

RMS TITANIC ▽ 15th April 1912

The infamous 269m-long 'unsinkable' ocean liner hit an iceberg five days into her maiden voyage

⚓ **Loss of life: 1,502**

What's the biggest loss of life at sea?

MV WILHELM GUSTLOFF ▽30th January 1945

The sinking of Germany's floating barracks, torpedoed by a Russian submarine while evacuating civilians, is the largest single loss of life in recorded maritime history

⚓ **Estimated loss of life: 9,400**

What's the biggest loss of life at sea in peacetime?

MV DOÑA PAZ ▽ 20th December 1987

This Philippine-registered passenger ferry sank after a collision with an oil tanker. The ship's passenger capacity was 1,518

⚓ **Loss of life: 4,374**

What's the biggest ship ever sunk?

SEAWISE GIANT ▽ 14th May 1988

Sunk by Iraqi jets in the Strait of Hormuz during the Iran-Iraq war – the 458m-long vessel was salvaged, renamed and eventually scrapped in 2010

⚓ **Loss of life: 14**

What's the biggest ocean liner ever sunk?

HMHS BRITANNIC ▽ 21st November 1916

Titanic's bigger sister – just over two metres longer – served as a hospital ship in World War I. Sunk by a mine off the Greek Island of Kea

⚓ **Loss of life: 30**

What's the shortest maiden voyage?

VASA▽ 10th August 1628

A Swedish warship, the largest wooden ship ever built, *Vasa* sank two kilometres outside Stockholm on its maiden voyage. The wreck was raised in 1956

⚓ **Estimated loss of life: 50**

Where are the world's most dangerous cities?

Statistically, the chances of being murdered are very small – the world's annual homicide rate is 5.78 per 100,000 people – but the odds are considerably worse if you live in certain cities...

Cities with the highest murder rate per 100,000 people

1. ✝X193 **San Salvador, SLV**
2. ✝X130.7 **La Ceiba, HND**
3. ✝X113.2 **San Pedro Sula, HND**
4. ✝X90.5 Tegucigalpa, HND
5. ✝X81.6 Soyapango, SLV
6. ✝X66.4 Belize City, BLZ
7. ✝X64.8 Guatemala City, GTM
8. ✝X64.8 Cali, COL
9. ✝X64.4 Santa Ana, SLV
10. ✝X54.3 Kingston, JAM
11. ✝X47.8 Salvador, BRA
12. ✝X47.5 Portmore, JAM
13. ✝X46 Escuintla, GTM
14. ✝X45.7 Bambari, CAF
15. ✝X33.9 Belmopan, BLZ

How it works: The chart shows the 15 cities with the highest annual homicide rate (number of victims of intentional homicide per 100,000 population). Figures shown are from the latest available year. Figures for global average from 2018

Source: United Nations Office on Drugs and Crime

Should I be worried about a plague of locusts?

Locust swarms didn't disappear after the Old Testament: in January 2020 the biggest one in decades was recorded in east Africa. Here is the size of the devastating cloud of voracious, crop-destroying insects in context

How it works: The circles below are sized proportionally to the urban areas represented and compared to the area covered by Kenya's largest recorded locust swarm

784km^2
Total area of
New York City

1,569km^2
Total area of
Greater London

2,400km^2
Estimated size of the
largest locust swarm ever recorded
in Kenya, reported by the UN in
January 2020

How much do locusts eat?

IN ONE DAY A 2,400-SQUARE-KILOMETRE SWARM OF LOCUSTS CAN CONSUME
ENOUGH FOOD FOR 84,000,000 PEOPLE
THE EQUIVALENT OF THE POPULATION OF GERMANY

Source: UN Food and Agriculture Organization

O (2005 ED224)

?▽ 2024-2056 **1 in 22,000**

O (2021 EU)

?▽ 2024-2120 **1 in 770,000**

O (2007 FT3)

?▽ 2029-2121 **1 in 91,000**

O (2010 MZ112)

?▽ 2030-2107 **1 in 14,000**

O (2005 QK76)

?▽ 2030-2119 **1 in 770,000**

O (2007 DX40)

?▽ 2032 **1 in 11,000**

O (2021 GX9)

?▽ 2044-2100 **1 in 31,000**

O (2008 UB7)

?▽ 2047-2050 **1 in 170,000**

O (2012 QD8)

?▽ 2062-2090 **1 in 19,000**

O (2008 EX5)

?▽ 2066 **1 in 220,000**

O (2021 MX)

?▽ 2022 **1 in 3,800**

What are the chances
of being hit by an asteroid?

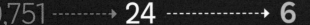

-crushing asteroids have long been a staple of science-fiction films, but how likely is a direct hit
ow much damage could it do? We analyse the data to find out

0,751 - - - - → **24** - - - - - → **6** - - - - → **13** - - - - → **5**

ar-Earth
cts being
itored by
SA's Jet
opulsion
boratory

potential Earth-impact
events identified by NASA's
Sentry collision monitoring
system. None is likely to
enter Earth's atmosphere,
but if any should...

should burn up
on entry but
fragments may still
hit Earth according
to the Earth Impact
Effects Program

could form a
bright fireball and a
strong airblast
capable of damaging
glass windows over
a wide area

could hit the
ground with
enough force to
form a crater.
The largest of
which is...

t works: We've illustrated the 24 potential future Earth-impact events NASA's Sentry collision monitoring system has identified
on currently available observations. The near-Earth objects identified are ordered in bands of probable impact and then by year
of closest approach. They are colour-coded to show what might happen in the unlikely case that they enter the Earth's
sphere, with impact predictions taken from UCL's Earth Impact Effects Program and based on asteroids being
of rock with a density of 3,000kg/m^3 and entering the atmosphere at a 45-degree angle.
orst-case scenario is based on the largest illustrated asteroid hitting the Eiffel Tower in Paris.

Center For Near-Earth Object Studies, Earth Impact Effects Program

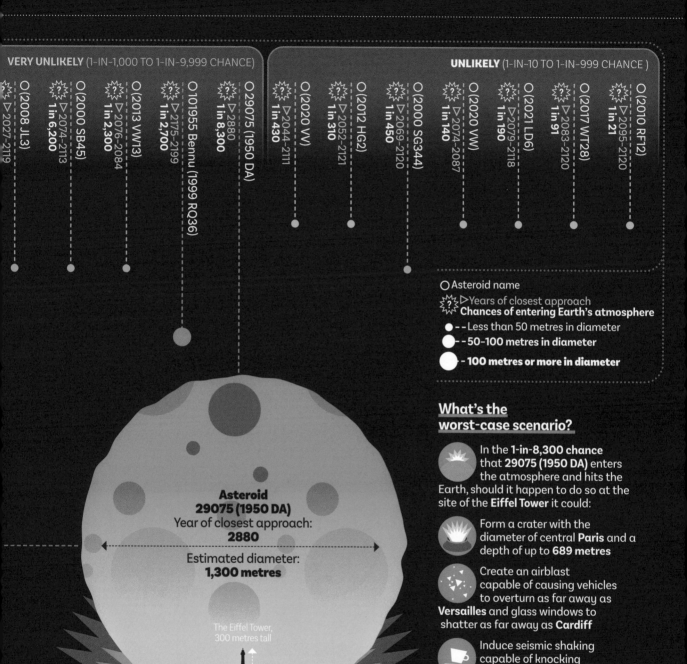

VERY UNLIKELY (1-IN-1,000 TO 1-IN-9,999 CHANCE)

O (2008 JL3)
▷ 2027-2119

O (2000 SB45)
▷ 2074-2113
1 in 6,200

O (2013 VW13)
▷ 2076-2084
1 in 2,300

O 101955 Bennu (1999 RQ36)
▷ 2175-2199
1 in 2,700

O 29075 (1950 DA)
▷ 2880
1 in 8,300

UNLIKELY (1-IN-10 TO 1-IN-999 CHANCE)

O (2020 VV)
▷ 2044-2111
1 in 430

O (2012 HG2)
▷ 2052-2121
1 in 310

O (2000 SG344)
▷ 2069-2120
1 in 450

O (2020 VW)
▷ 2074-2087
1 in 140

O (2021 LD6)
▷ 2079-2118
1 in 190

O (2017 WT28)
▷ 2083-2120
1 in 91

O (2010 RF12)
▷ 2095-2120
1 in 21

O Asteroid name
?▷ Years of closest approach
Chances of entering Earth's atmosphere
● – – Less than 50 metres in diameter
● – – 50–100 metres in diameter
● – 100 metres or more in diameter

What's the worst-case scenario?

In the **1-in-8,300 chance** that **29075 (1950 DA)** enters the atmosphere and hits the Earth, should it happen to do so at the site of the **Eiffel Tower** it could:

Form a crater with the diameter of central **Paris** and a depth of up to **689 metres**

Create an airblast capable of causing vehicles to overturn as far away as **Versailles** and glass windows to shatter as far away as **Cardiff**

Induce seismic shaking capable of knocking a cup over in **Stuttgart** and being felt in **Milan**

**Asteroid
29075 (1950 DA)**
Year of closest approach:
2880

Estimated diameter:
1,300 metres

The Eiffel Tower,
300 metres tall

1000

Holy Roman Emperor Otto III
Prediction made: 1000

Otto was convinced that the world would end in 1000. As predictions suggested that an emperor would rise to fight the Antichrist, he had the body of Charlemagne, who died in 814, exhumed on Pentecost ready to slay Satan

1000

Pope Sylvester II
Prediction made: 999

On becoming Pope, Sylvester II – AKA Gerbert of Aurillac – predicted that the world would end with the return of Jesus Christ 1,000 years after his birth. When the Saviour failed to turn up, Sylvester revised his prediction to 1033, the anniversary of Christ's death, but was once again happily proved wrong

circa 1247

Joachim of Fiore
Prediction made: 1187

Biblical scholar Joachim of Fiore believed that the end of the world would be brought about by the seven-headed dragon mentioned in the Book of Revelation. His predictions encouraged Richard the Lionheart to pursue the Third Crusade

1524

Astrologers
Prediction made: 1523

A group of astrologers in London predicted the world would end with a flood starting in the English capital on 1st February 1524. Twenty thousand Londoners left their homes and headed for higher ground in anticipation. They needn't have bothered: reports say it didn't even rain

1736

William Whiston
Prediction made: 1736

William Whiston was an early researcher into comets who attributed Noah's great flood to space rocks. He predicted that another would hit the Earth on 16th October 1736, bringing about its end. His prediction caused such panic that the Archbishop of Canterbury had to publicly denounce Whiston's prophecy

2011

Harold Camping
Prediction made: 2010

Californian Christian radio broadcaster Harold Camping predicted 'the Rapture' would occur on 21st May 2011 and advertised his forecast on more than 5,000 billboards. When Christians did not ascend as advertised, he revised his prophecy to 21st October 2011. Still nothing

2012

José Argüelles
Prediction made: 1987

José Argüelles believed that the end of the 13th baktun of the Mayan calendar in 2012 would prompt an alien invasion or the end of the world as we know it. To combat this he organised a mass meditation in 1987 with thousands joining in at sites including Central Park and Stonehenge

2021

Kenton Beshore
Prediction made: 1988

Having supposedly decoded the Bible, American pastor Kenton Beshore predicted 'the Rapture' would take place in 2021, before the country of Israel 'becomes an old man'

2038

Nostradamus
Prediction made: 1555

History's most famous forecaster, Nostradamus, had the world ending when Easter fell on 25th April. So far we've dodged Easter annihilation in 1666, 1734, 1886 and 1943. Next up is Easter 2038. Probably best not to save your Easter eggs, to be on the safe side

2038

Various
Prediction made: 1970

Time runs out at 3:14:0█ on 19th January 2038. Or at least it does for computers using the Un█ software system, whose internal clock can only count that high. Tech doom-mongers claim this will lead to satellite falling out of orbit, powe█ cuts and life-support systems failing

1806

Mary Bateman
Prediction made: 1806

In 1806 the Prophet Hen of Leeds started laying eggs emblazoned with the words 'Crist [sic] is coming'. People panicked. Christ didn't come. It turned out to be the work of local con artist Mary Bateman, who wrote on the eggs using vinegar before reinserting them into the bird

1843

William Miller
Prediction made: 1842

After intense study of the Bible, American William Miller predicted that the world would be destroyed by fire on 3rd April 1843. Believing the dead would get to heaven first, some of his followers reportedly killed relatives. One broke his arm trying to fly to heaven using turkey wings attached to his shoulders

1919

Albert Porta
Prediction made: 1919

Respected meteorologist Porta claimed that an alignment of six planets on 17th December 1919 would 'cause a magnetic current that would pierce the sun, cause great explosions of flaming gas and eventually engulf the Earth'. When the fireball failed to appear, Porta was cast out of academia. He spent the rest of his life working as a weatherman

1967

Anders Jensen
Prediction made: 1967

Anders Jensen, the leader of a sect known as the Disciples of Orthon, announced that a nuclear holocaust was coming on Christmas Day 1967 and invited people to spend the festive period in his bunker, The Ark. A few days into 1968 the 30 people who took him up on his offer sheepishly re-emerged

1976

George King
Prediction made: 1954

While drying dishes in 1954, British taxi driver George King claimed to have received a message from Venus saying the world would end 22 years later. King and his followers, the Aetherius Society, were apparently able to avert the end of days by piling 700 hours of prayer energy into a book and releasing it on the appointed day

2060

Isaac Newton
Prediction made: 1704

Isaac Newton was a keen decoder of the Bible, and private letters revealed he believed the second coming would arrive in 2060. Newton claimed Christ's comeback would be followed by a 1,000-year reign by the saints on Earth – of which Newton would be one

2126

Brian G Marsden
Prediction made: 1992

In 1992 British astronomer Brian Marsden claimed that Swift-Tuttle, a six-mile-wide comet – similar to the one many scientists believe wiped out the dinosaurs – could collide with Earth on 14th August 2126. Subsequent researchers have said that there's almost no chance it will hit our planet

Is the end of the world nigh?

The drawback with predicting the total annihilation of the Earth is that you're unlikely to have time to gloat when you're proved right. That hasn't stopped successive generations of doommongers from having a bash at it, though

How it works: The timeline shows the **predicted date** ☀ of the world's end according to a number of prophets, monarchs, scientists and astrological groups 👁

Sources: A History of the Apocalypse by Catalin Negru, American Physical Society, Cambridge University Press, Encyclopedia Britannica, history.com, Lancaster Gazette, New York Times, PBS, Sir Patrick Moore, Smithsonian magazine

How long have we got?

The Doomsday Clock, a symbolic measure of proximity to the apocalypse, creeps ever closer to midnight. Here are the key swings of its minute hand since the clock was first devised in 1947

How it works: We've visualised every key change to the Doomsday Clock, created and maintained by the *Bulletin of the Atomic Scientists* to 'warn the public about how close we are to destroying our world with dangerous technologies of our own making'
MIDNIGHT = THE END OF HUMANITY

1947 Seven minutes to midnight
Artist Martyl Langsdorf designs the clock for the cover of the *Bulletin of the Atomic Scientists*

1949 Three minutes to midnight
The Soviet Union develops and tests its first atomic weapon

1953 Two minutes to midnight
The US develops the hydrogen bomb. The USSR follows with a test of its own H-bomb

1960 Seven minutes to midnight
The US and USSR actively seek to avoid direct confrontation. US and Soviet scientists meet

1963 Twelve minutes to midnight
The US and USSR sign the Partial Test Ban Treaty, ending atmospheric nuclear testing

1968 Seven minutes to midnight
France and China develop nuclear weapons, US involvement in the Vietnam War intensifies

1969 Ten minutes to midnight
Most nations sign the Nuclear Non-Proliferation Treaty - Israel, India and Pakistan refuse

1972 Twelve minutes to midnight
The US and USSR sign treaties limiting ballistic missiles and anti-ballistic missile development

1974 Nine minutes to midnight
India tests its first nuclear weapon. The US and USSR appear to be modernising their nuclear arsenals

1981 Four minutes to midnight

The USSR has invaded Afghanistan. New US president Ronald Reagan scraps talk of arms control

1984 Three minutes to midnight

US-USSR relations reach a low point. The US considers space-based anti-ballistic missile defences

1988 Six minutes to midnight

The US and USSR sign a treaty banning intermediate-range nuclear weapons

1990 Ten minutes to midnight

The fall of the Berlin Wall and collapse of the USSR significantly reduce the threat of nuclear war

1991 Seventeen minutes to midnight

The US and USSR sign the Strategic Arms Reduction Treaty. The USSR is dissolved

1995 Fourteen minutes to midnight

Concerns arise about post-Cold War relations and the status of Russia's nuclear facilities

1998 Nine minutes to midnight

India and Pakistan carry out a series of nuclear weapons tests

2002 Seven minutes to midnight

The September 11th attacks in 2001 spark fears that terrorists could seek to acquire nuclear weapons

2007 Five minutes to midnight

North Korea has conducted a nuclear test and it is feared that Iran is developing its own weapons

2010 Six minutes to midnight

The US and Russia enter talks to plan further cuts in their nuclear arsenals

2012 Five minutes to midnight

North Korea continues to develop nuclear weapons under the new leadership of Kim Jong-un

2015 Three minutes to midnight

Multiple threats to international stability arise, from climate change to cyberwars and Ebola

2017 Two-and-a-half minutes to midnight

North Korea continues nuclear tests, technological change disrupts democracies

2018 Two minutes to midnight

North Korea has tested its first H-bomb. The Iran nuclear deal comes under threat

2020 One hundred seconds to midnight

The clock moves the closest it has come to midnight, as governments fail to tackle multiple planetary threats

WHY CAN'T WE ALL JUST GET ALONG ?

Questions about wars, guns and Eurovision

◁ CONFLICTS

2010 2011 2012 2013 2014 2015 2016 2017 2018 2019 ◁ YEAR

2009 2008 2007 2006 2005 2004 2003 2002 2001 2000 1999 1998 1997

Don't you know there's a war on?

Japan's surrender on 2nd September 1945 brought the horrors of World War II to an end. But peace on Earth has remained elusive ever since

How it works: Each explosion symbol represents a war that was taking place in that year. We've used the Uppsala Conflict Data Program's definition of war, as 'a conflict resulting in at least 1,000 battle-related deaths in a given year'. Wars are colour-coded by the geographic region in which the conflict predominantly took place

Sources: Pettersson, Therése and Öberg, Magnus (2020), Organized violence, 1989-2019, Journal of Peace Research 57(4); Pettersson, Therése (2020) UCDP Battle-related Deaths Dataset Codebook v 20.1

1996 1995 1994 1993 1992 1991 1990 1989 1988 1987 1986 1985 1984 19

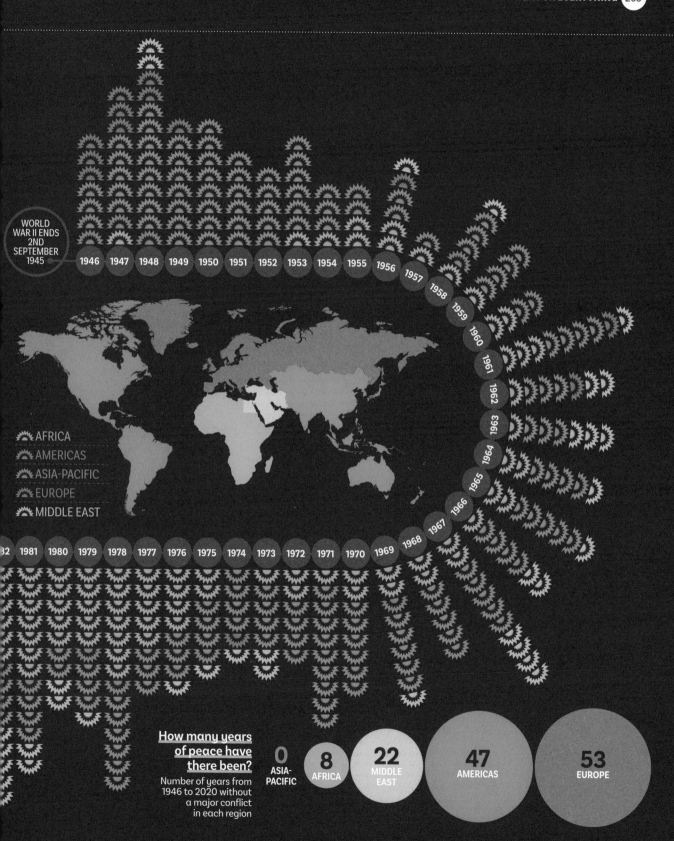

WORLD
WAR II ENDS
2ND
SEPTEMBER
1945

1946 1947 1948 1949 1950 1951 1952 1953 1954 1955 1956 1957 1958 1959 1960 1961 1962 1963 1964 1965 1966 1967 1968 1969

AFRICA
AMERICAS
ASIA-PACIFIC
EUROPE
MIDDLE EAST

82 1981 1980 1979 1978 1977 1976 1975 1974 1973 1972 1971 1970 1969 1968

How many years of peace have there been?

Number of years from 1946 to 2020 without a major conflict in each region

0 ASIA-PACIFIC

8 AFRICA

22 MIDDLE EAST

47 AMERICAS

53 EUROPE

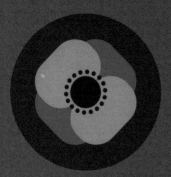

Where have people died in conflict?

NORTH AMERICA

SOUTH AMERICA

Over two-and-a-half million people worldwide have been killed as a result of conflict in the last three decades. This is where they fell

How it works: We have mapped the best estimate of conflict deaths from 1st January 1989 to 31st December 2019 according to the Uppsala Conflict Data Program (UCDP). The UCDP defines a conflict event as 'An incident where armed force was used by an organised actor against another organised actor, or against civilians, resulting in at least one direct death at a specific location and a specific date'. *Estimates of the death toll of the Rwandan genocide vary considerably **Data for the Syrian conflict are preliminary and may be significantly revised in future

Sources: Högbladh, Stina (2020) 'UCDP GED Codebook version 20.1', Department of Peace and Conflict Research, Uppsala University. Sundberg, Ralph, and Melander, Erik (2013); 'Introducing the UCDP Georeferenced Event Dataset', Journal of Peace Research, vol.50, no.4, 523-532

10,000+ casualties
Countries and territories in which over 10,000 people have died a result of conflict 1989–2019 (marked in black)

101-9,999 casualties
Countries and territories in which 101-9,999 people have died a result of conflict 1989–2019 (grey)

<100 casualties
Countries and territories in which fewer than 100 people have died as a result of conflict 1989–2019 (white)

How many people have died in conflict?
Between 1989 and 2019
2,546,751 people
have died as a result of conflict. The equivalent of
225 people a day

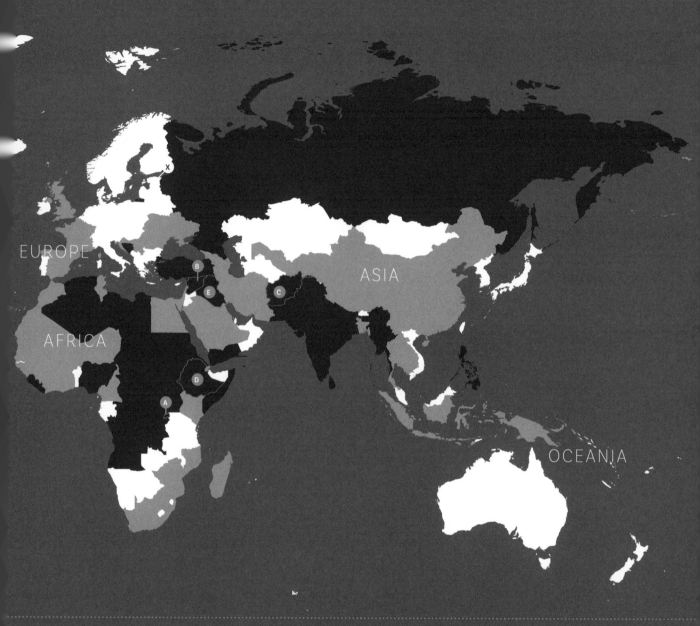

EUROPE

ASIA

AFRICA

OCEANIA

Which countries have seen the most conflict deaths? ☠

✝✗543,176*	**Rwanda**	A
✝✗359,843**	**Syria**	B
✝✗257,944	**Afghanistan**	C
✝✗178,169	**Ethiopia**	D
✝✗121,659	Iraq	E

WORST

Which has been the deadliest year in conflict since 1989?

WORST		
▲ 1994	✝✗570,862
2014	✗ 144,101
2015	✗ 122,348
2016	✗ 106,581
2013	✗ 99,993

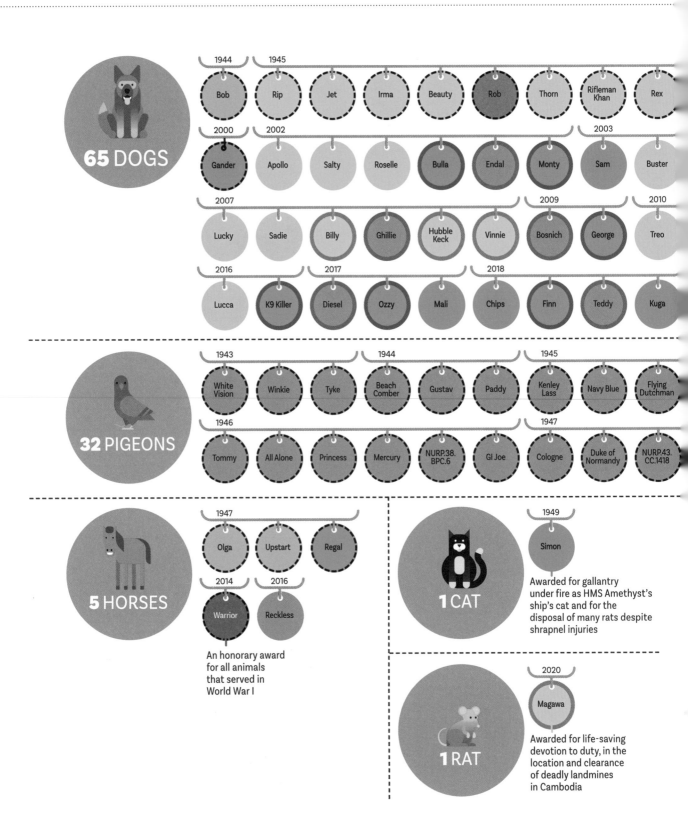

65 DOGS

1944	1945							
Bob	Rip	Jet	Irma	Beauty	Rob	Thorn	Rifleman Khan	Rex

2000	2002						2003	
Gander	Apollo	Salty	Roselle	Bulla	Endal	Monty	Sam	Buster

2007						2009		2010
Lucky	Sadie	Billy	Ghillie	Hubble Keck	Vinnie	Bosnich	George	Treo

2016		2017				2018		
Lucca	K9 Killer	Diesel	Ozzy	Mali	Chips	Finn	Teddy	Kuga

32 PIGEONS

1943			1944			1945		
White Vision	Winkie	Tyke	Beach Comber	Gustav	Paddy	Kenley Lass	Navy Blue	Flying Dutchman

1946						1947		
Tommy	All Alone	Princess	Mercury	NURP.38. BPC.6	GI Joe	Cologne	Duke of Normandy	NURP.43. CC.1418

5 HORSES

1947		
Olga	Upstart	Regal

2014	2016
Warrior	Reckless

An honorary award for all animals that served in World War I

1 CAT

1949
Simon

Awarded for gallantry under fire as HMS Amethyst's ship's cat and for the disposal of many rats despite shrapnel injuries

1 RAT

2020
Magawa

Awarded for life-saving devotion to duty, in the location and clearance of deadly landmines in Cambodia

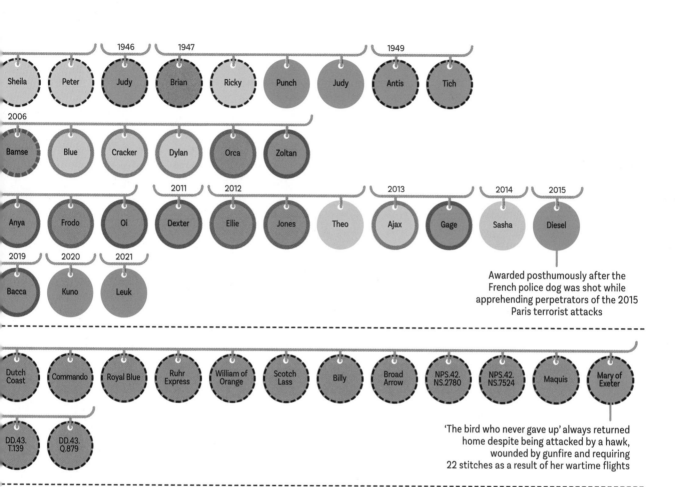

Awarded posthumously after the French police dog was shot while apprehending perpetrators of the 2015 Paris terrorist attacks

'The bird who never gave up' always returned home despite being attacked by a hawk, wounded by gunfire and requiring 22 stitches as a result of her wartime flights

What's the bravest animal?

Both the Dickin Medal, for military service animals, and the Gold Medal, for civilian creatures, recognise outstanding courage by our furry and feathered friends. We've charted every recipient of the animal equivalent of the Victoria and George Crosses to see which creatures are the most courageous

How it works: Listed above is every recipient of the PDSA Dickin Medal for military bravery by an animal and the PDSA Gold Medal for civilian bravery by an animal as awarded by veterinary charity the PDSA. Recipients are grouped by species

1944 denotes the year of the award and recipients are colour-coded according to the act recognised:
● Boosting morale ● Courage/fighting ● Delivering messages/supplies/raising alarm
● Finding/rescuing ● Honorary award ● Parachute missions ● Patrolling

 Awarded for service in WWII

 Awarded for civilian service

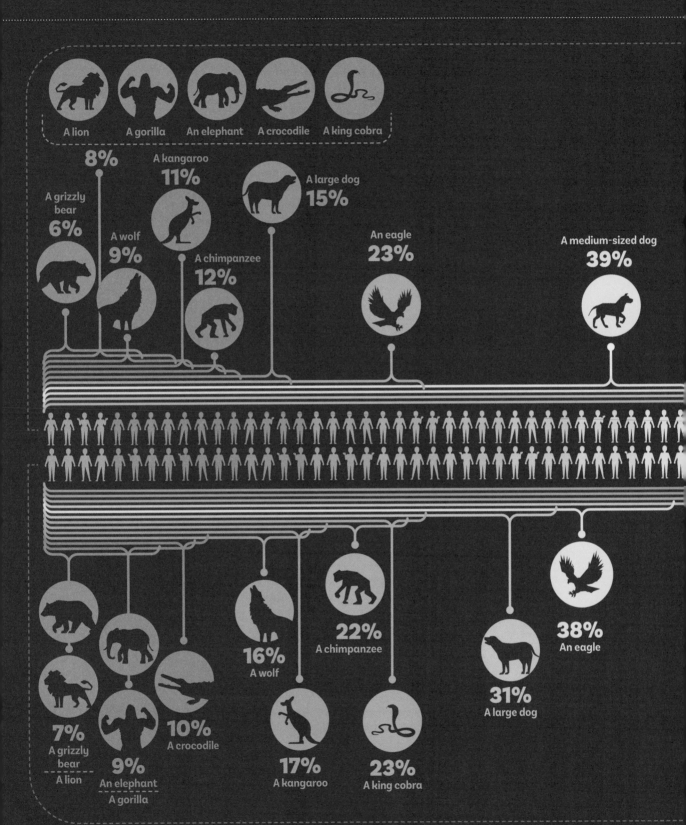

A lion
A gorilla
An elephant
A crocodile
A king cobra

8%
A grizzly bear **6%**
A wolf **9%**
A kangaroo **11%**
A chimpanzee **12%**
A large dog **15%**
An eagle **23%**
A medium-sized dog **39%**

7%
A grizzly bear
A lion
9%
An elephant
A gorilla
10%
A crocodile
16%
A wolf
22%
A chimpanzee
17%
A kangaroo
23%
A king cobra
31%
A large dog
38%
An eagle

Could you beat a goose in a fight?

A poll asked Americans whether they could defeat certain creatures in unarmed combat – and we've mapped the results. Disclaimer: We do not condone starting fights with animals, no matter how disrespectful a goose, eagle or gorilla has been to you

How it works: We've plotted the results of a poll of 1,224 US adults conducted in 2021 and split them by sex. The figures have been weighted to be representative of all US adults

Source: YouGov America

Proportion of US women who think they could beat...

A goose
51%

A house cat
64%

A rat
68%

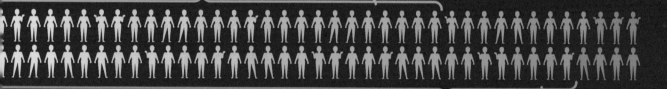

60%
A medium-sized dog

71%
A goose

74%
A house cat

76%
A rat

Proportion of US men who think they could beat...

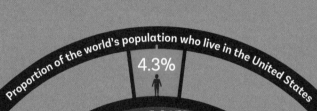

Proportion of the world's population who live in the United States

4.3%

46%

**Proportion of the world's civilian-owned guns
that are in the United States**

Who's got all the guns?

It is estimated that there are nearly 400 million guns in the US, which has by far the worst gun-violence problem of any developed nation. Changing the country's unique relationship with gun ownership will be an uphill task

How it works: Charts based on latest available data

Sources: BBC, Billboard, Centers for Disease Control and Prevention, Everytown, FBI, Flemish Peace Institute, IBISWorld, McDonald's, Small Arms Survey, Starbucks, US Department of Justice

21 Age at which you can legally buy a bottle of beer in the US

18 Age at which you can legally buy an AR-15 assault rifle in most US states

Millions of firearm background checks in the US in 2010

 14.4

39.7

Millions of firearm background checks in the US in 2020

Number of McDonald's and Starbucks outlets in the US combined

28,970

 **55,891**

Number of licensed gun traders in the US

Estimated number of Europeans killed annually by other Europeans with guns

 1,000

 **14,414**

Average number of Americans killed annually by other Americans with guns

Box office revenue in North America in 2019

$11.4 billion

 **$19.2 billion**

Average annual revenue of the US gun and ammunition manufacturing industry

US children and teenagers killed in car accidents in 2019

3,233

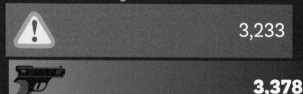 **3,378**

US children and teenagers killed by firearms in 2019, the leading cause of death for people aged 19 and under

How bad is the gun problem in the US?

Mass shootings have become a frighteningly regular occurrence in the United States. An analysis of mass shootings in 2017, a year in which the country experienced its deadliest ever such event, maps the trail of destruction left by gun violence across the nation

How it works: On the right we've charted all 427 mass shootings that were recorded in the US in 2017. A mass shooting is defined by crowd-sourced US database the Mass Shooting Tracker as an incident in which four or more people are shot. Numbers of fatalities are represented by the black bars on the outer ring; injuries from gunfire are represented in dark red. Days without a mass shooting are marked on the central ring in white

Source: Mass Shooting Tracker

How bad was America's worst mass shooting?

The deadliest mass shooting in US history took place on 1st October 2017, when a gunman fired into the crowd at the Route 91 Harvest festival from the 32nd floor of Las Vegas's Mandalay Bay hotel

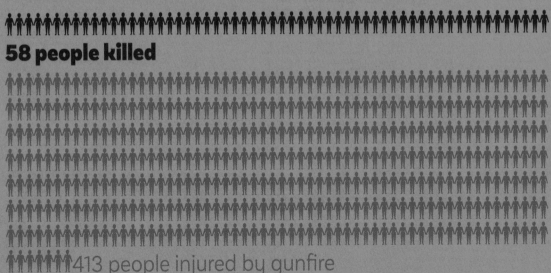

58 people killed

413 people injured by gunfire

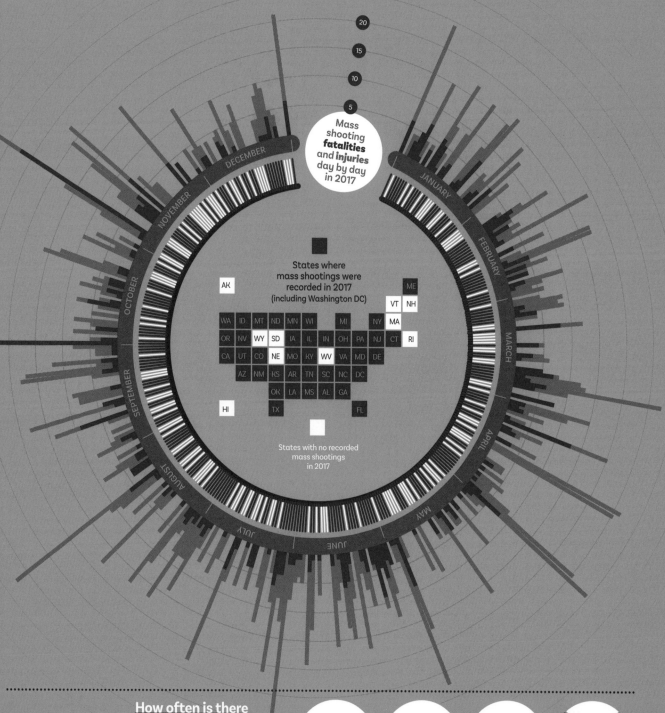

20
15
10
5

Mass
shooting
fatalities
and **injuries**
day by day
in 2017

DECEMBER
NOVEMBER
OCTOBER
SEPTEMBER
AUGUST
JULY
JUNE
MAY
APRIL
MARCH
FEBRUARY
JANUARY

States where
mass shootings were
recorded in 2017
(including Washington DC)

| AK | | | | | | | | | | ME |

| | | | | | | | | VT | NH |

WA	ID	MT	ND	MN	WI		MI		NY	MA
OR	NV	WY	SD	IA	IL	IN	OH	PA	NJ	CT	RI
CA	UT	CO	NE	MO	KY	WV	VA	MD	DE
	AZ	NM	KS	AR	TN	SC	NC	DC
		OK	LA	MS	AL	GA
HI		TX				FL

States with no recorded
mass shootings
in 2017

How often is there a mass shooting in the US?

While 2017 was the year with the worst single
incident, **days without mass shootings** have been
increasingly scarce in recent years:

135
IN 2017

123
IN 2018

116
IN 2019

86
IN 2020

Which war cost the US the most?

In April 2021 President Joe Biden announced that American operations in Afghanistan, the US's longest military engagement, would come to an end. But how does it compare to other wars in terms of Americans killed or wounded in action?

How it works: We've visualised the number of US troops who suffered non-mortal injuries or were classed as a 'battle death', 'other death (in theater)' or 'other death in service (non-theater)' by the US Office of Public Affairs in major conflicts (1,900+ US casualties) since 1861. The Gulf War = Operation Desert Shield and Operation Desert Storm; Afghanistan = Operation Enduring Freedom and Operation Freedom's Sentinel; the Iraq War = Operation Iraqi Freedom and Operation New Dawn. Civil War deaths and injuries are based on incomplete data

Sources: American Battlefields Trust, US Department of Defense, US Department of Veterans Affairs, US Office of Public Affairs

American Civil War
1861-1865

476,000
X498,332

What's the daily cost of war?

Average number of non-mortal injuries and deaths per day of warfare

Civil War	Vietnam War
326 X342	39 X23
World War I	**Gulf War**
349 X200	2 X9
World War II	**Afghanistan**
493 X298	3 X0.3
Korean War	**Iraq War**
92 X48	10 X1

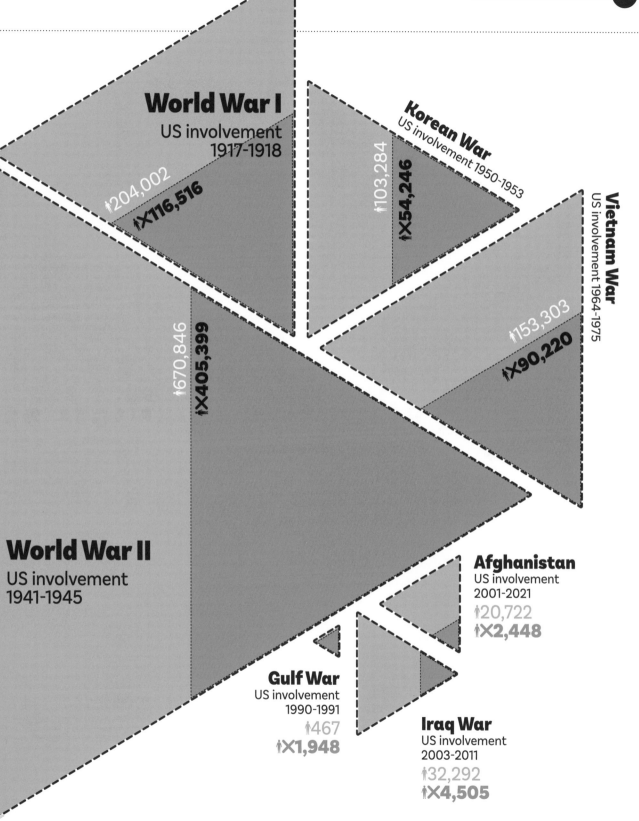

World War I
US involvement
1917-1918

↑204,002
↑X116,516

Korean War
US involvement 1950-1953

↑103,284
↑X54,246

Vietnam War
US involvement 1964-1975

↑153,303
↑X90,220

↑670,846
↑X405,399

World War II
US involvement
1941-1945

Afghanistan
US involvement
2001-2021

↑20,722
↑X2,448

Gulf War
US involvement
1990-1991

↑467
↑X1,948

Iraq War
US involvement
2003-2011

↑32,292
↑X4,505

Canned food

Struggling to deliver food to troops on the frontline in 1795 during the French Revolutionary Wars, the government of France held a competition to solve the problem. Chef Nicolas Appert won with his designs for mass-produced airtight glass jars and meat packed in tin cans

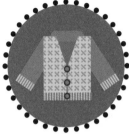

Cardigans

Produced to help British troops through the cold Ukrainian winter during the Crimean War, this staple of many a modern wardrobe was named after Lord Cardigan, who led the Charge of the Light Brigade

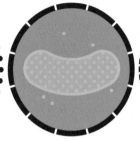

Cheetos

Investigating ways to reduce the weight and volume of food for troops during World War II, the US Army tried dehydrating foods, including cheese. The resulting powder was used for making sauces at the front and in 1948 was adapted to create the popular brand of cheesy crisp

Disposable sanitary pads

Developed by American manufacturer Kimberly-Clark, Cellucotton was an ultra-absorbent fabric used to dress wounds in World War I. Red Cross nurses soon began to use Cellucotton for menstrual hygiene and after the war Kimberly-Clark began mass-producing sanitary pads and tampons

Duct tape

In 1943, ammunition factory worker Vesta Stoudt, mother of two sons serving in the US Navy, realised that the seals on cartridge cases were time-consuming to open. Worried the delay would cost lives, she helped come up with a waterproof alternative that could be quickly and easily removed

War: what is it good for?

While wars have cost the lives of hundreds of millions of people, they have also led to the creation of a surprising array of everyday objects

Sources: BBC, Combat-Ready Kitchen by Anastacia Marx De Salcedo, Vice, Washington Post

Plastic surgery

The world's first cosmetic procedure was performed in 1917 by New Zealand surgeon Harold Gillies, who grafted skin over the cordite facial burns Walter Yeo suffered at the Battle of Jutland

Ready-made guacamole

Developed by the US Army with corporations including Mars and Unilever in the mid '90s, high-pressure processing preserves food for distribution to far-flung war zones. One of the first foods to undergo the process was the avocado, allowing for the creation of ready-to-eat guacamole that stays green

Salad in a bag

Developed by Whirlpool and the US Navy to send lettuce to troops in Vietnam, modified-atmosphere packaging extends the shelf life of food by substituting air inside its package with a gas mixture. Used in containers during the war, it was later adapted to individual packages, allowing for bagged salad to hit the shelves

Silly Putty

With US rubber supplies from East Asia cut off during World War II, American engineer James Wright attempted to develop synthetic rubber with boric acid and silicone oil. No practical military use could be found for the resulting gooey substance, but it was repackaged in a distinctive red egg and sold as a toy

Slinky springs

While looking for a way to keep breakable equipment steady on ships in 1945, American Navy mechanical engineer Richard James accidentally knocked a torsion spring off a shelf. Struck by the way it appeared to 'walk' off its perch, James was inspired to create the popular toy

EpiPens

Developed by American medical equipment researcher Sheldon Kaplan in the mid-1970s as a way of administering the antidote to new Soviet nerve agent, the EpiPen was approved for public use in 1987 and has come to the aid of countless allergy sufferers since

Insect repellent

Looking for a way to protect soldiers serving in the South Pacific against catching mosquito-borne diseases such as malaria during World War II, research scientists Lyle Goodhue and William Sullivan developed an aerosol which deployed a fine mist of insecticide

Memory foam

In 1966 at the height of the Cold War and the Space Race, inventor Charles Yost was charged by NASA with creating seats that would increase the chances of pilots surviving a crash. The result was memory foam, which is now used in everything from prosthetic limbs to mattresses

Microwave ovens

In 1945, while working on a wartime radar machine fitted with a magnetron, US engineer Percy Spencer noticed that a chocolate bar in his pocket had been melted by the microwaves it emitted. Intrigued, he began experimenting and patented the design for the first microwave oven a year later

Pilates

Interned on the Isle of Man as an enemy alien at the start of World War I, German bodybuilder Joseph Hubertus Pilates developed his own system of stretches to keep fit. After his release he taught his technique to the world

How it works: We've illustrated a selection of objects that can trace their origins back to military developments for specific conflicts. Inventions are colour-coded by category. The line around each invention denotes the era of conflict it came from

- ● Body and health
- ● **Clothing and comfort**
- ● Eating and drinking
- ● Manufacture and repair
- ● Toys and games

PRE-WORLD WAR I · WORLD WAR I · WORLD WAR II · COLD WAR AND VIETNAM · POST COLD WAR

Stainless steel

the search for harder alloys for weapons during World War I, the UK military called in English metallurgist Harry Brearley. His addition of chromium to molten iron produced a rustless metal that became stainless steel and changed cutlery the world over

Sun lamps

In 1918, when an estimated half of Berlin's children were suffering from rickets, German doctor Kurt Huldschinsky experimented with exposing sufferers to ultraviolet light. This provided them with much-needed vitamin D and eventually led to the tanning salon

Superglue

In 1942 American chemist Harry Coover was trying to develop a material that could be used for sights on military rifles. The resulting compound, cyanoacrylate, was too sticky for the job, but was repurposed as superglue, the saviour of many a smashed vase

TV dinners

Strato-Plates were complete frozen meals designed by America's Maxson Food Systems to be reheated on planes for troops heading to or from the front during World War II. Founder William L Maxson died before his idea could be developed for the retail market, but others took it and ran with it

Vegetarian sausages

To help combat Germany's wartime food shortages, in 1916 the mayor of Cologne, Konrad Adenauer (who would later become German Chancellor), invented the Kölner Wurst, a meat-free sausage made with soya, flour, corn, barley and ground rice. It was not well received

Do you love your neighbour?

The Eurovision Song Contest was launched to promote cooperation between European countries in the years following World War II, but do countries vote for the best song - or is regional solidarity a bigger vote-winner than a catchy chorus? We reveal who's given each other the most points in finals since the contest began in 1956

How it works: We've mapped all the countries that have ever competed in the Eurovision Song Contest into regional blocs:

- WESTERN
- NORTHERN
- EASTERN
- SOUTH EASTERN
- SOUTH-WESTERN
- THE OUTSIDERS (competing countries outside Europe)

The arrows point to the country each nation has given the largest number of points to between the first contest in 1956 and the 2021 event. Each arrow's weight denotes the percentage of available points that total represents.

 25-49% 50-74% **75% or more** of available points

If a country has historically given the largest percentages of its points to a country that no longer exists (eg Yugoslavia) then the second largest percentage is shown.

Source: The Eurovision Song Contest Database

 Mutual admiration society: Participants who are each other's all-time favourite country

Breaking rank: Countries whose favourite is outside their bloc

 Iceland

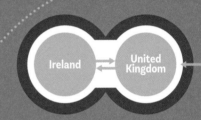 Ireland — United Kingdom

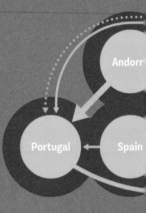 Andorra / Portugal / Spain

 Morocco

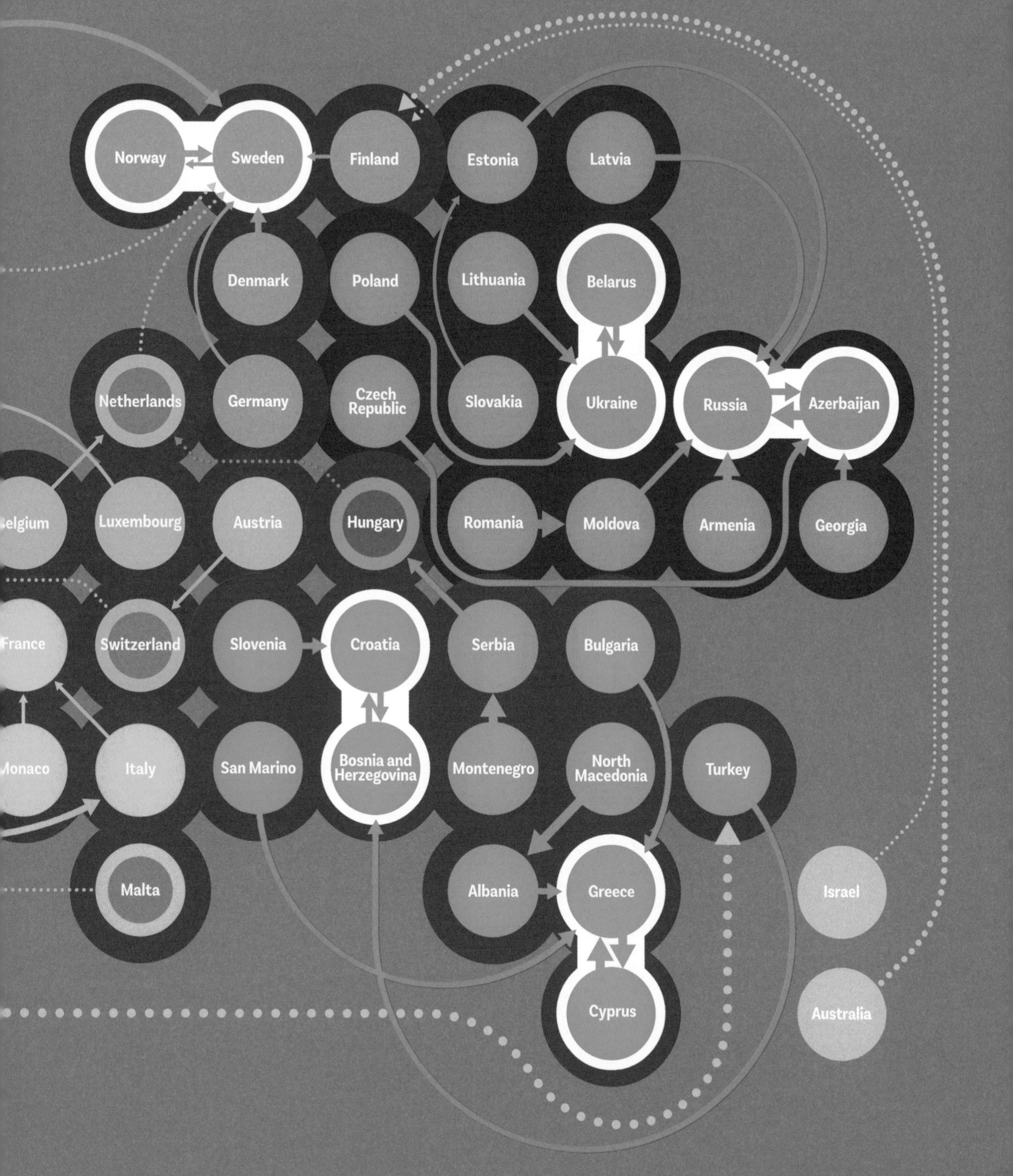

Norway
Sweden
Finland
Estonia
Latvia
Denmark
Poland
Lithuania
Belarus
Netherlands
Germany
Czech Republic
Slovakia
Ukraine
Russia
Azerbaijan
elgium
Luxembourg
Austria
Hungary
Romania
Moldova
Armenia
Georgia
France
Switzerland
Slovenia
Croatia
Serbia
Bulgaria
Ionaco
Italy
San Marino
Bosnia and Herzegovina
Montenegro
North Macedonia
Turkey
Malta
Albania
Greece
Israel
Cyprus
Australia

ANY OTHER QUESTIONS

Questions about odds, sods
and miscellanea

Apptimistic

(adj) Confident and hopeful that an app will work as it is supposed to

Beerboarding

(n) Attempting to extract information from a person by getting them drunk

Borringe

(v) To borrow something and then lose it: you then cringe every time you meet the lender

Carcolepsy

(n) A condition causing a passenger to fall asleep soon after a car journey begins

Carpet treader

(n) An estate agent's term for a time waster

What's a kiddle?

Every year Collins accepts online proposals for new words to be included in updates of its English dictionary: we've trawled through a decade of suggestions to find the finest neologisms that have been vying for inclusion

How it works: Words are colour-coded according to category:
● Animals ● Business ● Domestic and leisure ● Science and technology ● Society and politics

Source: Collins English Dictionary's online suggestions hub

Heircat

(n) When a cat inherits the wealth or property of its deceased owner

Hepeating

(n) When a woman's suggestion is overlooked, but accepted when repeated by a man

Idinnerary

(n) The schedule of evening meals for a holiday or business trip

Investigoogle

(v) To investigate or research using an online search engine

Jealivation

(n) Motivation that comes from jealousy, on account of others' success

Octogator

(n) An alligator with eight legs

Päntsdrunk

(n) Finnish practice in which one removes one's trousers and drinks alcohol in the comfort of one's home

Phub

(v) To snub someone by not giving them your full attention because you are looking at your mobile phone

Scurryfunge

(n) A hasty tidying of the house between seeing the neighbour coming and hearing them knock on the door

Shrobe

(v) To wear one's coat as a cape or draped off the shoulder

Chadults

(n) Children who have grown up to be adults

Chairdrobe

(n) A pile of clothes left on a chair. See also 'floordrobe'

Datachondriac

(n) A person who constantly thinks their computer is infected with some kind of virus

Dispunctional

(adj) Congenitally incapable of being on time

Epiphanot

(n) An idea that seems like an amazing insight to the conceiver, but is in fact pointless, stupid or incorrect

Factronise

(v) To patronise a person using facts. Can't believe you didn't know that

Floiter

(v) Of a flying insect or bird: to hover around an object for no reason

Gramping

(n) Camping with three generations of one's family

Granddog

(n) Canine with similar status to a grandchild

Handwavy

(adj) Of a proof, demo or explanation: missing important details or logical steps

Kayaktivist

(n) A protester in a kayak

Kiddle

(n) A kiss and a cuddle at the same time

Lukewarmer

(n) Person who believes in global warming, but not as a catastrophic phenomenon

Nonfrontational

(adj) Initially avoiding direct confrontation, but then posting your discontent on social media

Noseblind

(adj) Lacking the ability to use the sense of smell

Stagmin

(n) The admin involved in organising a stag weekend

Unfluencer

(n) Social media influencer who makes you want to stop doing something

Woemance

(n) A toxic relationship characterised by constant moaning about one's partner

Yote

(v) Past tense of yeet, to throw with force or lob eg I yote the bottle at the wall earlier

Youthanize

(v) To rebrand a product to appeal to a younger audience

How much for the Eiffel Tower?

While we aren't suggesting you steal the world's greatest metal monuments and sell them for scrap, we thought you might like to know what you could expect to clear from doing so

How it works: We've taken the weight of metal in a number of monuments and multiplied each tonnage by the latest available price you could receive for the materials at a metal-recycling centre. Monuments are drawn to scale against human figures (average human height 1.65 metres)

Sources: Arup, BBC, Encyclopedia Britannica, Flushing Meadows Park, Guggenheim Bilbao Museum, Indian Express, Musée Rodin, National Museum of the History of Ukraine in the Second World War, Queen Elizabeth Olympic Park, Quid Pro Quo: Assessing the Value of Berlin's Thälmann Monument by Kristine Nielsen, Société d'Exploitation de la Tour Eiffel, US National Park Service, Visit Falkirk Value information based on UK scrap prices from Reclamet Ltd as of 1st June 2021

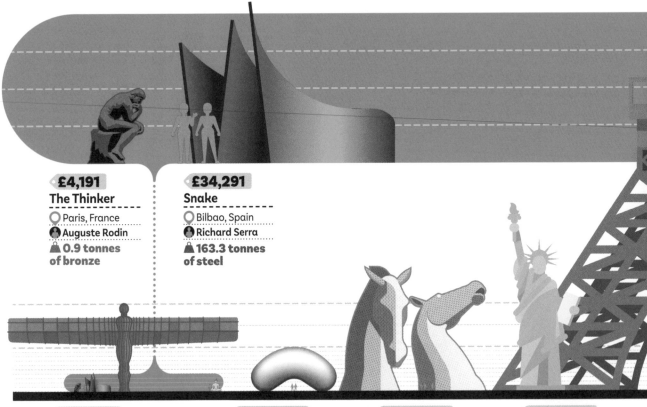

£4,191
The Thinker
Paris, France
Auguste Rodin
0.9 tonnes of bronze

£34,291
Snake
Bilbao, Spain
Richard Serra
163.3 tonnes of steel

£43,680
Angel of the North
Gateshead, UK
Antony Gormley
208 tonnes of steel

£110,000
Cloud Gate
Chicago, US
Anish Kapoor
100 tonnes of stainless steel

£126,000
The Kelpies
Falkirk, Scotland
Andy Scott
600 tonnes of steel

£170,005
Statue of Liberty
New York, US
Frédéric Auguste Bartholdi
28.1 tonnes of copper

£1,533,000
Eiffel Tower
Paris, France
Gustave Eiffel
7,300 tonnes of iron

£6,050,000
Spring Temple Buddha
Zhaocun, China
Unknown
1,000 tonnes of copper

£335,225,000
Phra Phuttha Maha Suwanna Patimakon
(aka Golden Buddha)
Bangkok, Thailand
Unknown
5.5 tonnes of gold

£180,480
The Motherland Monument
Kiev, Ukraine
Yevgeny Vuchetich
90 tonnes of stainless steel
and 388 tonnes of steel

£231,000
Ernst Thälmann monument
Berlin, Germany
Lev Kerbel
50 tonnes of bronze

£420,000
ArcelorMittal Orbit
London, UK
Anish Kapoor and Cecil Balmond
2,000 tonnes of steel

How much water is turned into wine?

A surprisingly large amount of water goes into the production of everyday foodstuffs. But how much went into your favourite tipple – and where did it come from?

How it works: We've proportionally represented the average global water footprint of food and drink items. National and local footprints will vary considerably, particularly for animal products, as different feed types contain different embedded water levels

- Total water footprint predominantly made up of 'green water' (from precipitation, stored in soil and incorporated by plants)
- **Proportion of footprint that comes from 'blue water'** (from surface or groundwater resources)
- **Proportion of footprint that comes from 'grey water'** (the water needed to assimilate pollutants)

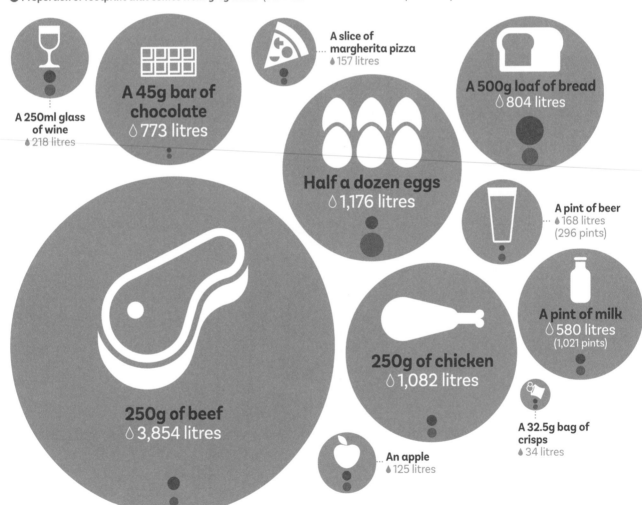

A 250ml glass of wine
◊ 218 litres

A 45g bar of chocolate
◊ 773 litres

A slice of margherita pizza
◊ 157 litres

A 500g loaf of bread
◊ 804 litres

Half a dozen eggs
◊ 1,176 litres

A pint of beer
◊ 168 litres
(296 pints)

250g of beef
◊ 3,854 litres

250g of chicken
◊ 1,082 litres

A pint of milk
◊ 580 litres
(1,021 pints)

An apple
◊ 125 litres

A 32.5g bag of crisps
◊ 34 litres

Source: Water Footprint Network and Arjen Hoekstra

How fast is the world's fastest computer?

In 2020 Japan's Fugaku supercomputer was officially declared the world's fastest. It's 2.8 times faster than IBM's Summit, which held the record from 2018 to 2020. But exactly how speedy is the new king of the petaflops?

How it works: Fugaku is illustrated below, alongside a mathematician trying to match its performance

Sources: BBC, Live Science

415.53 Speed of Fugaku in petaflops
(a petaflop = a quadrillion mathematical operations per second)

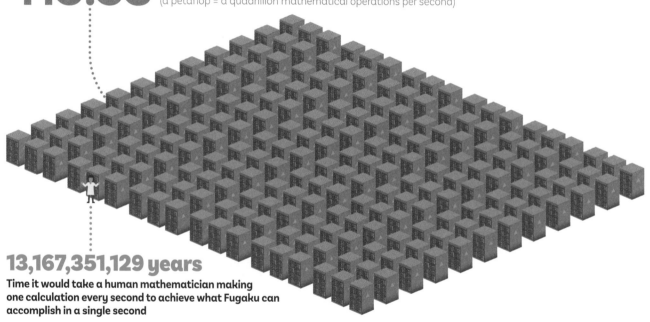

13,167,351,129 years
Time it would take a human mathematician making one calculation every second to achieve what Fugaku can accomplish in a single second

How fast is 5G?

China's new 5G networks have reported an average download speed of 125 megabytes per second. Here's how that compares to previous mobile-data generations

How it works: We've calculated the time it would take to download an average episode of *Friends* (333MB) over different generations of mobile network

Source: Digital Trends

1991	2000	2007	2009	2013	2019
2G	**3G**	**3G+**	**4G**	**4G+**	**5G**
7 hours 24 minutes	29 minutes 36 seconds	8 minutes 53 seconds	4 minutes 26 seconds	2 minutes 58 seconds	3 seconds

What's love got to do with it?

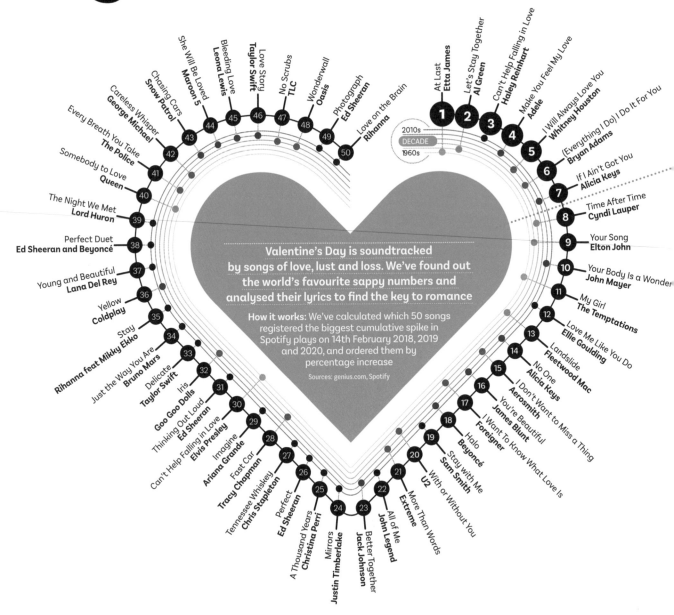

Valentine's Day is soundtracked by songs of love, lust and loss. We've found out the world's favourite sappy numbers and analysed their lyrics to find the key to romance

How it works: We've calculated which 50 songs registered the biggest cumulative spike in Spotify plays on 14th February 2018, 2019 and 2020, and ordered them by percentage increase

Sources: genius.com, Spotify

DECADE
2010s
1960s

1 At Last **Etta James**
2 Let's Stay Together **Al Green**
3 Can't Help Falling in Love **Haley Reinhart**
4 Make You Feel My Love **Adele**
5 I Will Always Love You **Whitney Houston**
6 (Everything I Do) I Do It For You **Bryan Adams**
7 If I Ain't Got You **Alicia Keys**
8 Time After Time **Cyndi Lauper**
9 Your Song **Elton John**
10 Your Body Is a Wonder **John Mayer**
11 My Girl **The Temptations**
12 Love Me Like You Do **Ellie Goulding**
13 Landslide **Fleetwood Mac**
14 No One **Alicia Keys**
15 I Don't Want to Miss a Thing **Aerosmith**
16 You're Beautiful **James Blunt**
17 I Want To Know What Love Is **Foreigner**
18 Halo **Beyoncé**
19 Stay with Me **Sam Smith**
20 With or Without You **U2**
21 More Than Words **Extreme**
22 All of Me **John Legend**
23 Better Together **Jack Johnson**
24 Mirrors **Justin Timberlake**
25 A Thousand Years **Christina Perri**
26 Perfect **Ed Sheeran**
27 Fast Car **Tracy Chapman**
28 Tennessee Whiskey **Chris Stapleton**
29 Imagine **Ariana Grande**
30 Can't Help Falling in Love **Elvis Presley**
31 Thinking Out Loud **Ed Sheeran**
32 Iris **Goo Goo Dolls**
33 Delicate **Taylor Swift**
34 Just the Way You Are **Bruno Mars**
35 Stay **Rihanna feat Mikky Ekko**
36 Yellow **Coldplay**
37 Young and Beautiful **Lana Del Rey**
38 Perfect Duet **Ed Sheeran and Beyoncé**
39 The Night We Met **Lord Huron**
40 Somebody to Love **Queen**
41 Every Breath You Take **The Police**
42 Careless Whisper **George Michael**
43 Chasing Cars **Snow Patrol**
44 She Will Be Loved **Maroon 5**
45 Bleeding Love **Leona Lewis**
46 Love Story **Taylor Swift**
47 No Scrubs **TLC**
48 Wonderwall **Oasis**
49 Photograph **Ed Sheeran**
50 Love on the Brain **Rihanna**

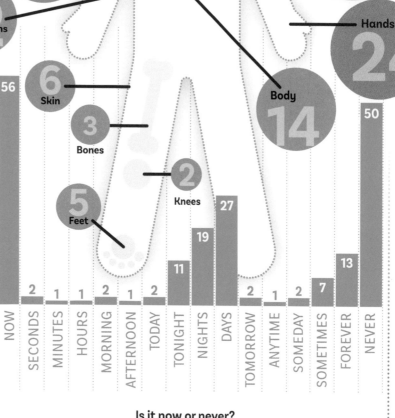

What are they singing about?

Number of references made to organs, limbs, assorted body parts and associated words in the lyrics of our top 50 songs

4 Tears

13 Brain/mind

5 Hair

33 Eyes

16 Head

19 Face

9 Breath

3 Lips

38 Heart

17 Smile

12 Arms

24 Hands

6 Skin

3 Bones

14 Body

5 Feet

2 Knees

Top 50 lyrical analysis

ME/YOU
7,513 | **930**

Is it you or me?

References to 'me', 'myself', 'I', etc vs references to 'you', 'your', 'yourself', etc

SHE 76 | **HE 40**

Who are they singing about?

Mentions of 'she', 'her', 'woman', 'girl' etc vs mentions of 'he', 'his', 'man', 'boy' etc

NOW	SECONDS	MINUTES	HOURS	MORNING	AFTERNOON	TODAY	TONIGHT	NIGHTS	DAYS	TOMORROW	ANYTIME	SOMEDAY	SOMETIMES	FOREVER	NEVER
56	2	1	1	2	1	2	11	19	27	2	1	2	7	13	50

Is it now or never?

Lyrical references to specific times and time periods in the top 50 songs

Who's your favourite royal?

The Queen's a popular head of state, but her subjects are more divided when it comes to other senior members of the House of Windsor. Although they're pretty unanimous about who they like the least...

MOST POPULAR OVERALL ♥

Senior members of the royal family	MOST POPULAR WITH MEN	MOST POPULAR WITH WOMEN	MOST POPULAR WITH BABY BOOMERS	MOST POPULAR WITH GEN X-ERS	MOST POPULAR WITH MILLENNIALS
Queen Elizabeth II	The Queen	The Queen	The Queen	The Queen	The Queen
Charles, Prince of Wales	William	Catherine	William	William	Harry
Camilla, Duchess of Cornwall	Catherine	William	Anne	Catherine	Catherine
Prince William, Duke of Cambridge	Anne	Anne	Catherine	Anne	William
Catherine, Duchess of Cambridge	Harry	Harry	Sophie	Harry	Meghan
Prince Harry, Duke of Sussex	Charles	Camilla	Charles	Charles	Anne
Meghan, Duchess of Sussex	Meghan	Sophie	Camilla	Camilla	Camilla
Prince Andrew, Duke of York	Camilla	Charles	Edward	Sophie	Eugenie
Princess Beatrice	Beatrice	Eugenie	Harry	Beatrice	Beatrice
Princess Eugenie	Edward	Edward	Eugenie	Meghan	Charles
Prince Edward, Earl of Wessex	Sophie	Beatrice	Beatrice	Edward	Edward
Sophie, Countess of Wessex	Eugenie	Meghan	Meghan	Eugenie	Sophie
Princess Anne	Andrew	Andrew	Andrew	Andrew	Andrew

1 The Queen
2 William
3 Catherine
4 Anne
5 Harry
6 Charles
7 Camilla
8 Meghan
9 Sophie
10 Beatrice
11 Edward
12 Eugenie
13 Andrew

How it works: The tables above rank the popularity of British royal family members according to different demographic groups in the UK in May 2021

Source: YouGov polling as of May 2021

Is brevity the soul of wit?

Every year an award is handed out for the top one-liner joke told at the Edinburgh Fringe. To allow you to judge whether brevity really is the soul of wit, we've placed the last ten winners in order of snappiness

How it works: We've listed the winners of the Dave's Funniest Joke of the Fringe award - awarded to the best one-liners performed at the Edinburgh Festival Fringe - between 2010 and 2019 and ordered them by the number of syllables each contains

Stewart Francis
◀ 2012
💬 13 syllables
❝ You know who really gives kids a bad name? Posh and Becks. ❞

Darren Walsh
◀ 2015
💬 16 syllables
❝ I just deleted all the German names off my phone. It's Hans free. ❞

Tim Vine
◀ 2014
💬 17 syllables
❝ I've decided to sell my Hoover... well, it was just collecting dust. ❞

Ken Cheng
◀ 2017
💬 17 syllables
❝ I'm not a fan of the new pound coin, but then again, I hate all change. ❞

Tim Vine
◀ 2010
💬 21 syllables
❝ I've just been on a once-in-a-lifetime holiday. I'll tell you what - never again. ❞

Nick Helm
◀ 2011
💬 21 syllables
❝ I needed a password eight characters long so I picked Snow White and the Seven Dwarves. ❞

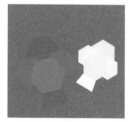

Olaf Falafel
◀ 2019
💬 23 syllables
❝ I keep randomly shouting out 'Broccoli' and 'Cauliflower'. I think I might have Florets. ❞

Masai Graham
◀ 2016
💬 24 syllables
❝ My dad has suggested that I register for a donor card. He's a man after my own heart. ❞

Rob Auton
◀ 2013
💬 29 syllables
❝ I heard a rumour that Cadbury is bringing out an oriental chocolate bar. Could be a Chinese Wispa. ❞

Adam Rowe
◀ 2018
💬 29 syllables
❝ Working at the job centre has to be a tense job - knowing that if you get fired, you still have to come in the next day. ❞

Source: Dave

Which are better, cats or dogs?

The world's furriest foes face off: which have the greater number of pedigrees, the most Instagram followers and the bragging rights on space travel?

Cats **v** Dogs

Cats		Dogs
VARIETY		
✕ 73	Number of pedigree domestic species	354 ★
★ 36	Number of wild species	35 ✕
AS PETS		
★ £12,000	Average lifetime cost of keeping one	£30,800 ✕
★ 10.9 million	Number of pets in the UK	10.1 million ✕
LANGUAGE & LITERATURE		
✕ 32	Mentions per million words in books*	58 ★
✕ 25	Appearances in popular idioms**	35 ★
PRICIEST		
✕ Cato, UK £29,678	Most expensive ever bought	£1,074,382 Big Splash, China ★
RECORD BREAKERS		
✕ 24	Most tricks performed in a minute	36 ★
✕ 1	Total number who have gone to space	7 ★
NOTABLE INDIVIDUALS		
✕ Blackie, UK £7 million	Recipient of largest inheritance	£43 million Gunther III, Germany ★
★ Creme Puff, US 38	Oldest ever	29 Bluey, Australia ✕
✕ nala_cat, US 4.3 million	Most Instagram followers	9 million Jiffpom, US ★

4 🐱 **v** 🐶 8

How it works: We've compared the latest available figures across 12 categories, awarding a point to the winner of each. The difference between cats and dogs is shown proportionally, with the winning total occupying the full bar. Cost of keeping is striped because the larger number represents a negative attribute

*Google Ngram, 1800-2019 **In Oxford Dictionary of English Idioms. Extra sources: BBC, Business Insider, Fédération Cynologique Internationale, Guinness World Records, The International Cat Association, IUCN, PDSA

What have Donald Trump and Jesus got in common?

Heavily edited Wikipedia entries. But whose pages have been tinkered with the most overall? And how many tweaks have they received since they were first created?

How it works: We've illustrated Wikipedia's most edited pages for individuals and groups. Total edits as of 11th March 2021 are listed below

THE TEN PEOPLE/GROUPS WITH THE MOST EDITED WIKIPEDIA PAGES

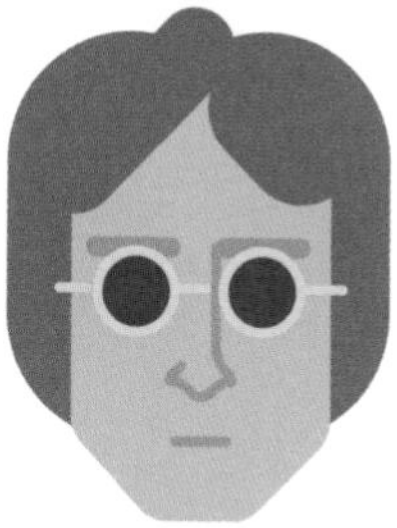

10

The Beatles

UK rock band

24,271

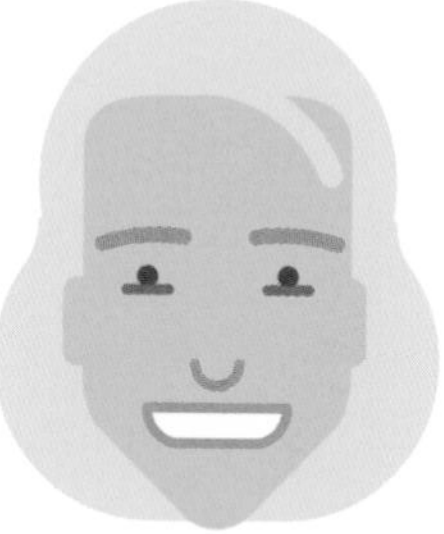

9

Britney Spears

US pop star

25,773

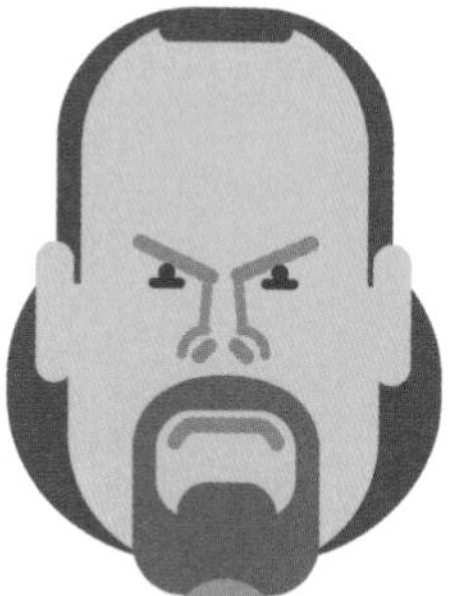

8

The Undertaker

US wrestler and actor

25,837

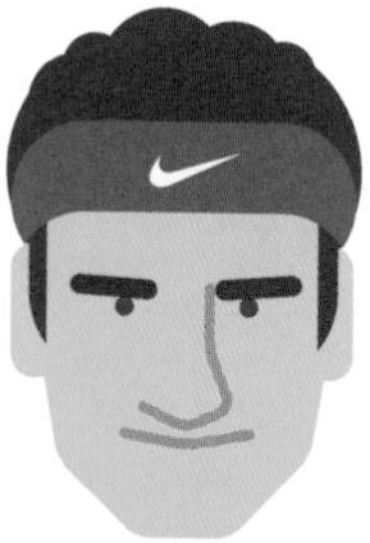

7

Roger Federer

Swiss tennis player

25,944

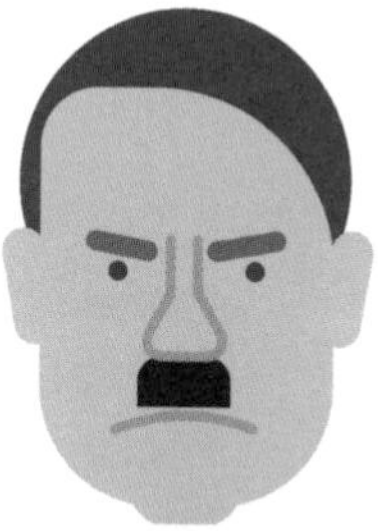

6

Adolf Hitler

Dictator of Germany

26,904

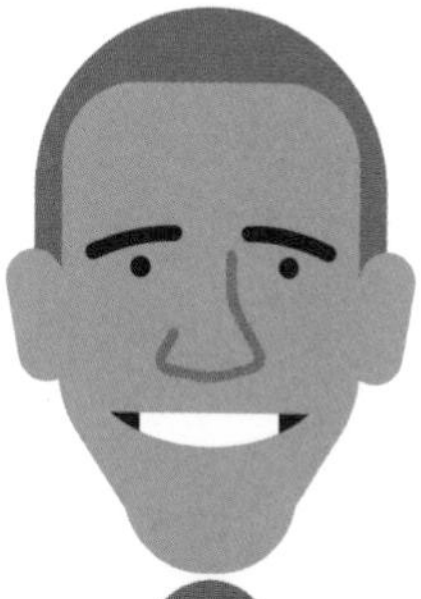

5

Barack Obama

44th US president

28,094

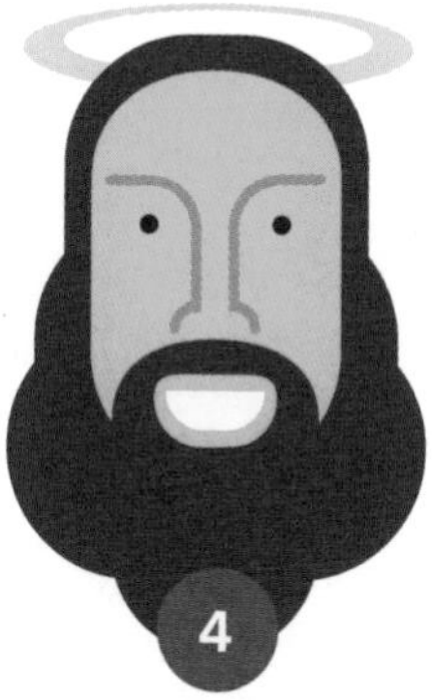

4

Jesus

Son of God

30,697

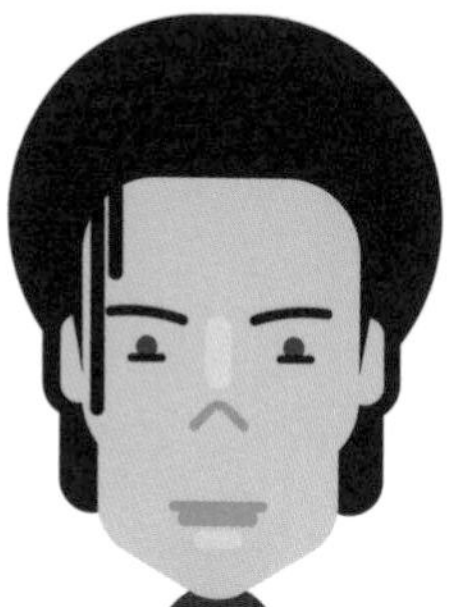

3

Michael Jackson

US pop star

31,324

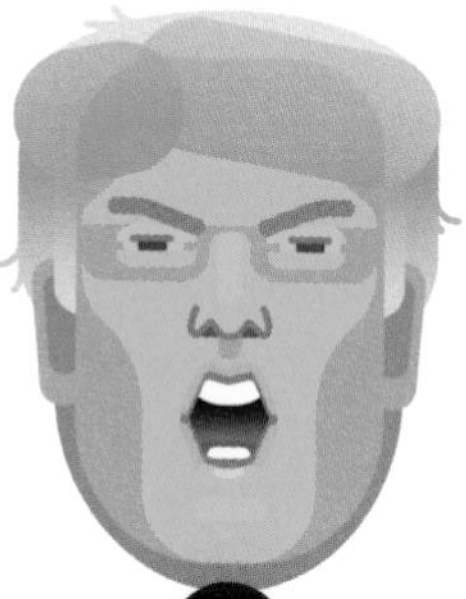

2

Donald Trump

45th US president

35,635

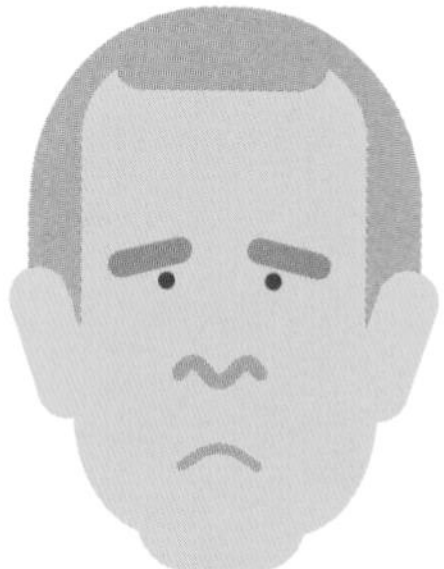

1

George W Bush

43rd US president

47,252

Source: Wikipedia

Aren't we all a little bit Irish sometimes?

To many in the United States, 17th March means only one thing: booze, and lots of it. But are Americans as Irish as their St Patrick's Day revelry would suggest?

Percentage of the US population with Irish ancestry

9.6%

Percentage of the US population who celebrated St Patrick's Day in 2019

55%

How it works: The pint glass is filled proportionately to illustrate figures taken from 2019, the last St Patrick's Day before festivities were curtailed by the Covid-19 pandemic

Sources: The National Retail Federation, US Census Bureau

Did you get your fingers burnt?

Three quarters of fireworks-related injuries in the US each year take place in the month around Independence Day. But what are people hurting?

Total number of injuries reported 21st June-21st July 2019:

7,300

How it works: The chart opposite represents the proportional breakdown of body parts hurt in firework-related, emergency-department-treated injuries

Hand/finger 30.1%
Leg 23.3%
Eye 15.1%
Head/face/ear 15.1%
Arm 9.6%
Trunk/other 6.8%

Source: Consumer Product Safety Commission

Is your cat ready for Halloween?

Halloween is big business in the US, with people decorating their homes, themselves and their pets

How it works: The ghostly figures are proportionally sized to represent estimated US spending on Halloween costumes in 2019

Adult costumes $1.51 billion
Children's costumes $1.16 billion
Pets' costumes $0.49 billion

Source: National Retail Federation

Do they know it's Christmas?

To answer Band Aid's tuneful question, we've mapped which countries mark Christmas with a national holiday. While we're on the subject of days off, we've also looked at which country gets the most annual nationwide public holidays – the UK's eight days a year seem quite meagre

How it works: We've marked on the map all countries and territories with a 2022 public holiday between 23rd and 28th December and/or between 6th and 8th January (Orthodox Christmas) in order to take account of any holiday being moved due to its falling on a weekend. Note that Christmas Day 2022 falls on a Sunday and that the number of holidays may change in years when this does not occur

For total public holiday days we have taken the average number of planned nationwide public holidays between 2021 and 2030. Holidays that fall on the local definition of a weekend are not counted

Source: The Oppstudio worldwide public holidays database

NORTH AMERICA

SOUTH AMERICA

 Has a national holiday on or near 25th December

 Has a holiday on or near Orthodox Christmas

 Has a holiday on or near both 25th December and Orthodox Christmas

 Does not have a holiday near 25th December or Orthodox Christmas

Who gets the most days off for Christmas?

Countries and territories with the most public holidays between 23rd and 28th December 2020 and between 6th and 8th January 2021:

Bulgaria – four days
Falkland Islands – four days

ASIA

EUROPE

AFRICA

OCEANIA

Who gets the most days off a year?

Countries/territories with highest annual average days
of nationwide non-weekend public holidays 2021-2030

Iran 24	A
Myanmar 23.6	B
Azerbaijan 18.4	C
Cambodia 18.3	D
Sri Lanka 17.9	E

Who gets the fewest days off a year?

Countries/territories with the lowest annual average days
of nationwide non-weekend public holidays 2021-2030

F Brazil 5.7
G Uruguay 5.6
H Eritrea 5.1
I **Pitcairn Islands** 4.7
J **Puerto Rico** 4.3

Eva Morris
 UK
8th Nov 1885
2nd Nov 2000
AGED 114
Oldest person for: **308 days**
? Whisky and boiled onions

Marie Brémont
FRANCE
25th Apr 1886
6th Jun 2001
AGED 115
Oldest person for: **216 days**
? Nothing divulged

Maud Farris-Luse
US
21st Jan 1887
18th Mar 2002
AGED 115
Oldest person for: **285 days**
? Going fishing

Grace Clawson
UK
15th Nov 1887
28th May 2002
AGED 114
Oldest person for: **71 days**
? Laughing a lot, coffee, no alcohol or tobacco

Adelina Domingues
CAPE VERDE
19th Feb 1888
21st Aug 2002
AGED 114
Oldest person for: **85 days**
? Vegetables and beans, no alcohol or tobacco

Mae Harrington
US
20th Jan 1889
29th Dec 2002
AGED 113
Oldest person for: **130 days**
? Nothing divulged

How can I live forever?

(Up to a maximum of 118 years)

If you're aiming to live beyond eleventy, why not take some advice from the most super of supercentenarians

How it works: We've listed every holder of the 'world's oldest person' title this millennium, colour-coded by 🌐 **birthplace**. We've included their **age at 💀 death**, **⏱ how long they held the title for** and the **❓reasons they gave for their longevity** in interviews. At the time of press the title holder was 118-year-old Kane Tanaka

Birthplace: ● **Africa** ● **Asia** (all Japan) ● **Caribbean/Latin America** ● **Europe** ● **North America**
Secrets: 🔆 Lifestyle/activities ✕ Food and drink ☺ Attitude 🚫 Abstinence ✝ Faith in God

Sources: BBC, CBS, The Guardian, Guinness World Records, LA Times, legacy.com, news.com.au, New York Times, The Daily Telegraph

WOMEN
MEN

Emma Tillman
US
22nd Nov 1892
28th Jan 2007
AGED 114
Oldest person for: **4 days**
? God's will

Yone Minagawa
JAPAN
4th Jan 1893
13th Aug 2007
AGED 114
Oldest person for: **197 days**
? Eating sensibly, plenty of sleep

Besse Cooper
US
26th Aug 1896
4th Dec 2012
AGED 116
Oldest person for: **1 year 166 days**
? Minding her own business, no junk food

Dina Manfredini
ITALY
4th Apr 1897
17th Dec 2012
AGED 115
Oldest person for: **13 days**
? Hard work, everything in moderation

Jiroemon Kimura
JAPAN
19th Apr 1887
12th Jun 2013
AGED 116
Oldest person for: **177 days**
? Sunbathing and avoiding large portions of food

Misao Okawa
JAPAN
5th Mar 1898
1st Apr 2015
AGED 117
Oldest person for: **1 year 193 days**
? Eating sushi, relaxing

Gertrude Weaver
US
4th Jul 1898
6th Apr 2015
AGED 116
Oldest person for: **5 days**
? Hard work, loving God, everybody and everything

Jeralean Talley
US
23rd May 1899
17th Jun 2015
AGED 116
Oldest person for: **72 days**
? Having faith in God

Yukichi Chuganji
- JAPAN 23rd Mar 1889
- 28th Sep 2003 **AGED 114**
- Oldest person for: **273 days**
- Healthy eating, being an optimist

Mitoyo Kawate
- JAPAN 15th May 1889
- 13th Nov 2003 **AGED 114**
- Oldest person for: **46 days**
- Custard cakes

Ramona Iglesias-Jordan
- PUERTO RICO 31st Aug 1889
- 29th May 2004 **AGED 114**
- Oldest person for: **198 days**
- Cooking with pork fat

Maria Esther de Capovilla
- ECUADOR 14th Sep 1889
- 27th Aug 2006 **AGED 116**
- Oldest person for: **2 years 90 days**
- Calm disposition

Elizabeth Bolden
- US 15th Aug 1890
- 11th Dec 2006 **AGED 116**
- Oldest person for: **106 days**
- Nothing divulged

Emiliano Mercado del Toro
- PUERTO RICO 21st Aug 1891
- 24th Jan 2007 **AGED 115**
- Oldest person for: **44 days**
- Eating boiled polenta, a sense of humour

Edna Parker
- US 20th Apr 1893
- 26th Nov 2008 **AGED 115**
- Oldest person for: **1 year 105 days**
- A good education

Maria de Jesus
- PORTUGAL 10th Sep 1893
- 2nd Jan 2009 **AGED 115**
- Oldest person for: **37 days**
- No tobacco, alcohol, coffee or meat

Gertrude Baines
- US 6th Apr 1894
- 11th Sep 2009 **AGED 115**
- Oldest person for: **252 days**
- God, no alcohol, tobacco or fooling around

Kama Chinen
- JAPAN 10th May 1895
- 2nd May 2010 **AGED 114**
- Oldest person for: **233 days**
- Regular exercise, avoiding stress

Eugenie Blanchard
- US 16th Feb 1896
- 4th Nov 2010 **AGED 114**
- Oldest person for: **186 days**
- Lifelong virginity

Maria Gomes Valentim
- BRAZIL 9th Jul 1896
- 21st Jun 2011 **AGED 114**
- Oldest person for: **229 days**
- A breakfast of bread, coffee, fruit and milk with linseed every day

Susannah Mushatt Jones
- US 6th Jul 1899
- 12th May 2016 **AGED 116**
- Oldest person for: **330 days**
- Lots of sleep, bacon and eggs, no alcohol or tobacco

Emma Morano
- ITALY 29th Nov 1899
- 15th Apr 2017 **AGED 117**
- Oldest person for: **338 days**
- Raw steak and brandy daily, leaving her husband aged 39

Violet Brown
- JAMAICA 10th Mar 1900
- 15th Sep 2017 **AGED 117**
- Oldest person for: **153 days**
- Working hard and having faith in God

Nabi Tajima
- JAPAN 4th Aug 1900
- 21st Apr 2018 **AGED 117**
- Oldest person for: **218 days**
- Eating and sleeping well

Chiyo Miyako
- JAPAN 2nd May 1901
- 22nd Jul 2018 **AGED 117**
- Oldest person for: **92 days**
- Sleeping for at least eight hours a night

Kane Tanaka
- JAPAN 2nd Jan 1903
- Oldest person for: **2+ years**
- Studying mathematics, having faith in God

What can you tell me about...?

An index to everything

G

H

K

L

What went into this book?

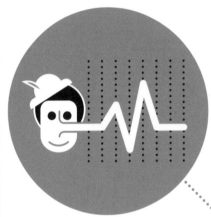

What gave you the idea?

It all began with *Delayed Gratification*, the Slow Journalism magazine we launched in January 2011. *Delayed Gratification* is dedicated to looking back on big events after the dust has settled to tell our readers what happened next and to seek out the stories that were missed or mistold the first time around.

Alongside *Delayed Gratification*'s longform features and photo essays, one of the big things that helped the magazine take off were the infographics we'd created for it since the first issue. As well as looking pretty, they helped us show the long-term impact of big stories, uncover new insights and strip out bias by focusing on facts.

In April 2020, wanting a project to work on during the UK's first Covid-19 lockdown, we started bringing together updated versions of the best infographics we'd published in *Delayed Gratification* to date with a host of new creations to create *An Answer For Everything*.

Have you been lying to me?

No - but we should have a quick chat about data. In this book we've used the latest and most credible data sets available, but they do have their limits. Many are compiled by people with limited resources, incomplete access and hidden biases, and the best sources don't always agree with one another.

Not just that, but when choosing data sets to use - to identify the best country in the world (p060) and best sportsperson of all time (p040), for example - each selection can alter the outcome. We've tried to be as fair and logical as possible when making these choices.

And then there's simple human error - we've checked and rechecked the data sets in this book but there are an awful lot of them, and the laws of Murphy and sod mean that errors will have crept in. If you spot one and want to let us know, email us at infographics@slow-journalism.com and we'll take it on the chin.

Who needs thanking?

Our colleagues and friends at *Delayed Gratification* - Chris Bourn, Vicky Burgess, Jeremy Lawrence, Matthew Lee, James Montague and Loes Witschge. Long-term supporters including Cathy Runciman, Kerin O'Connor and Janey Elliott. Tim Bates and Daisy Chandley at PFD, Rowan Yapp and the team at Bloomsbury.

All the people who helped us compile and check the data: Francesca Adkins, James Cary-Parkes, Will Coldwell, Frankie Lister-Fell, Joe Lo, Esther Marshall, Ian Morris, Penny Woods, Dr Joeri Rogelj, David Shaw, Anthony Smart, Dr Paul Taylor, Laurens Vreekamp, Phil Webb, and Chris Zimmermann.

And last but not least, Dr Tom Almeroth-Williams, Olivier Beltrami, Frida Berg, Gareth Collins, Rebecca Downie, Stephen Edridge, Gina Fullerlove, Robert Marcus, H Jay Melosh, Andy O'Keeffe, Therese Pettersson, Prof Richard Rex, Rishi Sharma, Nicky Thompson and Eliot Van Buskirk.

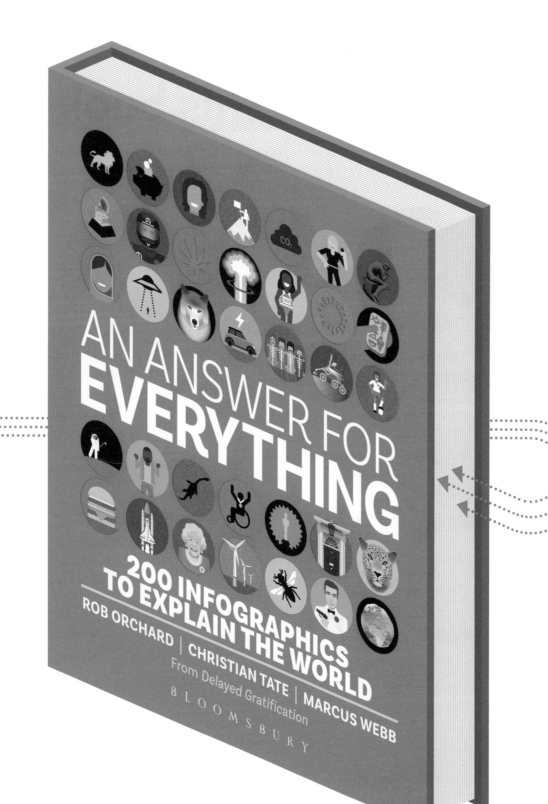

AN ANSWER FOR EVERYTHING

200 INFOGRAPHICS TO EXPLAIN THE WORLD

ROB ORCHARD | CHRISTIAN TATE | MARCUS WEBB

From Delayed Gratification

B L O O M S B U R Y

Who made this book?

A huge number of people contributed (see previous page) but the stories and data were brought together by Rob and Marcus, the editors of *Delayed Gratification*, and the book was designed and illustrated in its entirety by Christian, the magazine's art director

Rob Orchard

Christian Tate

Marcus Webb

What's your favourite infographic in the book?

As someone whose worldview swings wildly between pessimism and optimism, my favourite infographics include 'Is everything getting worse?' (p238) and 'Is anything getting better?' (p240).

A decade ago we crammed everyone who's been to space onto two magazine pages – I loved updating it as an eight-page spectacular for the book (p170), plotting the whole history of humans in space.

'How much would you get for the Eiffel Tower?' (p286) was the last thing that we created for the book and the latest thing we make together is always my favourite infographic.

What's your favourite fact that you discovered while making this book?

There is a back-up Earth we can all escape to should everything go wrong, but it will take us 324,843 years to get there (p102).

I was happily surprised to find I'd read 32 of the 100 best books ever (p162). Just need to carve out 709 hours, 4 minutes and 12 seconds to finish the rest.

That, by our calculations, Warwick Davis is the most popular supporting actor in movie history (p134). It took a 4,086-line spreadsheet to bring you that nugget.

Who couldn't I have done it without?

Jess, Freddie, Oscar, Charlie, dad and Mels

James and Arthur, Lisa, Eddie, Heather and my parents

B, Miller, Barney, mum and dad (plus Bobby and CT, naturally). But mostly B

If you'd like to learn how to make your own infographics, we run regular workshops, with discounts for *Delayed Gratification* subscribers.
To find out how to join one and to see more of our work, visit

slow-journalism.com

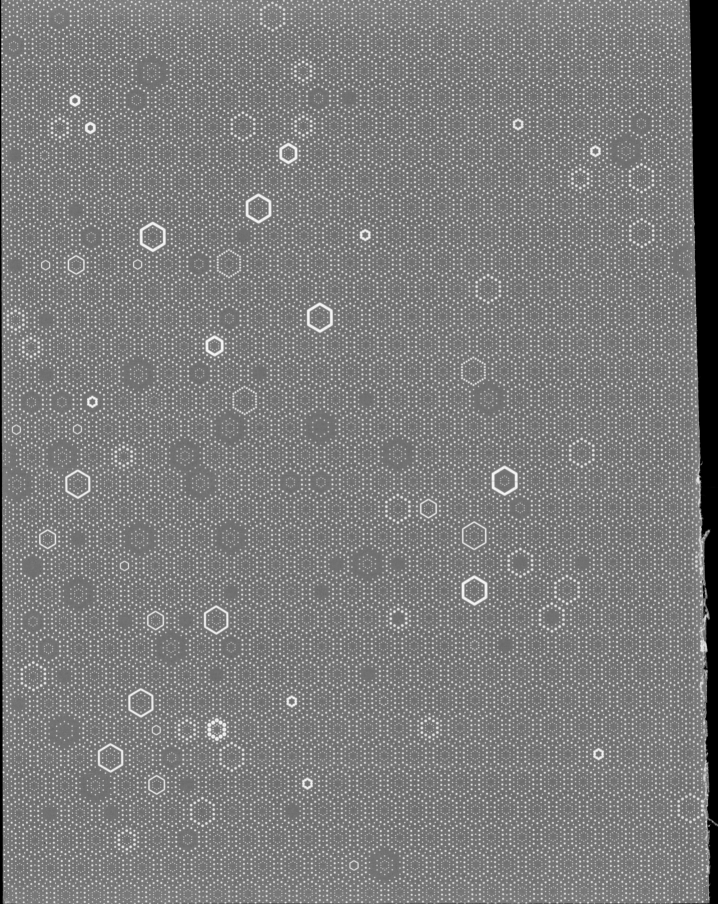